BLACK GOLD

BLACK GOLD

THE NEW FRONTIER IN OIL FOR INVESTORS

GEORGE ORWEL

WILEY

John Wiley & Sons, Inc.

Published by John Wiley & Sons, Inc., Hoboken, New Jersey.
Published simultaneously in Canada.

For general information on our other products and services or for technical support, please contact our Customer Care Department within the United States at (800) 762-2974, outside the United States at (317) 572-3993 or fax (317) 572-4002.

Wiley also publishes its books in a variety of electronic formats. Some content that appears in print may not be available in electronic books. For more information about Wiley products, visit our web site at www.wiley.com.

Library of Congress Cataloging-in-Publication Data:
Orwel, George, 1968–
    Black gold : the new frontier in oil for investors / George Orwel.
        p.   cm.
    Includes bibliographical references.
    ISBN-13: 978-0-471-79268-0 (cloth)
    ISBN-10: 0-471-79268-3 (cloth)
    1. Petroleum industry and trade.   2. Petroleum products—Prices.
    3. Speculation.   I. Title.
    HD9560.5.O77 2006
    338.2'7282—dc22

                                        2006004856

Printed in the United States of America.

10   9   8   7   6   5   4   3   2   1

Contents

PART THREE   The Oil Boom

Acknowledgments

Many friends and colleagues gave encouragement in one form or another during the writing of this book, and they all deserve my thanks regardless of whether they are mentioned here. Special mention goes to Tom Wallin, Sarah Miller, and John van Schaik, all at Energy Intelligence, for the intellectual debates we had on energy issues as well as for the encouragements they offered; my friends Juliette Fairley, Patrick Osewe, and David Bogoslaw were all very supportive and gave one form of advice or another for which I'm very grateful.

Bogoslaw, Jeff Tompkins, Ivan Weiss, and Matt Simmons read parts of this book and suggested corrections, for which I'm enormously grateful, but I'm ultimately responsible for any errors that made it to the final copy you are reading now.

Special thanks go to four people who worked tirelessly to publish this book: my editor Debra W. Englander, assistant editor Greg Friedman, senior production editor Todd Tedesco, senior marketing manager Nancy L. Rothschild, and Jesica Church, associate director of publicity. A huge debt of gratitude is owed to my partner Sheryl Sorensen who, as always, was very supportive and understanding during the writing process.

Finally, I want to dedicate this book to Anne Nelson, Sig Gissler, and Robert MacDonald, all of Columbia University Graduate School of Journalism, because they changed my life in various ways.

Introduction

"THE WEALTH OF NATIONS" . . . AND OURS

Oil and natural gas are part of what are known as fossil fuels. Scientists believe they were formed by organisms—plants and animals—that died, decayed, and were transformed into solid rock thousands, perhaps millions, of years ago as a result of high level heating. That natural process took place deep under the earth and resulted in what is now called petroleum, a finite mixture of hydrocarbon molecules that is not easily replaceable. Oil and natural gas have high net energy and, beyond the fact that one is a fluid and the other is vaporous at surface condition, their only other difference relates to the extent of the heating the rocks endured and their molecular weight.

Deposits of oil and gas are found in certain parts of the world where the formation process occurred, and most of these places have extreme weather conditions. Petroleum is recovered by drilling deep into the earth, between 7,500 and 15,000 feet down, then processing and transporting it to storage terminals and eventually to the consumer (though it first goes to refineries that use it to produce gasoline, diesel, kerosene, and other products). The first processing typically is done at the well site, where sophisticated technology separates oil from water and gas. Transportation is either by underground or above ground pipeline systems, sea tankers, and road trucks. Natural gas is typically liquefied, or transformed into liquid form, before being transported in specially designed tankers.

Fossil fuels are the dominant energy source fueling the modern economy, and at least in the short term they will continue to shape our society in the new millennium. As we move forward amid concerns about availability and cost of oil, we must ask some fundamental questions that will define our future—questions that will touch on economics, politics, population, philosophy, and even military issues.

1

Recent opinion polls have shown that energy security and affordability are among issues of the most immediate concern to Americans. That's because the availability and cost of energy dramatically impact our quality of life and our well-being, the health of our economies, and global stability. With profound apologies to Adam Smith, energy is actually the *wealth* of nations . . . and ours, too.

OIL HERALDS A BRIGHT NEW WORLD
AT THE TURN OF THE TWENTIETH CENTURY

The future couldn't have looked brighter for the United States at the dawn of the twentieth century, as industrialization gathered pace. The growth of automobile transportation made it easier to move people and goods across boundaries thanks to the emergence of gasoline as the best power source, about 1910. Today gasoline is the single most important product of oil, which itself was known even during ancient times and in fact as far back as the time of Herodotus.[1]

History shows that ancient Persians used oil in 480 B.C., as did Native Americans years later, mainly as medicine, not as a fuel, and the Bible makes reference to oil being used for cementing walls in Babylon. But in its pure form, oil is formed from organic matter that has decayed and stayed in rocks for hundreds or thousands of years. In the United States, oil first flowed from springs near Titusville, in northwestern Pennsylvania, and was harvested by the Seneca Indians.

The first oil well anywhere was drilled in Pennsylvania by a former New York, New Haven and Hartford Railroad conductor known as Edwin L. Drake in August 1859. The well was 69 feet deep and produced 15 barrels a day. The area quickly boomed and the modern oil industry was born. More than half a century later, in the 1930s, Texas and Oklahoma became the centers of U.S. production, but after World War II the Middle East became a major supplier to the United States.

Before the discovery of oil in Pennsylvania, Americans used whale oil, vegetable oil, and coal oil for lighting. But oil products—kerosene and gasoline—later proved far superior and have since dominated the market. Oil's biggest use, however, came with the development of the automobile. Today almost all forms of locomotion—cars, trucks, buses, trains, ships and airplanes—are fueled by oil, diesel, or gasoline. Fuel oil and natural gas have also been burned to produce electricity, although historically that had always been mostly coal's job.

Starting from Pennsylvania in 1859 and later in the Gulf Coast states, U.S. oil production grew sharply, with supply far surpassing demand during much of the 1930s, causing prices to fall to as low as four cents per barrel until the federal government, using its interstate commerce legislative authority, stepped in. To save the industry from collapse, the government set production quotas for each state and also instituted tariffs on imports from foreign suppliers like Venezuela.

Nonetheless, oil was on its way to becoming a global commodity with a global market, while at the same time, domestically local producers were in dire need of a stable market. In any case, with so much oil available, Detroit car makers were spitting out fleets of automobiles at a high rate, and the automobile began to have an enormous influence across America by the mid-twentieth century.

A lot has changed since then. The twenty-first century is starting out with a wake-up call: We must get prepared for an impending catastrophe. We've enjoyed cheap oil for far too long, and now there are signs we may be headed for a global "oil peak"—the point at which oil production worldwide will start declining at the rate of 2 percent per year. When the oil peak will occur is a matter of speculation and there's already an intense debate going on, but at least this much is certain: Our lifestyle will have to undergo drastic changes.

How prepared are we, and what do average investors need to do, are the subjects of this book. My understanding is that with better technology we might be able to squeeze some more oil out of old wells, perhaps through improved water treatment, or we may be able to prospect for oil in the deep underbelly of the Atlantic off the Gulf of Guinea in West Africa and in the Russian side of the frigid Black Sea; we may even be able to increase our use of natural gas to generate power, or churn out fuel from Canada's eastern Alberta tar sands and from Venezuela's heavy crude oil, found north of the Orinoco River.

However, those would be temporary measures and they wouldn't much change the equation. So, we stop here to ponder the issue, and knowing full well the grave consequences to our civilization, we ask the same question as Samuel Beckett's Vladimir:

> Let us not waste time in idle discourse. Let us do something, while we have the chance! It's not every day that we are needed. Nor in-

deed that we personally are needed. . . . To all mankind, they are addressed, those cries for help still ringing in our ears! But at this place, at this moment of time, all mankind is us, whether we like it or not. Let us make the best of it before it is too late! Let us represent worthily for once the foul brood to which a cruel fate consigned us! It is true that when with folded arms we weigh the pros and cons we are no less a credit to our species. The tiger bounds to the help of his congeners without the least reflection, or else he slinks away into the depth of the thicket. But that is not the question. What are we doing, that is the question.[2]

Why not accept the fact that fossil fuels are not the energy of the future and start developing alternatives? Oil executives already know this, but they have chosen to be quiet about it. There are reputations to protect and shareholders to please. That's the underlying story about the reserves scandal—companies depend on their reserves to keep up with Wall Street expectations. As one expert said, the 2004 reserve scandal involving the Royal Dutch Shell company was just a tip of the iceberg. Shell was forced to restate its reserves for several years. Ditto Repsol. Fortunately, for the investors, there's a silver lining: There is a lot of money to be made in this business. If you ever wanted to get a piece of the oil boom, this is your opportunity.

You shouldn't depend on oil executives to tell you anything more than they want you to know. That's just not going to happen. As a matter of fact, industry people only talk about "oil peak" when they want to shoot down the whole idea, but you can read between the lines when they express worries about maintaining their supply levels and replacing their reserves.

Certainly, the oil peak debate has a long history. It started in 1956 when Shell geophysicist Marion King Hubbert correctly predicted that U.S. oil production would peak in 1969–1970 and drop rapidly thereafter. Hubbert used the same theory that was already being used for the study of population, but he applied it to oil growth.[3]

The theory is based on how population growth is influenced by the environment. It argues that when a new population of a species starts growing in a resource-based area, the rate of growth increases by the same fraction each year. But once the population gets bigger than the resource available for its existence, the growth rate of that population starts to slow.

The same is true of oil, Hubbert said, adding that the chance of discovering new oil decreases when there's less new oil to find. Based on that analysis, he added, once we begin to discover less oil, it's possible that a time will come when we won't get any new oil. As such, the only amount of oil we'll have to depend on is that which is already in the reserves, which we are now slowly depleting. His whole point is that oil is finite.

There are an close to two trillion barrels of proven oil equivalent (boe) stored in rocks around the world, both onshore and offshore. That figure includes natural gas deposits of about 0.8 trillion barrels, which means global crude oil reserves are just about 1.2 trillion barrels. However, it is important to point out from the outset that these reserves data aren't very definitive because even the three most respected publications that analyze global oil reserves—BP's *Statistical Review of World Energy*, *Oil & Gas Journal*, and *World Oil*—have different numbers. For instance, BP puts proven global reserves at 1.188 trillion barrels, while *Oil & Gas Journal* puts the figure at 1.29 trillion and *World Oil* puts it at 1.08 trillion.

Since it is impossible to know who is right among them, I've decided to come up with the average of all these data for the purposes of this book. That gives us 1.19 trillion barrels, or roughly 1.2 trillion barrels, as the global oil reserves. Of that, about 6 percent is in North America, 9 percent in Central and Latin America, 2 percent in Europe, 4 percent in Asia Pacific, 7 percent in Africa, 6 percent in the former Soviet Union, and about 66 percent in the Middle East, including Libya and Algeria: Saudi Arabia (25 percent), Iraq (10 percent), Iran (8 percent), United Arab Emirates (9 percent), Kuwait (9 percent), Libya (2 percent), and Qatar (1 percent), Algeria (about 1 percent), and Oman, Syria, and Yemen combined (1 percent).

In terms of consumption, the United States uses 20 million barrels per day, or 25 percent of the world total, and imports about 60 percent of its oil needs, mostly from Canada, Saudi Arabia, Venezuela, Mexico, and Nigeria, in that order. That shows how we stack up against others with regard to demand and supply.

Other geologists have since pointed out that the rate of oil discovery has been declining for decades. Princeton geologist Kenneth S. Deffeyes, who worked with and became a friend of Hubbert at Shell, says global oil production growth has dwindled to 0.6 percent annually since 1998.[4] His point is that production growth has ceased. But because oil is produced in so many different parts of the world, it's misleading to talk about a global oil peak without looking at what's happening in different regions.

Looking at each region, we see that U.S. production peaked in 1970, Russia's in 1999 (except on Sakhalin Island, which is yet to be developed), and the North Sea in 2000. Mexico's largest oilfield, Cantarell, is on the decline after 30 years of production, while Nigerian oil production is expected to start falling by the end of this decade.

That will leave us with the Middle East as the sole source of oil in the future, but already a few Middle East producers, such as Kuwait, have seen some of their oilfields getting exhausted. No one knows with any accuracy the situation in Saudi Arabia other than what the government says. The kingdom has tried to scuttle any such debate, and although they insist there are more than enough oil reserves, that assessment is now seriously being questioned.

As a member of the Organization of Petroleum Exporting Countries (OPEC), the kingdom of Saudi Arabia has been playing politics with its reserves data. For example, many experts were surprised when OPEC's reserves data doubled within a short time during the 1980s. That some former Saudi Aramco experts are now questioning some of the company's own data and the fact that the kingdom's spare capacity is seriously restricted—now at 1.5 to 2 million barrels per day—have only added to speculations that there's more than the Saudis are publicly saying.

Because reserves outside the Middle East are being depleted much more rapidly, their overall reserves-to-production ratio, which indicates how long proven reserves would last at current production rates, is much lower (15 years for the rest of the world compared with 80 years for the Middle East).

If production continues at today's rate, many of the largest producers in 2002, such as Russia, Mexico, the United States, Norway, China, and Brazil will cease to be relevant players in the oil market in less than two decades, according to the Institute of the Analysts of Global Security (IAGS), a Washington, D.C., group of former national security officials who are currently trying to raise awareness about the need for energy security. At that point, the Middle East will be the only major reservoir of abundant crude oil. In fact, Middle Eastern producers will have a much bigger piece of the pie than ever before, the IAGS adds.

Just like now, at the time Hubbert came up with his contrarian forecast, he found it extremely difficult to get anyone to listen to him. He was criticized and his employers tried to suppress the publication of his study. It wasn't until 1970, when his prediction came true, that some people began to pay attention. Still, automobile manufacturers and oil executives mounted counterarguments in the years that followed, supported by government officials.

His detractors argued that his analysis didn't account for the growing production from other producers, especially from members of Organization of Petroleum Exporting Countries (OPEC), which accounts for almost a third of the current global oil supply. Up until that time, the United States was the world's leading oil producer, and the nation's industrial growth owes much to that locally produced oil and the subsequent consistently cheap supplies from the Middle East.

In recent years, the oil peak debate has got even louder. But what is important now is that perception is slowly changing among some of the industry's leading experts. Those who still refuse to accept the view that oil production will start declining at some point are locked in a time warp and there's nothing you can do about them. These optimists have marshaled all sorts of arguments.

The bottom line, however, is that serious people are getting concerned, and even some people at the U.S. Department of Energy are paying attention. Dr. Herman Franssen, a former chief economist at the Department of Energy, has reportedly said that the "concept [of peak oil] is realistic and most people would agree, but we disagree on the timing."[5] On that one, most geologists say oil will peak in five to ten years, but most economists give it about 30 years or more.

They both seem to be missing something. I think that the peak could come in about 15 years from now. I say this not because I have worked out the intricate mathematical formula the way Hubbert did, but because as an independent writer I have had time to scrutinize much of the information available on oil production and projections and the theories advanced by various oil peak experts. I'm neither a geologist nor an industry economist, but I have covered the industry for many years and talked to those who should know.

One of the many tricks I learned in this business is that whenever there's an agreement on an issue, the truth always lies in the middle. In this case, economists are downplaying the problem, while geologists are overplaying it. It doesn't mean they are wrong, but literally nobody knows until it shall come to pass, and that's the tragedy. There are so many assumptions built into every argument for or against the oil peak, in part because both camps represent certain specific interests.

It is essential to understand how important oil is to our way of life. We know that oil provides gasoline that powers our automobile engines, but it's also true that our lives today are dependent on oil for other things as well. About 90 percent of the organic chemicals we use are made from petroleum; think of pharmaceuticals, agricultural chemicals, and plastics—they all are byproducts of oil.

Power plants that supply our electricity are run by coal, fuel oil, and natural gas, and we know that electricity has become so much a part of our daily lives that without it there would be no civilization as we know it today. Hospitals wouldn't function, our military would be immobilized, and our transport network, including subways and airlines, wouldn't operate.

Just about everything that depends on electricity, like refrigerators and telephones, would be rendered useless—at least in the United States, where hydropower is no longer in much use. Given such potential problems, think of what our lives will become when we eventually run out of oil. Unemployment and inflation would follow.

Today's relentless surge in oil prices because of rising demand and a lack of spare capacity suggests the tough road ahead. Oil prices soared to $75 per barrel in April of 2006, and the upside remains a possibility. Indeed, none other than Goldman Sachs, New York's top investment bank, has forecast oil prices rising to $100 at some time, which I don't think is far off.

Oil prices started their steep climb in 2004 because of four factors that will remain relevant for a while: first, rapidly growing demand from China and India is putting a strain on the global supply system. What's happening in those two Asian powerhouses, with a combined population of 2.3 billion and oil demand growth rate of more than 6 percent, is a fundamental concern to the world, especially those who follow the financial markets.

China and India, or Chinindia to some, are thirsty for oil to power their rapid industrial growth, and they are now competing with the United States for oil and other scarce fossil fuels everywhere in the world. Little wonder that last summer the Chinese National Offshore Oil Company (CNOOC) engaged Chevron in a bid war for California-based oil explorer Unocal, for which the Chinese company offered to pay $18.5 billion.

Secondly, the world's major oil producing countries, most of them in the politically volatile Middle East, have almost maximized their output and have no spare capacity. The only producer able to flex its muscles is Saudi Arabia, but it too has only a paltry 1.5 to 2 million barrels per day of spare capacity, which isn't worth much. That means they are powerless to contain any additional oil demand pressures, and the fear resulting from that situation is fueling even bigger concerns about a future supply crunch, which in turn pushes up fuel prices.

Third, geopolitical tensions have become common, disrupting supply from Venezuela, Nigeria, Russia, and the Middle East. All of this started with a two-month strike in Venezuela in early 2003 that severely crippled exports and had ripple effects throughout the global oil market. In Russia, the Kremlin's brutal attack on Yukos and the eventual renationalization of the Russian oil industry were a signal that supply from Russia wouldn't be reliable, and a confirmation of that came in the frosty winter of 2006 when the Russians cut off gas to Ukraine, and in the process affected gas supply to Western Europe.

In Nigeria, community disturbances of the 1990s have evolved into well-organized militancy in the oil-producing Niger Delta region. In early 2006, the militants abducted a few expatriate oil workers and forced foreign oil companies—Royal Dutch Shell, Chevron, and Eni—to suspend production of close to 500,000 barrels a day of oil for several weeks. Nigeria remains so politically unstable that the government is unable to rein in the militants. Observers believe the situation there could worsen if President Obasanjo, who is in his second and final term of office, decides to change the constitution to allow him to run for a third term.

But of all the geopolitical issues, the standoff over Iran's nuclear ambition promises to be most problematic. That's because Iran is the world's fourth largest exporter of oil, supplying the market with about 2.5 million barrels a day, a huge volume that can't easily be covered by other producers in the event that Tehran decides to use its oil as a weapon against the West. Iranian leaders look determined to continue with their nuclear program and the question now is whether the United States will allow that to happen. The reason why this is scary is that hawks on both sides are moving the agenda, leaving little or no room for compromise.

Fourth, oil and gas are increasingly becoming viable investment vehicles for those seeking wealth, and this trend will only accelerate in the coming years. In the past two years, deep-pocketed hedge funds and mutual funds have dominated trading on the energy markets in New York and London. Now, ordinary investors may have to join in after the introduction of exchange-traded funds on the American Stock Exchange in April 2006.

As oil prices rise, so do the prices of oil products, such as gasoline, diesel, heating oil, and jet fuel—and even inflation. As a result, you'll spend more money to fuel your car for going to work each morning, to buy an airline ticket, and to keep your house warm in the winter, and more still to buy anything imported and then shipped across the country by truckers that use diesel. Or worse, you may lose your job.

You may think that you don't buy imported goods. Actually, you do. In the course of dressing for work, try looking for where your shirt is made.

Chances are you'll see China or the Philippines written on the shirt collar. The United States imports more than it exports. The trade deficit reached a record $617.1 billion in 2005.

Consumer spending accounts for two-thirds of the nation's economic activity. That spending, though, left Americans' savings rate—savings as a percentage of after-tax income—at 1.2 percent in 2004, the lowest since 1934. That means an increase in gasoline prices hit most people really hard in the wallet.

And don't even think there will be adequate alternative fuel when we finally run out of oil. We have got used to a type of lifestyle made easier by cheap oil, and we assume that by the time oil runs out, oil companies will have found some replacement. The reasoning goes this way, "We are an innovative people by nature and we always come up with solutions to the world's difficult problems."

Here's my favorite solution to the problem as espoused by TV experts: "We can use hybrid cars and hydrogen-powered machines." I don't buy that, and so shouldn't you. Remember, the previous oil shocks of 1973 and 1979 were man-made crises that had an easy answer—i.e., just pump more oil supply to the market. Those crises were political to the extent that Islamic governments in the Middle East were using their oil to score a political point against the West.

In response, our government started buying oil in the open market and keeping it in storage for a rainy day. The result was the creation of the US Strategic Petroleum Reserve (SPR), which is managed by the Department of Energy. SPR has storage tanks in Louisiana and Texas, but they can only carry a maximum of 700 million barrels, enough to last us slightly more than one month in case all other sources of supply are interrupted. We also have a heating oil reserve in the Northeast—enough to last ten days.

Are you kidding me? That's not enough in case of a serious long-term supply problem.

Other countries are doing the same. China has just established an emergency oil reserve that will store 100 to 150 million barrels by 2008, enough to cover 30 days of refinery demand. By 2010, China expects that it will have expanded its SPR capacity to 300 million barrels. That additional Chinese demand for oil will put extra pressure on the world's already thin supply system.

The oil market pressures are also partly fundamentally driven. They are market-inspired changes that we all appreciate as free marketers. But they are hurting most of us nonetheless, and we have to do something about it. The biggest change in the oil market over the last 20 years or so is a steady shift to a seller's market.

Demand is outpacing supply and sellers dictate prices. Those sellers are producers such as Saudi Arabia, Iran, and Libya, among others. We in the United States are the buyers—meaning the oil market is skewed against us. We have to pay more to get a barrel of oil from the Middle East, for example, and that additional expense translates into a cutback on our other budgets or savings. You would think that a simple solution to that problem would be for us to start using natural gas, say, to power our electric generators.

However, natural gas prices also spiked nearly three times in the past decade and they will continue to soar. The reason is that natural gas now accounts for 22 percent of U.S. energy use, but its supply is limited—mostly from domestic production, with no imports. Natural gas is a difficult commodity to import, unless you liquefy it first.

None other than Alan Greenspan, the recently retired chairman of the Federal Reserve Board, has expressed concerns that continued high prices are a "very serious problem" that could hurt the economy, singling out natural gas for his worries.

There is no easy answer for all these problems right now. All major systems that depend on oil here and abroad are expected to be destabilized a little. In fact, that process may already have begun, as oil price and demand data appear to have become incongruent in recent years.

The oil industry depends on reliable data on expectations and actual demand and supply and on reliable prices as well. But because the world is headed down the path of oil supply tightness, geopolitical fights and culture wars are frequently going to interrupt fuel supply in the coming years.

Eventually, economic growth as we know it will stall. We can push back these problems for a while by militarily taking control of oil producing Middle East and West Africa, but I wonder whether we can afford to do that. It will require a lot of financial and military capital, something the United States doesn't have enough of right now.

As everyone knows, the Middle East is a geopolitical minefield, as the Iraq war shows. In fact, some believe the Iraq war was part of a struggle to ensure we have access to one of the world's largest oil reserves, currently estimated at 112.5 billion barrels, or about 11 percent of the world's total.

With time Iraqi reserves, when fully developed, may actually rival Saudi Arabia's. What's more, Iraq's oil is of high quality for gasoline and is cheaper to produce than oil in the Gulf of Mexico. But Iraq is a mess right now, unable even to police itself, let alone move ahead with reconstruction.

Oil facilities there are dilapidated after 20 years of neglect, and Iraq needs about $30 billion to put things back together. When all that is done, nationalism will ensure continued problems with the private industry that is expected to help develop new oilfields.

A CHANCE ENCOUNTER AND A TOUGH QUESTION TRIGGER A SEARCH FOR THE TRUTH

I started thinking about writing this book in late 2004 after a chat with my neighbor, Madeline Brainard—one of those scholars who read *The Nation* regularly. She was thin and looked worried most of the time, just like most intellectuals, but she was brainy. Although she has a doctorate degree from Princeton, she quit teaching at a college in upstate New York to devote herself full time to teaching yoga in New York City.

One evening I was picking up my mail in the lobby of my apartment building when she came in and we started chatting. It was our first meeting, and after I told her that I was an oil markets reporter, she asked what I knew about the coming peak in global oil production. I told her that was a lie, that we always have and always will have oil. She refused to accept my explanation. She had read an article in *The Nation* suggesting we were on the verge of running out of oil.

I knew at once where she was heading, so I politely disagreed, but I promised to investigate the issue later. Up to that point, I had depended pretty much on sanitized information provided by oil companies about their assets and reserves. It didn't occur to me that the industry could keep secret the fact that they had less oil reserves than what they were actually telling the public. Neither did I expect the industry's media to let that happen.

However, in much of the news media these days, there's a symbiotic relationship between the seekers of news and the suppliers of news (in this case, oil industry leaders and the reporters who cover them), so adequate scrutiny is lacking. The problem with modern media is that they consider themselves part of the establishment, and they generally don't want to bite the hand that feeds them.

After all, in today's journalism few reporters get promoted for not seeking the truth (whatever that means), but for getting exclusive interviews and keeping everyone entertained. A regular interview with a company executive shows that the executive trusts the reporter, but he wouldn't be giving his time to a scoundrel bent on making things tough for him.

Meanwhile, I started to do more research on the issue, asking hard questions, and privately investigating what industry leaders knew, when they knew it, and what they intend to do. It didn't take long before I found out part of the answer.

A senior editor told me about a meeting he had with oil executives where that topic was discussed, and their consensus was that global oil output would soon be peaking. The meeting was private and no one wrote about it, but it showed rare candor by the industry executives.

On hearing that, I immediately became skeptical of anything oil executives said. Their primary goal is to protect themselves and their shareholders. This book is a product of my eight-year experience covering and talking to some of the industry's leaders and experts, among them: British Petroleum chairman and chief executive John Browne; Royal Dutch Shell chairman and chief executive Jeroen van der Veer; Premcor chairman and chief executive Tom O'Malley; and former Halliburton chief executive and current U.S. vice-president Dick Cheney.

While shedding some light on the prospects for global oil peak, in this book I have devoted more time to discussing the consequences to our lifestyle and what we could do to prepare ourselves. In addition, I have discussed some investment choices for investors to investigate in the wake of the oil boom.

Anyone who follows Wall Street (even a little) knows that oil and refinery stocks have been rising like there's no tomorrow. Even the worst performers among oil stocks are making huge profits. Oil companies now occupy a lofty perch that would have been impossible just a few years ago. If the 1990s was the decade of technology, the first decade of the new century is one of oil boom.

Major oil companies such as Exxon Mobil, BP, and Valero have displaced Microsoft, AOL Time Warner, and General Electric from the high table of capitalism. For instance, Valero's outlook for 2005 was even better than the previous year, when many refiners posted record profits. Valero's stock price increased by more than 50 percent in 2005 to $80 per share. Like other refiners, Valero's earnings have exceeded expectations every quarter for the past two years. "The best is yet to come," is how Valero's senior vice-president for refining operations put it.

You already know that the oil boom coicides with debate about "oil peak oil," but my view is that instead of mourning the impending tight market, investors like you and me should actually embrace it, at least for now, because we have many years ahead of us to enjoy the boom. The question is whether you—as an investor—are going to be part of that blessed group of people. Oil stocks, whether you invest in oil exploration or refining companies, are doing so well that market analysts discount any possibility of a meltdown.

Wall Street has re-rated the oil sector, suggesting that this rally has a staying power and is a good buy. Current and future supply-demand fundamentals support this bullish view. Big oil investors need a sector large enough for them to invest in, and they don't get any bigger than oil. Large institutional investors, as well as hedge funds and private equity firms, have piled into oil.

For a start, listen to this: Goldman Sachs, the scion of Wall Street investment banking, has teamed up with a private equity firm, Kelso & Co., to acquire Coffeyville Resources LLC, which owns a 100,000-barrels-per-day refinery in Kansas. This action is part of a recent trend of Wall Street banks to buy physical energy assets, because they believe energy markets will remain stout for a while.

Goldman Sachs also has an investment commodity index, which means it manages a pool of money from ordinary investors by buying and selling energy stocks as well as trading energy futures. Energy futures are paper contracts or agreements to buy or sell physical oil and gas cargoes in the future, but the cargoes are never actually delivered. Instead, the traders buy and sell those contract instruments, making a profit on the price differential between the contracts.

For instance, if I buy a prior contract between A and B to sell one cargo (300,000 barrels) of oil at $18 million, and then proceed to sell that same contract to C for $20 million, the price difference between those two transactions—$2 million—is my profit. Taken together, all of the energy futures contracts traded in New York and London by commodity indexes like Goldman Sachs Commodities Index (GSCI) and Dow Jones AIG Commodities Index (DJAIGC) amount to $1 trillion.

Finally, exchange-traded fund securities, which track the price of light sweet oil on the New York Mercantile Exchange (Nymex), the commodities trading floor in lower Manhattan, have also proved very rewarding. They can buy and sell an oil contract on behalf of an investor when the price is right, and then sell that contract at a profit, which goes to the investor, whose only obligation is to pay a transaction fee.

PART ONE

THE END OF OIL

CHAPTER 1

The End of an Era?

"I once set up a debate between the geological optimists and pessimists for the IEA with Morie Adelman, Mike Lynch and Peter O'Dell on the one side, and Colin Campbell and John Laherrere on the other. The optimists won."

—David Knapp, senior editor,
Energy Intelligence Group

AN OIL CRISIS CREATES DEBATE THAT
MAY DETERMINE WHO IS THE TOP DOG

With oil prices on a stratospheric flight, many traders and investors are finally taking notice. The stock market already is: Oil stocks are higher than other equities in 2006. In 2005, oil stocks rose while the rest lagged. Oil has had a negative effect on the market ever since it went above $35 a barrel just two years ago. Since then, on days when oil has risen, the stock market has dropped, and on days that oil has fallen, stocks have gone up.

The oil stock gains have been seen all around the world, not just in the United States alone. Last year, one hedge fund manager who has benefited from higher oil prices by purchasing oil stocks was among those touting investments in refiners as well as Canadian oil royalty trusts. Everyone, from professional economists on Wall Street to ordinary consumers, has been wondering why oil prices are so high and continue to rise. For an answer, they should look no further than economics, geology, and politics.

As everyone is aware by now, there has been a tremendous increase in oil demand—and ultimately fuel consumption—since 2003, primarily from China and India, but also from the United States. Oil demand is tied to economic growth, which has been going from strength to strength in the years since the September 11 terrorist attacks on the United States. The explosive economic growth in China has proved more of a shock to the oil markets because as late as the early 1990s China was self-sufficient in oil. But its gross domestic product (GDP) rate took a flight by the end of that decade and doubled to about 9 percent by 2005—the fastest of any country. China's economic boom is still on track and it has to import more oil to support that rate of growth, with construction projects—hotels, bridges, and apartment buildings—going up every day ahead of the 2008 Olympic Games in Beijing. China's demand for oil products is only going to increase as its large population gets more motorized. Ditto India, Asia's other economic powerhouse.

And while all that oil demand is rising, supply is struggling to keep pace. The availability of cheaply exploited oil has been reduced. Of course, there are still a lot of oil reserves in some parts of the world, like in the deep waters off West Africa, in arctic Russia, and in the Middle East, but there are problems as well: The cost of drilling in unreachable areas like the offshore Black Sea, the Gulf of Guinea, and the Gulf of Mexico is sometimes prohibitive and superior technology is required; security is tenuous at best in places like Iran, Iraq, and Saudi Arabia; and most of the readily available oil is of the low-quality heavy, sour type, which is expensive to process into gasoline and other products. High-quality light, sweet oil, which yields more gasoline, is in short supply, and most of the old refineries we have around the world have not been fitted with coking units that can process heavy, sour crude.

Moreover, since the early 1990s, oil companies have not invested enough in expanding their infrastructural capacity, both in oil production and in refining. Oil executives say they couldn't invest because they had no money, as oil prices were low until the shock demand of 2004 boosted prices. They say the high oil prices have, in fact, given them a shot in the arm, and a number of projects are in the pipeline. Most of these projects started in early 2006 in the United States, in Asia, and in the Middle East. Saudi Arabia, for example, plans to invest $50 billion in various projects over the next several years both in production as well as in refining. However, these projects will take time to come onstream. In the meantime, the world is becoming not only less safe, but also "flat,"[1] or smaller, so that political and security problems in one part of the world—like Venezuela, Nigeria, Russia, and Iraq—affect people elsewhere. The global nature of the oil market makes it even more susceptible to geopolitical tension, and that typically adds something like a 15 percent premium to the actual oil price.

Just about everyone I know believes that high oil prices are here to stay because world oil production may be nearing its peak, after which we shall see a decline of about two percent per year for the foreseeable future. That's unfortunate because demand for oil, meanwhile, is traveling the other direction—rising. The signs are everywhere of a potential huge problem in the near to long term: Our fuel supply system is already failing to keep up with demand, a situation that, as every economist knows, could lead to a total breakdown of free market economy. Since supply represents how much the market can offer, the quantity supplied refers to the amount of a certain good producers are willing to supply when receiving a certain price. In basic economics, the correlation between price and how much of a good or service is supplied to the market is the supply relationship, and so price is a reflection of supply and demand. The relationship between demand and supply underlies the forces behind the allocation of resources. In a market economy like ours, therefore, we depend on demand and supply of commodity goods like oil to allocate resources in the most efficient way possible.

A bigger debate is raging on how fast oil deposits around the world are getting depleted, and increasingly that debate is getting politicized. Broadly speaking, that debate pits geologists, who have been dubbed pessimists, against economists, who are seen as optimists. I'm not sure if these labels help the debate, but here's what I have to say: By the very nature of their profession, traditional free market economists are an optimistic lot, and often their views are in conflict with traditional scientists, who, by the nature of their professions, aren't as optimistic, though not necessarily pessimistic. It might be more accurate to call most scientists cautious. This debate, now dubbed the "peak oil," has drawn a fault line between the business community, particularly the oil industry, and the environmental community, particularly geologists. The stakes are huge and, since most governments don't know what to do, some have chosen to align themselves with the oil industry—no surprise. There are many other characters with less than adequate understanding of the issue, particularly journalists and other think-tank paid commentators, who have also chosen to partake in the debate and they are spread all over the map, with nothing much to offer but their own political ideologies.

We have to be careful and say this debate isn't new, but its intensity is. The first phase of it started in the United States during the First World War, in which the allied victory became known as the victory for oil. That probably was a better way to put it because, given the heavy casualties on both sides, the actual victory was pyrrhic, and it was achieved mostly through the use of army trucks following the discovery of petrol, or gasoline. As Pulitzer-Prize-winning energy writer Daniel Yergin tells us in his seminal 1991 book, *The Prize: The Epic Quest for Oil, Money and Power*, the fuel shortage in 1917 came in the middle of the war and caused a great deal of panic, particularly in Britain, but that was caused by nothing more than the ability of the German forces to block supplies to Britain. During the Second World War, for which oil remained crucial, U.S. officials became more concerned about a dwindling supply of its oil reserves. Yergin makes it clear that, even then, U.S. officials had come to recognize oil as the most critical resource that would separate top dog from underdog in international politics.[2]

Yergin writes: "The precipitous decline in new discoveries transfixed and frightened those responsible for fueling a global war," and goes on to quote senior U.S. government officials as saying, "The time will come sooner or later when the supply is exhausted.... If there should be a World War III it would have to be fought with someone else's petroleum, because the United States wouldn't have it. America's crown, symbolizing supremacy as the oil empire of the world, is sliding down over one eye." The allied military strategy in the Second World War was guided by oil more than anything else. As the U.S. almost alone fueled the allied war effort, using most of its own oil supply, fear of a shortage grew with each passing day. To skeptics, these fears might have had no legs to stand on, but government officials considered them real and justified, because the U.S. became a net importer of oil rather than an exporter some 30 years later.

Along the way, in 1956, Shell geologist Marion King Hubbert mathematically calculated a U.S. oil peak production in 1969, angering his employers and sparking an even greater debate on "oil peak." In any case, he was right, for his prediction was confirmed in 1972 when the Texas Railroad Commission abandoned rationing oil production. The commission had been mandated from the time of the Great Depression to ration how much oil would be transported, which meant that production in the Gulf Coast was also rationed. Now, there was no longer any need to do that because production was on the decline. Proving that nothing is as good as success, the confirmation of the U.S. oil peak, which was now narrowed to 1970, vindicated Hubbert—who became a celebrity—and gave birth to what is now known as the "Hubbert Curve" theory.

The current oil peak debate started around 1995 but stayed off the radar because it was drowned by the tech boom of that decade. It was started by geologists who used Hubbert's theory to determine global oil peak, something far more difficult than what Hubbert did. It was difficult because it depended on a larger volume of data, some of which are either difficult to find or are unreliable, especially data from the Organization of Petroleum Exporting Countries (OPEC).

For the most part, these geologists and energy economists fought it out in the pages of scientific journals—*Nature*, *Science*, and *Scientific American*—before they found publishers willing to give them a larger audience through books. First to fire a salvo was Craig Bond Hatfield, who in 1997 published in *Nature* a commentary article entitled "Oil Back on the Global Agenda,"[3] which argued that "a permanent decline in the global oil production rate is virtually certain to begin within 20 years," adding that "serious planning is needed to deal with the economic consequences." A year later, Richard A. Kerr published an article in *Science* entitled "The Next Oil Crisis Looms Large—and Perhaps Close,"[4] which pretty much made the same points, although in much more alarming language. Kerr was the first to brand the debate as a conflict between economists, who argue that technological advances would expand production for another 40 or 50 years, by which time alternative fuel sources would have matured, and geologists, who warn that oil will begin to run out much sooner than we expect because there's just no more oil to be found even with advanced technology. Kerr's 1998 prediction for peak oil was 10 years, which would be in 2008. The debate took off in earnest after Colin Campbell and Jean H. Laherrère wrote a joint article in *Scientific American* arguing for the end of cheap oil.[5] The article touched off a huge debate in the oil industry because Campbell and Laherrère are both highly respected geologists and have worked for major oil companies in senior production positions. More recently, Kenneth S. Deffeyes, a Princeton geologist who worked at Shell with Hubbert and later became a disciple of the man who has become the patron saint of "global peak oil" proponents, joined the debate as a pessimist.

A few years ago, these followers of Hubbert did what has become common in our troubled world. They formed a lobbying group, the Association for the Study of Peak Oil (ASPO), to create public awareness of the impending problem and convince everyone that we have reached a fork in the road and must decide which way to take. Campbell, an Irishman with a doctorate from Oxford, chairs the group, with Kjell Aleklett, a Swede who is a professor at Uppsala University, acting as president. Also joining the group were American professors Deffeyes, David Goodstein of California Institute of Technology, Brian J. Skinner of Yale, and Houston-based energy banker Matt Simmons.

Those who have tried to understand the processes involved in determining, indeed predicting an oil peak, know just how scientific it is. Hubbert used a great deal of intricate mathematical formulae, which no one understood at the time and economists have struggled to disprove, not so much with any new scientific evidence as by arguing that rising demand would prompt scientists to come up with new technologies that would get more oil. That's hardly a thoughtful approach; it's more like relying on hope. One of Hubbert's critics, American economist Michael C. Lynch, has argued that oil is not a finite resource and that recoverable reserves can be expanded by using better technology, if the price is right, by which he meant that higher oil prices would prompt producers to use advanced technology to increase oil supply. Although some writers have misunderstood Lynch, his position is actually quite simple, as it is based on nothing more than demand and supply principles of economics.

Lynch, who runs his consulting firm, Strategic Energy and Economic Research, Inc. (SEER) in Winchester, Massachusetts, told me during an interview on February, 28, 2006, that peak oil proponents "ignore most of the data and the reality" that disprove their point of view. The data Lynch was referring to are those published by industry publication *Oil & Gas Journal* that revised global reserves upward some years ago on the basis of better technology. While agreeing with oil peak proponents that reserves recovery was declining at an increasing rate, the journal argued that better technology would eventually enhance the recovery factor of existing reserves. "They pretend that revisions don't exist, but they [revisions] are there and secondary oil recovery is also occurring in some fields," Lynch said, and then went on to challenge the view that recovery in some major oilfields has been less than previously expected. "One field recovery problem does not mean that all the other fields are going to have a similar problem," Lynch told me in that interview. To the argument that modern technology can only address how much oil can be recovered sooner and doesn't expand the reserve base, Lynch said: "No. With super technology, you can produce faster and more of the reserves. When people go into deeper seismic areas, the recovery factor increases by 5 to 10 percentage points. On a global level that translates into hundreds of billions of oil barrels, something like a 30 to 50 percent increase in production, which is recoverable for over 50 years."

And that's where Campbell comes in. Picking up from where Lynch left off, Campbell used an analogy that is familiar to all. "Understanding depletion is simple," Campbell said. "Think of an Irish pub. The glass starts full and ends empty. There are only so many more drinks to closing time. It's the same with oil. We have to find the bar before we can drink what's in it."[6]

Campbell's group, ASPO, is growing fast around the world and its view about oil depletion is becoming mainstream, especially as oil prices continue to skyrocket. It's not a useless organization, as some in the oil industry are trying to portray it, and its members are not just crying wolf. It's very credible and its members include people who should know, including some from the Middle East, such as Ali Bakhtiari, head of strategic planning at Iran's National Oil Company (NOIC). Campbell himself is a former executive vice president of Total, the French oil company, and Simmons was an adviser to the controversial Bush-Cheney energy plan.

ASPO members don't think much of the argument advanced by Lynch and Leonardo Maugeri, an executive for Italian energy company ENI, that high oil prices would spur development of additional oilfields because the cost of developing some of the known reserves could be too high to be economically feasible. "The figure I'd use is around $182 a barrel," says Simmons. "We need to price oil realistically to control its demand. That is because global production is peaking. If we price oil correctly, it could give us time to find bridge fuels, fuels to fill the gap between an oil economy and a renewable economy. But I don't see that happening."[7] Moreover, oil peak theorists warn that the decline of world oil output will force oil prices higher for good, the effects of which could be catastrophic. "In my opinion, unfortunately, there will be no linear change," says Bakhtiari. "There will only be sudden explosive change."[8]

All of this debate misses the point. As Simmons told me during an interview on February 28, 2006, the issue of reserves is too complex for any meaningful discussion here, because proven reserves are known in a field only when its last barrel of produced oil is removed. "From the time an oil and gas field is first discovered, the process of guessing what amount of hydrocarbon can be recovered waxes and wanes," says Simmons. "As more knowledge of the field is gained, it sometimes leads to seeing that the field is much larger than first thought. As more wells are drilled, the opposite can also happen and does all too often."

The amount of oil that is recoverable under normal conditions also varies by each type of field. Some fields end up recovering as much as 65 to 80 percent of oil in place, while others get as little as 10 to 20 percent recovery. The total reserves also include high-quality light, sweet oil commingled with low-quality heavy, sour oil. In a way, it's like commingling wines ranging from jug wine to extremely expensive merlots.

Since the mid-1990s, most oil and gas companies have tended to add more than 100 percent reserves each year compared to what they produce, meaning they have been able to more than replace what they take out of their reserves. That's important because Wall Street values oil companies based on their reserves as well as their earnings. "BP, for instance, had a five-to-seven-year period when its reserves additions were 150 percent of production. But few of these companies found a way to grow production. This raises a serious question as to whether the industry systematically overbooked proven reserves," Simmons told me.

But the companies are not alone. In the 1980s, OPEC members almost doubled their reported proven reserves in a burst of revisions, without any new discoveries. Then the numbers didn't change for the next 15 years. Canada also revised upward its reserve numbers by adding unconventional oil reserves—the tar sands—so it could brag that it was the Saudi Arabia of heavy oil; that's to say, Canada is the king of low-quality sour crude. Does the data mean much? "I argue not much," says Simmons. Does the data prove that peak oil will not happen for decades? "The data is meaningless as a guide to addressing when oil supply peaks and when it begins to decline," adds Simmons.

But to investors, the dire scenarios and the higher oil prices present an opportunity to get a piece of the boom for the next few years. "Oil investments have been a profitable component for any portfolio and I believe that soon people are going to see them as a must," says Mike Swanson, a fund manager who also writes a regular online column on energy investment.[9]

So, whom should you believe if we are really running out of oil? You should know from the outset that whenever experts talk of an oil peak, what they generally mean is that from then on, production will gradually slide down the slope toward the last drops at the rate of about 2 percent annually. Those who reject the oil peak theory have a lot of faith in technology; they argue that new technologies—and higher prices—are going to make it possible to suck oil out of unconventional places. For instance, they say, extracting oil from tar sands was once thought to be prohibitively costly, but today oil from Canadian tar sands sells for $20 per barrel or more. Indeed, Canada puts its reserves at 300 billion barrels, higher than even Saudi Arabia, but much of that is unrecoverable. That's a fair point. But in my view, there is no denying that oil is a finite commodity, and even new sources would only prolong the downward slide for so long.

That's why along with debate about oil peak, there should be proposals to promote renewable fuel sources—the so-called "green energy." As anyone might expect, wind and solar power are the darlings of people who are environmentally conscientious. But they only provide supplemental solutions that have limited impact at a time when we need adequate and lasting solutions. We could line the Atlantic coast with windmills and still not make much of a dent in electricity demand. Solar and wind power are unreliable sources. If we were to switch en masse to hybrid cars, the cut in oil consumption would be dramatic. But those vehicles are not in large supply and are relatively expensive. Biofuels—diesel-like liquids from corn or garbage—are promising, but would require a mass switch to diesel car engines and a new distribution infrastructure.

Should we revisit nuclear power? That may be necessary. Europe and Japan, where oil products are more expensive, produce most of their electricity from nuclear power plants. The United States, where people are averse to nuclear power, produces less than 20 percent of its electricity from it. Although modern nuclear designs have few safety problems, the disposal of spent nuclear fuel is a political hot potato. There is currently a very strong opposition to dumping nuclear wastes in the Yucca Mountains of Nevada.

What is the way forward? There's no shortage of advice on that from everywhere, including the comedian Bill Maher, who urges us to trade in big sport utility vehicles for smaller ones. Others say you should move closer to your job or car-pool to work. Or don't buy a bigger house than you need; use public transport if you can. The truth is these are small solutions to a much bigger problem. Many have observed that, unlike Europe, the United States has been trapped in a pattern of suburban living tied to the highways since the 1950s, which is supported by tax incentives and cheap fuel. Long Island is a typical example and it will be hard to reverse course. High oil prices may well be the shock we need to change course.

THE FUTURE OF OIL AND THE AMERICAN DREAM

Although oil is known mostly for producing transportation fuels, it's not an exaggeration to say that it literally drives our planet. It's the key source of heat and a critical component of virtually millions of products, from clothing to construction materials. But given that the supply is finite, there are two inescapable facts about oil and other fossil-based fuels: The supply eventually will be depleted, and at some point in the not too distant future demand will outstrip production capacity.

Increasing demand, along with supply problems, has already begun to drive energy prices upward. Recent oil price volatility serves as a warning: Just as we've seen in the past two years, the price of energy, in particular the price of oil, will increase as time goes by. Consumers should expect to pay substantially more at the pump in coming years, while investors should consider the pain at the pump an opportunity to profit on energy equities.

How soon the world's supply of oil and oil equivalents will be exhausted is open to debate. There are a number of economic, political, and environmental factors at play, including global economic growth, Middle East violence, terrorism, and conservation efforts. Moreover, as prices rise, new supplies of oil emerge as do efforts to reduce consumption. At current consumption levels, experts say, the world's known oil supply could be exhausted within the next 30 years, but my guess is that the oil peak could come in the next 15 to 20 years.

My 15- to 20-year estimate may even be optimistic as demand from emerging markets, particularly China and India, is driving up global consumption quite dramatically. In addition, that guess is based on an estimate of known oil reserves, which is still suspect because oil producers—both companies such as Royal Dutch Shell Group and countries such as Saudi Arabia—have an incentive to overstate their reserves. On the other hand, the estimate does not take into account undiscovered or unproven reserves because it's simply unrealistic to assume that everything will be fine at a time when we have real problems. Exploration and advances in production technology will obviously bring to light additional reserves, but those new reserves may also just replace what is being depleted, and in some cases, the high cost of drilling in the offshore deep waters or Arctic areas may be prohibitive. In fact, even some economists admit that OPEC reserve estimates would have to be significantly inflated and new reserve discoveries surprisingly low for my estimate to be an overstatement.

While oil is the most known form of fossil fuel, coal and natural gas are part of the same group, and all can be measured in terms of barrels of oil equivalent (boe). One boe equals six thousand cubic feet of natural gas, or 0.2 tons of hard coal, or 0.4 tons of light coal. There are an estimated two trillion barrels of oil equivalent (boe) in proven reserves around the world today, including 885 billion boe of natural gas.

For natural gas, by some estimates, the supply at present rates of consumption would be exhausted in about 60 years, while the current known supply of coal would last 180 years.

Energy Economics

I have talked to many economists on this oil issue, and despite their claims to the contrary, there's a wide belief that energy is an elastic commodity, meaning consumption and production behaviors change in response to price changes. There is normally a lag in consumption change as a result of price changes. For instance, it takes time for car owners to shift to more energy-efficient vehicles in response to higher fuel prices. A similar lag can occur in other conservation efforts because manufacturing plants require time to change production methods or shift to alternative sources of energy. And despite the spike in the price of oil and the claims by some analysts that it has reached an all-time high, viewed on an historic basis, oil is not exceptionally expensive.

Since 1972, the inflation-adjusted price for a barrel of oil has averaged $34, and while higher oil prices will depress demand, even in classical economic model, the price of oil has to average an inflation-adjusted $60 per barrel before oil consumption/production actually declines year over year. Between 1980 and 1984 oil output declined for four consecutive years as the inflation-adjusted price averaged $69 per barrel. In 1984, as the price declined to an average of $50 per barrel, output once again began to increase and has increased each year since. Yes, demand hasn't suffered in the current situation because family incomes are just as high and energy now represents only a tiny bit of family spending in the United States. All of this makes estimating the remaining lifespan of the world's oil and equivalents supply a tricky business. But my view is that energy prices are going to rise toward a $100 per barrel benchmark at some point in the next year or two, in large part due to simple supply and demand forces.

Supply and Demand

There are 38 major oil producing countries, of which only 11 are OPEC members. These 38 producers and many other minor producers are sitting on the 1.2 trillion barrels of oil and 885 million boe of natural gas reserves. Of course, there is no real agreement on how large these oil reserves really are. However, what is uncontestable is that we are finding reserves now at a much lower rate than we are consuming them. Even more important is the fact that current daily supply and demand for oil are so tightly matched that there's no room for error. You could almost call it an oil demand growth shock. In 2003 demand from the developed world, especially the United States, was just as robust as China's, and that trend intensified in 2004, flattened in 2005, and recovered in 2006. Moreover, oil demand from the rest of Asia, particularly India, South Korea, Taiwan, Thailand, and Singapore, soared as well.

On the supply front, there are three things to consider. First, the rate of non-OPEC production capacity is growing, and that's a good thing. In recent years, the former Soviet Union supply has began to increase after a few years of flat growth. This resurgence, however, has been principally from repairing tired infrastructure, and such a growth rate is likely to be hard to sustain. Now, here's the problem: Development is likely to be slow because of what appears to be renationalization efforts by the Kremlin. No foreign investors are willing to spend money where there are no strong laws to protect their assets. Additionally, West Africa,

Canada, and Brazil have seen another 0.5 million barrels per day annual growth in production capacity, but as in the former Soviet Union, this growth does not look easy to maintain. In fact, Nigerian production could peak by the end of this decade. Meanwhile, outputs from the United States and the North Sea are shrinking.

Second, the potential for growth in OPEC production capacity is becoming increasingly smaller. At the moment, most of OPEC members, with the exception of Saudi Arabia, are operating at near capacity, although it is difficult to ascertain what is really happening because OPEC production numbers are often inaccurate. The Saudis recently announced plans to raise output to 12 million or 15 million barrels per day in 2009, but several experts with deep knowledge of the Saudi oil industry have noted that the kingdom can't meet those supply levels. One of those challenging the Saudi estimates is Sadad al-Husseini, Saudi Aramco's former upstream chief engineer, who said in 2005, both at an oil conference in London and in separate interviews with Reuters news agency, that such a sharp increase would deplete reserves much faster than the kingdom would like.

Third, we have to look at how effective OPEC has been in managing supply. Since 1998, OPEC has been surprisingly effective in keeping supply well matched with demand, effectively keeping the world oil supply a little tight. This combination of strong demand, slow non-OPEC production growth, and effective OPEC supply management should get some credit for helping to drive world oil prices in recent years.

Long-Term Outlook

Over the last 30 years daily oil consumption has risen by approximately 30 million barrels, just under one million barrels per day each year, according to the International Energy Agency (IEA). In recent years, over one-half of the growth in demand has come from Asia. Asian demand—particularly China, India and South Korea—has grown by 10 million barrels daily in the last 17 years. Looking ahead, Asia is going to continue to be the engine of global oil demand growth. It is hard to see how it will not grow by at least a similar amount, if not more, over the next 17 years. In fact, growth is more likely to accelerate as Asia goes through the energy intensive stage of economic liftoff. If Asian oil demand were to grow at the same rate over the next 17 years, it will have grown by 27 million barrels per day by 2021.

To illustrate this point, you simply need to examine the potential for growth in the Chinese automobile industry. At the moment, domestic Chinese automobile demand is rising rapidly toward two million vehicles per year. There is a remarkable parallel between U.S. automobile demand in 1910 to the Chinese automobile demand today. Here are some statistics: China is producing one car for every 600 people, which equates to the U.S. automobile penetration in 1910. By 1920, U.S. car production and consumption jumped tenfold to one car per 60 Americans. If China's car production follows that same trajectory, it would equate to 21 million additional cars per year in a decade's time. That means China's automobile ownership would be about 210 million by 2015, and approaching the number of vehicles owned by Americans at 217 million. Given that U.S. gasoline consumption is about nine million barrels per day, it is easy to see how China's consumption can rise dramatically.

Based on 2005 data, the world is consuming approximately 83 million barrels of oil per day, with production at about 84 million barrels per day. That leaves a cushion of one to two million barrels per day, which typically gets lost in the event of a supply disruption, like the Venezuelan strike in 2003, the Yukos-Kremlin problem in 2004, and the Hurricane Katrina impact in 2005. I think that oil consumption worldwide, at current price levels, will reach at least 100 million barrels per day in 20 years. In fact, if my view of an increase in demand from Asia alone in the next 17 years will add an additional demand of 27 million barrels per day, then the daily demand will equate to 107 million barrels per day without any increase in demand from the rest of the world. The question is whether production will be able to keep up with that kind of demand. Not surprisingly, capacity can increase not only as prices rise to support additional production, but also as demand for oil slows with the

TABLE 1.1 Oil Demand Growth

Year	China	Asia exChina	Rest of World	Total World
2005	4.10%	0.79%	1.23%	1.39%
2004	16.88%	−2.90%	4.61%	4.40%
2003	13.84%	−4.50%	2.32%	2.01%
2002	5.78%	−0.74%	0.54%	0.65%
2001	1.58%	0.24%	1.11%	1.00%

Source: Oil Market Intelligence Numerical Data Source.

surge in alternative fuels. Further, the Hubbert Curve would suggest that at some point in the next few years the oil peak will occur whatever the price of oil, meaning that year-over-year declines of production are on the horizon.

The Hubbert Curve

As a framework for thinking about the world's oil production and supply, it is useful to understand the work of Hubbert, the Shell geologist who in 1956 correctly predicted that U.S. oil production would peak around 1966–1972. Oil analysts have applied Hubbert's methodology to world oil production and are predicting that world oil production will peak within the next several years, though they disagree on the precise timing. Essentially, Hubbert's technique was based on the prediction that the production level for oil as it was utilized would follow a normal distribution. Thus, if the United States had 200 billion barrels of reserves when 100 billion barrels had been extracted, U.S. production would begin to decline.

Assuming that the world originally had three trillion barrels of oil reserves, if two trillion has been discovered thus far and one trillion has already been consumed, then one trillion barrels would remain to be discovered. A peaking of oil production would occur after another one-half trillion barrels had been consumed, and this would probably occur in about 15 years, according to this analysis.

It is worth noting that Hubbert's methodology is based on a purely statistical analysis of exploration and production data. It does not take into account new developments like tar sands, which could potentially prolong oil supplies for a few decades, nor does it take into consideration emerging advanced production technologies. Still, Hubbert's theory is important because it provides a road map for the oil market; if demand is set to rise to 100 million barrels per day and there isn't the production capacity to match, oil prices can only move in one direction: up.

THE FUTURE OF ENERGY

As the world faces dwindling supply—and higher prices—for oil, there is a tremendous appeal to the idea of inexpensive, nonpolluting, re-

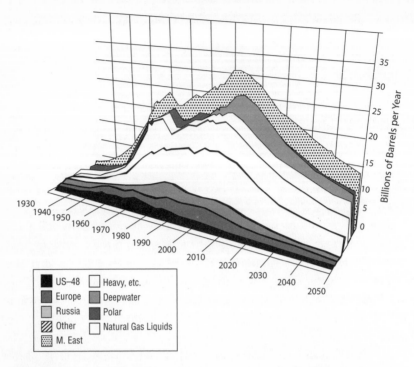

FIGURE 1.1   In the fashion of Hubbert, Dr. Colin J. Campbell, of the Association for the Study of Peak Oil and Gas in Sweden, has produced the above graph showing his estimate of the peak production year at 2008. Most economists think somewhere in 2035 to 2045 is the likely time for the oil peak. My estimate is about 2015 to 2020, which I got by simply calculating the midpoint of the predictions by geologists and economists.
Source: The Association for the Study of Peak Oil and Gas, C.J. Campbell, June 2004.

newable energy. As the cost of conventional fuels continues to rise, more attention will inevitably be paid to alternative forms of energy, all of which currently suffer from a combination of economic and technical drawbacks. Fossil fuels account for approximately 89 percent of world energy consumption, nuclear and hydroelectric account for about 10 percent, with wind, solar, and biomass accounting for about 1 percent. None of these alternative fuels represents a threat to the dominance of fossil fuels—at least not yet.

However, over the coming decade, as hydrocarbon fuel costs rise and as better technology reduces the cost of producing energy from non-conventional sources, alternative fuels will gradually become economically viable and may present investment opportunities. But until we reach that point, oil will continue to drive the planet. So if there's anything you'd want to get from this book, it is this: Tightening supply and demand for oil and other fossil fuels will nudge oil prices ever higher, creating perhaps the greatest opportunity for investors to acquire wealth in the new millennium—the equity ownership of the world's dwindling hydrocarbon.

"Saint" Hubbert to Disciples: Go Ye and Spread the Gospel

The current debate about oil peak is quite interesting. Because Hubbert's prediction came to pass, he became a patron saint among oil peak advocates. But most of his opponents have switched their argument. It's now not a question of whether he was right, but of how his theory applies in a global context. Does Hubbert's Curve matter in the wider global oil production matrix, and even if so, have new technologies not made his theory irrelevant?

Yet, some experts now agree that even taking all these issues into consideration does not change the central basis of Hubbert's argument: that oil is a tangible, finite commodity that must come to an end some day. What's really hard to pin down is when exactly we may run out of oil. There are many wild guesses that fall into two categories: Most economists who dispute the oil peak theory present the best case scenario, arguing that if it happens at all, then it could be 30 or 40 years away. On the other hand, independent geologists who support the theory, the so-called disciples of Hubbert, present a very bleak scenario, suggesting that the peak could be as early as 2008.[10]

The two most prominent disciples of Hubbert are Colin Campbell and Princeton University geologist Kenneth S. Deffeyes. The oil industry calls them pessimists because they are predicting "a permanent state of oil shortage." Of the two, Deffeyes is the greater pessimist because he argues that maybe in 2007—almost certainly by the end of the decade—the world's oil production, having grown exuberantly for more than a century, will peak and begin to decline.[11] Matt Simmons, a banker in Houston who knows much about the oil business, believes we are at peak already in 2006. After that, it really will be all downhill. The price of oil will increase drastically and major oil-consuming countries will experience crippling inflation, unemployment, and economic instability.

According to these scientists (and now a very few economists), it will take a decade or more before conservation measures and new technologies can bridge the gap between supply and demand, and even then the situation will be touch and go. Of course, none of this will affect vacation plans this summer, so Americans shouldn't fret much—you can plan beach weekends for a little while. Though gas prices are up, they are expected to remain relatively affordable to middle class Americans if incomes keep rising, at least for the next decade. Accounting for inflation, current gasoline prices, at an average of $2.50 per gallon, are pretty comparable to what motorists paid in past decades; it only feels expensive because gasoline was unusually cheap between 1986 and 2003.

As anyone would expect, the analysis by Campbell and Deffeyes is way off the much more optimistic official figures. The U.S. Geological Survey states that reserves in 2000, the year of its latest figures, of recoverable oil were a lot, and that peak production will not come for about 30 years. The International Energy Agency (IEA) believes that oil will peak between "2013 and 2037," and Saudi Arabia, Kuwait, Iraq, and Iran, four countries with much of the world's known reserves, report little if any depletion of reserves. Meanwhile, the oil companies (which do not make public estimates of their own peak oil) say there is no shortage of oil and gas for the long term. These conflicting views show that nobody knows the answer. "The world holds enough proved reserves for 40 years of supply and at least 60 years of gas supply at current consumption rates," according to BP.[12]

The industry is asking the public to trust it, arguing that every year for more than 100 years it has produced more than it did the year before, and predictions of oil running out or peaking have always been proved wrong. Today, the industry says, global production has hit 84 million barrels per day, with big new fields in Azerbaijan, Angola, Algeria, Nigeria, and the deep waters of the Gulf of Mexico and elsewhere soon expected to be onstream. But as everyone knows, the business of estimating oil reserves is contentious and political. According to Campbell, companies seldom report their true findings for commercial reasons, and governments, which own 90 percent of the reserves, often lie. Most official figures are grossly unreliable: "Estimating reserves is a scientific business. There is a range of uncertainty but it is not impossible to get a good idea of what a field contains. Reporting [reserves], how-ever, is a political act," Campbell recently told the *Guardian* newspaper in London.[13]

The two most widely used estimates of world oil reserves, drawn up by the *Oil & Gas Journal*, an industry publication, and BP's own annual sur-vey, *Statistical Review*, both rely heavily on reserve estimates provided to them by governments and industry, and, from what I hear, they do not question the accuracy of these data. Companies typically underreport their new discoveries to comply with strict U.S. stock exchange rules, but then revise them upwards over time, partly to boost their share prices by releasing good news later on. It's a form of cheating and they know it, but since it's industry-wide, no one bothers to question the practice. "I do not think that I ever told the truth about the size of a prospect. That was not the game we were in," says Campbell. "As we were competing for funds with other subsidiaries around the world, we had to exaggerate."[14]

Most serious of all, he and other oil depletion proponents, most of whom have been in the industry for years, accuse the U.S. Geological Survey of using questionable statistical probability models to calculate global reserves. They also accuse OPEC countries of drastically revising upwards their reserves in the 1980s. "The estimates for the OPEC coun-tries were systematically exaggerated in the late 1980s to win a greater slice of the allocation cake. Middle East official reserves jumped 43 per-cent in just three years despite no new major finds," Campbell says.[15]

Still, there are many who doubt the doomsday scenario presented by the likes of Campbell. Many economists, who comprise the majority of oil industry analysts, think production will continue growing for at least another 30 years. By then, substitute energy sources will be avail-able to ease the transition into a post-petroleum age. Daniel Yergin, who runs a consulting firm in Boston called Cambridge Energy Re-search Association, and Michael C. Lynch, who runs his consulting business, the Strategic Energy and Economic Research (SEER) in Winchester, Massachusetts, are two vociferous critics of the oil peak. They are considered stars by many in the oil industry in part because they are such prolific writers on energy, but also because they are well connected and run successful consultancies. They offer very strong ar-guments for their point of view, too. In the wake of Hurricane Katrina, however, the tone of the debate seems to be changing. Oil companies—particularly BP and Chevron—have released TV commercials that pretty much acknowledge the fact that we may be on the homestretch as far as oil supply is concerned. The main points they make are that they are doing something, they are concerned about oil depletion and global warming, and they are looking for new production as well as trying to come up with alternative fuels.

The interesting thing about this debate is that it's become political. Where you stand depends very much on which forces you consider dominant in controlling the oil markets. Is discovering more oil the only way to increase production capacity? And what about the fact that not much remains to be discovered, besides a few areas in arctic Russia, offshore West Africa, and Brazil. "The economists all think that if you show up at the cashier's cage with enough currency, God will put more oil in ground," Deffeyes told the Associated Press a while ago.[16]

One of the reasons this debate has become more intense is the fact that oil prices are high, which is a warning sign of what is to come, and it won't be pretty. Prices will rise dramatically and become increasingly volatile. And with little or no excess production capacity, minor supply disruptions—political instability in Venezuela, hurricanes in the Gulf of Mexico or labor unrest in Nigeria, for example—will send the oil markets into a panic buying and the prices will shoot into the stratosphere. So will periodic admissions by oil companies and petroleum-rich nations that they have been overestimating their reserves.

Here's the good part: oil producers—companies and countries—won't lose out. Instead, their boom will grow. On the other hand, because the price of oil ultimately affects the cost of just about everything else (and the economy in general), inflation like the kind we saw in the 1970s will return. If you've been paying close attention to the news lately, you may be feeling a little nauseated already. Does that mean that $6-per-gallon gas is right around the corner? You bet. We saw $5 gas already in the wake of Katrina in some parts of the country such as Georgia and the Midwest.

During Hubbert's time, he started his analysis by collecting data on how much oil had been discovered and produced in the Lower 48 states, both onshore and offshore, between 1901 and 1956. Alaska's oil wealth was still not known to petroleum geologists at the time. His data showed that U.S. oil reserves had risen rapidly between 1901 and 1930, then more slowly after that. When he graphed that pattern it appeared that

U.S. oil supply was about to peak. Soon, U.S. petroleum reserves would reach an all-time maximum. Then they would begin to shrink as oil companies extracted crude from the ground faster than geologists could find it. That was all right.

Hubbert knew that some oil fields, especially the big ones, were easier to find than others. Those big finds would come first, and then the pace of discovery would decline as the remaining pool of oil resided in progressively smaller and more elusive deposits. The production figures followed a similar pattern, but it looked as if they would peak a few years later than reserves. That also was convincing. In any case, oil can't be pumped out of the ground the instant it is discovered. Lease agreements have to be negotiated, wells drilled, pipelines built; the development process can take about 10 years or more.

When Hubbert extended the production curve into the future it looked as if it would peak about 1969 or 1970. Every year after that, the United States would pump less oil than it had the year before. If that prediction wasn't daring enough, Hubbert had yet another mathematical trick up his sleeve. Assuming that the reserves decline was going to be a mirror image of the rise, geologists would have found exactly half of the oil in the Lower 48 when the curve peaked. Doubling that number gave Hubbert the grand total of all recoverable oil under the continental United States: 170 billion barrels.

At first, critics objected to Hubbert's analysis, arguing that technological improvements in exploration and recovery would increase the amount of available oil. They do, but not enough to extend production beyond the limits Hubbert had projected. Even if you throw in the unexpected discovery of oil in Alaska, U.S. petroleum production history has proceeded almost exactly as Hubbert predicted it would. Contemporary critics of Hubbert dismiss the oil peak at their peril. "Even in 30 to 40 years there's still going to be huge amounts of oil in the Middle East," said Daniel Sperling, director of the Institute of Transportation Studies at the University of California, Davis.[17]

Yet the critics are missing the larger point. A few years ago, geologists began applying Hubbert's methods to the entire world's oil production. Their analyses indicated that global oil production would peak some time during the first decade of the twenty-first century. And so in the wake of China's robust demand growth, signs of global warming, and current high oil prices, the debate has intensified and probably shifted significantly from "if" there is actually going to be a global oil peak to "when" there will be one.

Wall Street should get concerned. Energy consultants John S. Herold, Inc. recently compared the stated reserves of the world's leading oil companies with their quoted discoveries and production levels, and predicted that the seven largest oil companies will all begin seeing production declines within four years. Deutsche Bank reported recently that global oil production could peak in 2014.

In 2005, The *Guardian* newspaper in London wrote about a U.S. government report on oil shale and unconventional oil supplies that seems to indicate concern among some government officials. The *Guardian* story quoted the report:

> World oil reserves are being depleted three times as fast as they are being discovered. Oil is being produced from past discoveries, but the reserves are not being fully replaced. Remaining oil reserves of individual oil companies must continue to shrink. The disparity between increasing production and declining discoveries can only have one outcome: a practical supply limit will be reached and future supply to meet conventional oil demand will not be available. . . . Although there is no agreement about the date that world oil production will peak, forecasts presented by USGS geologist Les Magoon, the *Oil & Gas Journal*, and others expect the peak will occur between 2003 and 2020. What is notable . . . is that none extend beyond the year 2020, suggesting that the world may be facing shortfalls much sooner than expected.[18]

I find it more useful to approach this global peak debate from a different angle, by looking at different producing regions, or oilfields, and when they are likely to peak individually. We know that by the same Hubbert analysis, the U.S. production, both onshore and offshore, has peaked. Similar patterns of peak discovery and production have been found throughout all the world's main oilfields, including in the North Sea. The first North Sea discovery was in 1969, discoveries peaked in 1973, and the British portion of the basin passed its production peak in 1999. The British portion is now in serious decline, while production from the Norwegian portion has leveled off.

Chris Skrebowski, editor of *Petroleum Review*, a monthly magazine published by the Energy Institute in London, says that conventional oil reserves are now declining about 4 to 6 percent a year worldwide. He says 18 large oil-producing countries, including Britain, and 32 smaller ones, have declining production; and he expects Denmark, Malaysia, Brunei, China, Mexico, and India all to reach their peak in the next few years. "We should be worried," he told the *Guardian* in 2005.[19] "Time is short and we are not even at the point where we admit we have a problem," he says. "Governments are always excessively optimistic. The problem is that the peak, which I think is 2008, is tomorrow in planning terms." Bill Powers, editor of the *Canadian Energy Viewpoint*, an investment journal, adds: "There is a growing belief among geologists who study world oil supply that production is soon headed into an irreversible decline. . . . The U.S. government does not want to admit the reality of the situation. Dr. Campbell's thesis and those of others like him are becoming the mainstream."[20]

Thus what seems to be indisputable is the fact that world oil demand is growing while supply isn't growing as fast. In the long term, the International Energy Agency (IEA), a Paris-based energy watchdog for rich countries, which also collates national figures and predicts demand, says developing countries could push demand up 47 percent to 121 million barrels per day by 2030, and that oil companies and oil-producing nations must spend about $100 billion per year to develop new supplies to keep pace. The IEA reckons that demand rose faster in 2004 than in any year since 1976; that may be due to additional demand growth from China and India.

China's oil consumption, which accounted for a third of extra global demand last year, grew 17 percent and is expected to double over 15 years to more than 10 million barrels a day, half of current U.S. demand. India's consumption is expected to rise by nearly 30 percent in the next five years. If world demand continues to grow at 2 percent a year, then almost 160 million barrels per day will need to be extracted in 2035, twice as much as today. That kind of demand is almost impossible to satisfy.

According to industry consultants IHS Energy, 90 percent of all known reserves are now in production, suggesting that few major discoveries remain to be made. Shell says its reserves fell last year because it found only enough oil to replace 15 to 25 percent of what the company produced. BP said recently that it replaced only 89 percent of its production in 2004. And Repsol downgraded its reserves estimate in early 2006 because of political problems in Latin America, where it has many assets.

All across the industry, reserves growth is falling below expectations. It seems that companies had better luck during the 1990s than today. In 2004 and 2005, publicly traded oil companies with reserves of over one billion barrels of oil had their reserves replacement ratio falling below 100 percent for the first time since 1991. That means they failed to get enough new oil to replace what they pumped out of the earth, which is the first sign of falling production. This is frustrating to many companies, and some of them no longer want to drill for new oil.

As a result, major companies find it easier to add reserves by acquiring smaller companies rather than through new drilling. In fact, the latest data from one drilling consulting firm, Evaluate Energy, shows that just 10 percent of all wells drilled worldwide in 2005 by large oil companies were exploration wells; that's a decline of about 10 percent from the 1990s, and the trend continues. Analysts say the reserves decline started in 1998.[21]

Moreover, oil supply is increasingly limited to a few giant fields, with 10 percent of all production coming from just four fields and 80 percent from fields discovered before 1970. Even finding a field the size of Ghawar in Saudi Arabia—by far the world's largest, which is said to have another 125 billion barrels—would meet world demand for only about 10 years. On the other hand, Equatorial Guinea, Sao Tome, Chad, and Angola are all expected to grow, although by how much is still unknown. There may still be more fields left in Africa, and probably one or two big ones in Russia, but these would have little bearing on world supplies. Unconventional deposits like tar sands and shale may merely slow the production decline.

Having talked to a number of economists and geologists, and based on what I know, I do believe the peak will be just a few years later than 2010 and earlier than 2030—and that puts my prediction at about 2015 to 2020. But I also think the exact date doesn't really matter and the fight between scientists and economists isn't worth it. That's because it's already too late for fights. The median lifetime of an American automobile is 17 years. That means even if the government immediately mandated a drastic increase in fuel efficiency standards, the conservation benefits wouldn't fully take effect for almost two decades. And while conservation would certainly be necessary in a crisis, it wouldn't be enough.

In an analysis done for the U.S. Department of Energy (DOE) in February of 2005, an independent energy consultant concluded that it will take more than a decade for the U.S. economy to adapt to declining oil production. "You've got to do really big things in order to dent the problem. And if you're on the backside of the supply curve you're chasing the train after it's already left the station," the consultant told the Associated Press.[22]

Still, mitigating the sting of decreasing oil supplies would require developing alternate sources of energy—and not the kind that politicians and environmentalists have in mind when they promise pollution-free hydrogen cars and too-cheap-to-meter solar power. If oil supplies really do decline in the next few decades, U.S. energy survival will hinge on the last century's technology, not this century's. The consultant's report for the DOE concludes that compensating for a long-term oil shortfall would require building a massive infrastructure to convert coal, natural gas, and other fossil fuels into combustible liquids. Those who support coal liquefaction, which creates synthetic oil by heating coal in the presence of hydrogen gas, refer to the process as "clean coal" technology. It is clean, but only to the extent that the synthetic oil it produces burns cleaner than raw coal.

Synthetic oil still produces carbon dioxide, the main greenhouse warming gas, during both production and combustion (though in some scenarios some of that pollution could be kept out of the atmosphere). And the coal that goes into the liquefaction process still has to be mined, which means tailing piles, acid runoff, and other toxic ills. Even so, nobody wants a "clean coal" plant in the backyard. Shifting to new forms of energy will require building new refineries, pipelines, transportation terminals, and other infrastructure at a time when virtually every new project faces intense local opposition.

CHAPTER 2

Consequences of an Oil Peak

IT WAS GOOD FOR A WHILE; NOW CIVILIZATION WILL BE TESTED

Our civilization has got to a point where it is almost impossible for us to imagine life without cars, air-conditioned rooms, hot showers, and electric appliances. And yet, there's a growing realization that such habits need to change because it takes a lot of limited resources to produce and run all the machines that make our lives easy and comfortable. All of our advances and problems are now manifested in rising fuel prices. We feel the strain at the gasoline pumps and in our home heating bills.

At the moment, about 89 percent of all of the energy used in the U.S. comes from fossil fuels—oil, coal, and natural gas. Nuclear power provides 10 percent of our energy and the remaining 1 percent comes from renewable fuels—sun, wind, and water, according to the U.S. Department of Energy. Our travels—and other forms of transportation—depend mostly on gasoline (for cars), with diesel fuel (for farm trucks), bunker fuel (for sea vessels), and jet fuel playing supplementary roles. But reliance on these fuels comes, literally, at a steep price. Oil prices, which skyrocketed from $18 to $75 per barrel in just four years, are not likely to get much lower in the long run, so we might as well get used to them.

Despite the irony, however, in time we may learn to love the aftermath of the pain. That's because as investors we are going to make money out of the situation, and in the long run we'll also find other ways of living without Middle East oil. If there is a silver lining in this petroleum gloom, it's the potential that high oil prices may spur individual and collective initiatives to reduce our insatiable appetite for oil. The consuming public, industry executives, and politicians all can contribute in equal measure to cutting back on our oil use. In addition, they all can help us tap new energy sources, consider alternative fuels, and promote cutting-edge technologies for more efficient fuel use.

We'll all be better for it. In the heat of the debate about energy security, a lot of things get mixed up. The question each one of us wants answered is pretty obvious, but the answer or answers are not, and often they will make us more uncomfortable because none of them provides the simple solutions we want. Still, we must face up to the challenge. Why are oil prices so high? Basically, it's Economics 101. Oil is a freely traded commodity, subject to the law of supply and demand. The global market, not the U.S. oil industry, sets the price.

In recent years, demand has steadily outstripped supply. For that, blame the mushrooming industrial growth of China and India. China is sucking up as much oil as she can get, and will soon use more than the United States, the world's largest consumer today. But that's just part of the story; it doesn't explain the problem in its entirety. There are also issues to do with a lack of adequate capital investment and, as we have seen in Chapter 1, resource scarcity.

Oil companies must also do their part, in light of recent huge profits, if they expect to stop conspiracy theories perpetrated by people who often know very little about the industry. Current absurd talk of a dark conspiracy by oil cabals to impoverish U.S. drivers and homeowners is unfortunate, but it is feeding off a historically negative public perception, which will only continue unless the industry and the government step up and address the problem before it's too late.

Today, the oil market is as good as it can be. With literally thousands of oil traders negotiating prices all over the world and demand hotter than ever, oil companies are raking in tons of money, and commodity investors are benefiting as well. Individual investors also should benefit. We can blame the Chinese for wanting to drive more cars, or blame ourselves for buying big gasoline-guzzling sport utility vehicles. But for the U.S. investor, what will help most is to invest in oil stocks.

NEGLECTING FUTURE PROBLEMS IS
A FAILURE OF LEADERSHIP

Since we are voters, the U.S. government should be responsible to us. We all have a right to ask certain things of it. On that note, we can ask Congress to take a few actions, including raising fuel-efficiency standards for cars and trucks as part of a broader effort to control explosive demand growth. I'm told that just a 10 percent gain in fuel efficiency would cut two million barrels a day from the nation's consumption by 2025. Moreover, tax incentives for businesses to purchase gas-guzzling trucks should be replaced with subsidies for fuel-efficient or hybrid vehicles. And Congress should push for more refineries—not one has been built in the United States since the mid-1970s, leading to higher gasoline prices.

Far more important, though, is for the government to come up with a more imaginative and creative national energy policy that would not only encourage energy conservation and diversify supply, but would also jump-start a major national initiative to cut our dependence on foreign oil. The federal government's inability to enact a broad energy policy to create alternative energy sources at least three decades ago has been justifiably called the biggest single U.S. policy failure of the past half-century. It has made the United States vulnerable to oil shocks from abroad.

I have often been reminded of a Chinese saying that basically translates into something like this: Long is not forever. In other words, everything comes to an end; it doesn't matter how long it takes. I've been covering the oil industry for a long time and I often talk with many economists about the status of the market. They are a very optimistic lot. I think that's fairly good because they deal with issues of wealth creation, except that when they let unreasonable optimism to color their thinking in such a sway that their only concern is the short-term financial benefits, then they run the risk of losing their credibility.

I say that because something new is happening in the modern world. For a long time, we've been used to classical economics championed by the likes of Milton Friedman. But there is a new breed of what one might call renegade economists whose focus is not based merely on competition alone, but also on community good. These economists, just like scientists, are now debating the consequences of a world with reduced petroleum supplies. They are asking, "Why can't we start preparing for the time when we probably won't have it?" Like geologists who are now calling our attention to an oil peak, these skeptics think the oil industry is taking itself for a ride by being overly optimistic that natural resources will stay abundant. Very soon, we shall see a shift in mainstream economic thinking from unbridled, red-hot free markets to something grayish.

Let's get back to the debate about peak oil and just assume that world oil production peaks in about 15 years. What will that mean to us, in concrete terms? It won't mean we'll run out of oil right away. It only means that net oil availability will decline at an annual rate of about 2 percent thereafter, and we should expect that supply will be down by 20 percent by about 2035, when world population will be doubled, along with fuel consumption. This is still speculative and things might turn out differently, including development of new technologies that would make life a little easier, but it's going to a huge problem. It's safe to say that the general progression of events points to a scary future.

In the last two years we have already seen a preview of this movie, in the form of oil supply not being able to keep up with demand. The result has been high fuel prices and a dent in the economy and in consumer confidence. It's important to remember that current high fuel costs aren't bad compared to what we should expect in the future. It will be a crisis when supply is so drastically reduced that it won't matter whether you have the money to pay for the fuel. As anyone knows, when money loses meaning because there's nothing you can buy with it, what you are left with is primordial existence.

It's going to be tough to deal with the impact on transportation, health, agriculture, and other development issues. In the event of a general power outage, think of what would become of our metropolitan subways, our hospitals, our farms, our offices, and our houses. Our economy depends so much on fossil fuel that a lack of oil without any alternative fuel sources would lead not only to a virtual crash of the economy but to total chaos. As James Howard Kunstler points out in his book, *The Long Emergency: Surviving the Converging Catastrophes of the Twenty-First Century*, the U.S. economy has gradually evolved from the use of solar energy to the artificial patterns of living subsidized by cheap fossil fuel.[1]

I'm typically an optimist and my view is that living off oil may not be as artificial as Kunstler puts it, but I have to appreciate his central point. He says that we depend on computers for work, for learning, and for shopping. That we are used to microwaving our food and using gas to cook is not in doubt. The systems we have developed in the West, he argues—systems that are supposed to improve efficiency—can't survive without some kind of energy, mostly fossil fuel energy.

Others have also noted that the financial boom of the early to mid-1920s was spurred by oil. The economy was propelled by automobiles as well as by the first great wave of suburban expansion.[2] Both generated enormous business activity in other sectors, from real estate to manufacturing. Some 8 percent of American households had electricity in 1907, and that number jumped to 35 percent by 1920. Car production rose from 45,000 units in 1907 to 3.5 million in 1923. Most important, the United States met its own oil needs from domestic production. The fact that oil was cheaply available here in the United States saved us a ton of money, which we invested in Wall Street.

But that oil boom also meant trouble for the farm economy, which got neglected as we moved toward industrialization during the mid-twentieth century, with exports of manufacturing goods to Europe just as the Second World War got under way. U.S. farms, which had done well by exporting grains to Europe during the First World War, began to hurt in the 1930s as mechanization led to an oversupply of farm products such as grains. Grain prices crashed, and the financial depression of the early 1930s gave way to farm depression later in that decade. The system we had depended on collapsed during the Great Depression. Some think the current scarcity of energy sources could push our economy toward a similar situation.

POTENTIAL COLLAPSE OF PUBLIC DELIVERY SYSTEM AND OTHER URBAN RUIN

Up until now, we haven't started thinking of what we can do to keep these systems running in the event that we run out of fossil fuels. In Kunstler's view, the reason we haven't invested in alternative fuels is simple: we have left the decision to neoclassical economists who don't think a crisis is looming. The result, he says, is that our economy will stop growing at some point in the near future.[3] In the past two years, high energy costs have cut growth by a small percentage, lowered consumer confidence, and impacted earnings of both the automakers and airlines. When the U.S. economy takes a major hit, we are likely to feel it—not only in our pocketbooks, but also in the social structures we have built—because of the potential collapse of services.

Change isn't going to happen overnight. The automobile industry is one of the most energy-intensive modes of transportation ever created. Car ownership in the United States, at 217 million, is the highest in the world. Because of urban sprawl in the south and west, in places such as California and Arizona, we have a social dependency on car transportation. The highway system, which was built in the 1950s, has only encouraged this urge to drive in a huge car alone. Millions of gallons of gasoline are being used in the process. In the decades ahead, there may be no need to build more highways because there won't be many cars to use them. We might be well advised to start moving toward a mass transit system even in cities that currently don't have one. The reason is simple: the need to conserve fuel is becoming greater by the year.

A study several years ago by Randall G. Holcombe of Auburn University in Alabama shows that the automobile industry would sustain by far the most significant damage in the event of an oil shock, due to either an embargo by producers or other supply shortages. Also, a large part of the economic damage is from a decline in the demand for output rather than as a direct consequence of reduced petroleum supplies. Holcombe considers this significant for two related policy reasons. First, it implies that even if policy makers could replace all of the embargoed oil, major economic disruptions could still result from an embargo or just from limited supply. Secondly, policies designed to minimize demand disruptions can achieve significant benefits at low cost, and should have a high priority in policy matters pertaining to embargoes. That's a powerful argument for early planning.

At the same time, modern passenger jets are getting bigger to allow airlines to carry more passengers on each trip. As the cost of jet fuel rises to a level that would make the airline business unprofitable, more airlines are likely to start using hydrogen. Some agencies have long-term plans, but they need more support. The National Aeronautics and Space Administration (NASA) is currently supporting research on hydrogen-powered aircraft. Experts say that if that research is successful, hydrogen potentially could become a standard fuel source for the commercial airline industry within the next two decades, although I have my doubts as to whether hydrogen, with its low energy, would ever be a better replacement for jet fuel. In any case, many airlines are going to go bankrupt in the meantime, taking down with them global trade. Airlines have been making nothing but huge losses in recent years because of high fuel prices. That could also affect how many products China would export.

A bigger problem would most likely hit the food industry. Currently, millions of Americans rely on cheap, mass-processed food. Ours is an overfed society, although the quality of the food we eat isn't great. We super-size every meal, and throw away more in a year than the continent of Africa would ever get to eat. All of that is because food prices are way too cheap, in part because cheap oil and gas changed the way we farm, by promoting mass production through mechanization—from the farm to food packaging.

U.S. government data show that since 1940, U.S. farm productivity has grown at the rate of 2 percent per year, roughly the same as the growth in oil consumption. Modern industrial agrobusiness has become more mechanized and is very energy intensive. As a result, the efficiency of food production has lowered the cost of food. But that's about to change, as the higher cost of diesel means farming and processing raw materials for our industries will be more expensive. A reversal to traditional solar-based farming would be less efficient, time consuming, and very costly.

Home heating during the winter and home cooling during the summer are mandatory things we are forced to do in North America, Europe, and Asia for our own safety. We don't have a choice over these because a lack of either can be fatal. Unnecessary deaths could occur in a hospital in the event of a power outage, or at a nursing home during a hot summer without air conditioning, or in apartment buildings during a cold Northeast winter if there's no home heating oil. In that light, serious and persistent fuel shortages could lead to an increase in mortality rates from extreme temperatures.

According to the Energy Information Administration (EIA), a statistical unit of the U.S. Department of Energy, residential energy use accounts for 21 percent of total national energy consumption, of which 51 percent is for home heating, 19 percent for water heating and meal preparation, and 4 percent for air conditioning. The rest powers lights and appliances such as refrigerators. We seem to take some of these things for granted because they are so easy to forget, but it's important to remember that fuels are piped and electrical power is wired to our homes and every other private and commercial building in North America and elsewhere. These pipes and wirings aren't ordinarily seen when we look around our homes; they work silently and predictably at the switch of a button or turn of a knob.

Home and office air conditioning is the product of natural gas or fuel oil powering power plants. Natural gas is also widely used in industrialized countries for cooking, heating, and producing hot water, and so limited supply would increase the cost of such services. In the developing world, most of the energy supply comes from coal, wood, and dry animal waste or biofuel.

Would we in North America be really happy with such an inefficient energy supply? That's very unlikely. How about our information systems that have created a service economy over the past two decades? In modern society, computers and the Internet have become essential to everyday life, whether in schools, at work, in hospitals, or in the military. Computers and the Internet are indirectly powered by fossil fuels, so a lack of oil would shift demand away from oil and to other sources, eventually causing the alternative fuel prices to go up. In the long run, therefore, information systems would be more difficult to expand and to maintain.

In the end, however, we'll all have to find some new ways of doing things without fossil fuel. We might want to make changes in our transportation systems and other forms of support infrastructure, according to Richard Heinberg, author of *The Party's Over: Oil, War and the Face of Industrial Societies*.[4] He adds that an energy-led collapse of the global economy is assured, starting with recession of a new kind—one that will last for a long time. As part of that economic ruin, the nation's electricity grid will also collapse because there won't be any funds to improve it. "The ultimate consequence will be a global depression worse than that of the 1930s," he says.

Other energy experts agree with him. Colin Campbell, a follower of Marion King Hubbert and one of the proponents of the oil peak theory, puts it this way:

> The scene is set for the Second Great Depression, but the conservatism and outdated mindset of institutional investors, together with the momentum of the massive flows of institutional money they are required to place, may help to diminish the sense of panic that a vision of reality might impose. On the other hand, the very momentum of the flow may cause a greater deluge when the foundations of the dam finally crumble. It is a situation without precedent.[5]

Campbell blames commodity investors, who are interested in making a quick profit out of the current tight market, for creating a condition whereby no one wants to prepare for the consequences of an oil peak. I'm not sure that's really the problem because even alternative fuel investments are becoming profitable as time goes. Nonetheless, I agree with the central point he's trying to make: that to survive the looming crisis, urban authorities will have to find cheaper ways to maintain water treatment and waste management to ensure high standards of public health.

Moreover, governments may be forced to cut their defense budgets so as to secure funding for more important social services. If and when we reach that point, all our social and economic infrastructure will collapse unless alternative renewable fuel sources have been found and developed.

There you have it; the oil peak will be marked by the decline of oil and all that depends on it, unless we find and exploit alternatives. It heralds the collapse of our financial system. Being an optimist, however, I'm focusing on the silver lining, which is that we may rediscover peaceful rural living, regionalism, diversity, and local markets, learning to live in better harmony with ourselves, each other, and our natural environment. The transition will be hard, of course. International and locals tensions will most likely arise as consumers compete for dwindling supplies and as city life becomes impossible.

I'd love to be encouraging and cheer you up with a hopeful future, but at this point it seems to me that the only good news is that you could make a ton of money from the current oil boom. Whether money alone will help you survive the impending energy crisis is difficult to tell. What is certain is that the coming oil crisis will not be temporary and it will have far-reaching implications for our social fabric—affecting our transportation system, our social services, our economy, and even our national security.

CHAPTER 3

Alternative Fuels

WHILE ALTERNATIVE FUELS ARE NOT THE PANACEA, PROMOTING THEM IS KEY

Last summer Jeffrey Immelt, chief executive of General Electric, came up with an idea quite revolutionary for an American business executive. Saying he wanted to change the way GE does business, Immelt introduced what he called "eco-imagination," an initiative focused on clean energy, which would make GE the first green conglomerate in the United States. GE executives would henceforth be judged by their efforts to save the planet as well as their zeal to make money for shareholders. Every GE business unit will be required to cut its emissions of carbon dioxide (CO_2), the main greenhouse gas that causes global warming.

The goal for the company is to cut overall emissions to 1 percent below the level of 2004 by the year 2012. The company will double its research funding by 2010 to come up with new technologies that will still allow the company to grow while cutting emissions. Immelt's plan came after a lot of research, but it was also forced by the realities of a changing marketplace—rising fuels costs, tightening environmental regulations, and growing consumer expectations that will spur demand for cleaner technologies, especially in the energy industry. All of these events have led to concerns about energy security throughout the Western world.

General Electric is not alone. British Petroleum (BP) and Royal Dutch Shell (Shell) were the first to stake a claim to alternative energy sources, and both have established big renewable fuels divisions. They have since been joined by a host of other companies, mostly in Europe. Wall Street is cheering them on, which itself is a 360-degree change from just a few years ago. Improved technology and an oil boom have created the best investing environment. The International Energy Agency (IEA), an energy watchdog for industrialized countries which is based in Paris, estimates that over $1 trillion will be invested in nonhydro renewable technology worldwide by 2030. That figure may be too low because by then renewable fuel use may be way up. Moreover, demand will increase as renewable fuel prices come down with better technology.

Right now, low net energy from renewable fuels and the high cost of producing them are the greatest impediments to renewable fuel growth. For instance, the cost of generating electricity from wind turbines is five cents per kilowatt hour and 20 cents per kwh for solar, compared with just three cents for conventional oil and gas. Better technology is increasingly closing that gap by making it cheaper to use renewable fuel even without government subsidies. In other words, renewable fuels are becoming marketable.

Oil still has an edge—it is a valuable commodity because it is versatile. It has more net energy than any other fuel and is easily transportable. In addition, it can be refined into many products—gasoline, diesel, heating oil, bunker fuel, propane, and fuel oil, among others. Oil fuels the modern world, and at this moment no other substance comes close to even replacing it. In its various product forms, it has a unique combination of many desirable and useful characteristics, including the fact that it's the basis for the manufacture of plastics, medicines, and paints. It's also true that the amount of energy we can command determines our living standard. Yet, in a world worried about global warming, high fuel prices, and the prospect of oil depletion, isn't it necessary for us to develop alternative fuel sources?

Surely that's part of risk management. Indeed, there are many nonfossil fuel sources we can tap—including renewable fuels. I once heard someone say that renewable energy is nature's gift to the world. I agree with whoever said that and here's why: They say we get it for free. It's not exactly that simple—we have to use money to make it commercially available for use. There is no clear definition of renewable energy, but it generally includes energy derived from natural processes that do not involve the consumption of exhaustible sources such as fossil fuels and uranium.

Many activists in the environmental movement have been touting renewable fuels as the key to our energy security, but business people don't agree. I should point out, however, that energy security—a euphemism for ending reliance on Middle East oil—is an illusion. And so we probably need to search harder for other solutions. We get so much oil from the Middle East that it would take many years before an alternative is found, perhaps in West Africa. The United States consumes about 25 percent of the world's total oil supply or about 20 million barrels per day, of which 55 percent comes from all over the world, including the Middle East. Meanwhile, renewable fuels account for less than 1 percent of our energy supply, and that percentage can be only modestly accelerated, which would have limited impact because renewable fuels have not yet proven to be economically successful.

You can see we still have a long way to go with renewable fuels. Large-scale hydropower is not a renewable, but hydro, wind and wave power, solar and geothermal energy, landfill gas, waste incineration, and biomass are. Environmental experts tell us that the resource potential of renewable energy, as set out in the United Nations World Energy Assessment, is more than sufficient to meet the world's energy needs. They talk of sustainability. That's a very popular word, but it needs to be clearly defined within a context to be meaningful. Business executives use it to champion their interests, just as environmental activists use it for their own purposes. Ideally, in our context, it should mean moderation, as in balancing the use of oil along with other alternatives.

One thing we need to acknowledge is that the transition to alternative fuels is necessary, but it won't be easy. It will involve more financial resources and time. Not all fuels are interchangeable, and most renewable fuels have lower fuel yields than fossil fuel. There is still no battery that can move farm machinery in the fields. Some sources of oil such as tar sands, found in Canada, and heavy oil in Orinoco, Venezuela, require a lot more energy to produce, so much that in the end their net energy recovery is considerably less.

In some places where I lived as a child, our lighting came from hydroelectric power generators, and I still think that's pretty good although rare in the United States, as most power companies switched to cheaper fuel oil and natural gas a long time ago. That only reflects the fact that the economics of renewable energy are still unfavorable compared to the cost of conventional technologies utilizing fossil fuels.

A large share of renewable fuel is noncommercial in the sense that its production and consumption do not involve a market transaction. Such noncommercial energy, typically in the form of firewood, charcoal, crop residues, and animal waste, is especially important in the Third World and accounts for the vast majority of the world's renewable energy use. Since it is very difficult to collect data for this sort of energy, it is typically not accounted for in conventional energy statistics. Commercial renewable energy is better measured, especially energy used in the production of electricity and fuel oil for home heating. The International Energy Agency estimates that such energy accounted for around 2.5 percent of commercial energy in 2002.

Some forms of commercial, renewable energy are well established and relatively mature. According to the IEA, global geothermal power generation capacity grew by only 1.8 percent per year between 2000 and 2003, with global capacity reaching 8.4 gigawatts; growth over the previous decade was a modest 3 percent per year (1990 to 2000). In recent years, significant growth in capacity in Indonesia and Mexico has been partly offset by the continued decline in U.S. capacity. Geothermal energy is used as a source of direct heat for industry or in uses such as district heating. Geothermal capacity of this kind is estimated to be almost double that involved in power generation.

Consumption of biofuel—which comprises ethanol and biodiesel or vegetable oil—in transport has risen in recent years; ethanol in particular is expanding in Brazil and the United States. Consumption of ethanol in the United States—roughly 220,000 barrels per day in 2004—is counted in U.S. oil consumption in BP's *Statistical Review of World Energy* as it is blended into gasoline. Ethanol use in the United States is only going to increase with a transition from MTBE-blended gasoline to ethanol-blended gasoline starting May 5, 2006. Brazilian ethanol (production reached about 250,000 barrels per day in 2004) is used as a pure transport fuel or blended with gasoline; it is not counted in Brazilian oil consumption in the *Statistical Review*. Biofuels in other countries, particularly in Europe, generally are blended into conventional fuels and are not separately accounted for.

Some other renewable fuels are relatively recent, but are now fast growing: for instance, wind power and solar energy. The rapid growth of wind and solar is being driven by a combination of technology advances and supportive government policy, which create a virtuous circle of expanding markets and falling unit costs. Data on renewable energy are not included in the main in *Statistical Review* because of problems with the

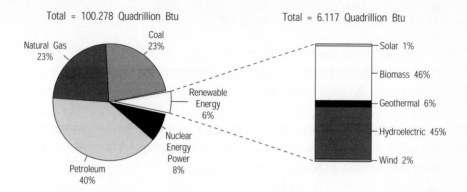

FIGURE 3.1   The Role of Renewable Energy Consumption in the U.S. Energy Supply, 2004
Source: Energy Information Administration, a unit of the U.S. Department of Energy.

completeness, timeliness, and quality of the data. However, the data on capacity included here help to illustrate some of the key trends in renewable energy. Renewable fuel use is growing because of government support and increasing private sector investment. Global investment in renewable energy hit a record $30 billion in 2004, accounting for 20 to 25 percent of all investment in the power industry, with solar power the fastest-growing energy technology, according to the nonprofit group, Worldwatch Institute. Technologies such as wind, solar, biofuel, and geothermal now provide up to 6 percent of the world's total energy, according to the U.S. Energy Information Administration. That's still very small, but it's a step in the right direction. On the frontlines of the alternative energy industry, business has been brisk lately. See Figure 3.1.

TYPES OF RENEWABLE FUELS

Solar Energy

This is the energy radiated to the earth from the sun. Solar thermal devices use direct heat from the sun, concentrating it in some manner to produce heat at useful temperatures. The amount of energy that reaches the earth and can be tapped for our use depends very much on time and geography. What that means is that there'll be more solar energy during the day than during the night, and also that the tropics—such as Africa and the Caribbean—will have more heat than polar areas in the northern hemisphere.

The modern solar industry has a long history, but began in earnest with the OPEC oil embargo of 1973 to 1974 and was strengthened in 1979 during the Iranian revolution, which took out of the market about six million barrels per day of oil from Iran. The growth of the U.S. solar industry during this period of fuel shortages and high prices (1974 to 1984) soared from 45 solar collector manufacturing firms to 225 firms, according to the U.S. Department of Energy. The solar market was helped during this period by federal and state government assistance. Currently, solar thermal devices do everything from heating swimming pools to creating steam for electricity generation. Photovoltaic devices use semiconducting materials to convert sunlight directly into electricity. Solar radiation, which is nearly constant outside the Earth's atmosphere, varies with changing atmospheric conditions—clouds and dust—and the changing position of the Earth relative to the sun. Nevertheless, almost all U.S. regions have useful solar resources that can be accessed.

Major U.S. oil companies haven't fully embraced renewable energy sources because of their low economic returns. It takes almost four to five times as much money to produce the same amount of energy from the sun as from conventional oil and gas. Moreover, solar has a lower net energy than oil and gas. Still, European companies are way ahead on this front. A good example is British oil giant BP, which is committed to creating a sustainable solar business that is both profitable and environmentally beneficial. In 2004 BP Solar took a major step toward this goal when it made a profit for the first time. It's important to note that happened because BP has a lot of experience—over 30 years—and installations in more than 160 countries. BP Solar is one of the world's largest solar companies—designing, manufacturing, and marketing solar electric systems for a wide range of applications in the residential, commercial, and industrial sectors.

Since 2004, BP has focused on key growth markets, particularly the United States and Germany, where it has rolled out new products and engaged in high-profile marketing campaigns. Sales of solar capacity have grown by more than 30 percent globally, consolidating BP's position as a leading player in the global photovoltaic market. This refocusing has given the company a new base from which to grow. In 2004, BP announced that it would be able to increase its renewable fuel supply capacity from 90 megawatts to around 200 megawatts by 2006. That's a re-markable achievement considering that the company's capacity was only 32 megawatts in 1999. BP Solar operates four major manufacturing plants in the United States, Spain, Australia, and India.

Wind Energy

This is produced when kinetic energy from the wind is harnessed by tur-bines to generate consumer electricity. Winds are created by uneven heating of the atmosphere by the sun, by irregularities on the Earth's sur-face, and by the rotation of the Earth. As a result, winds are strongly in-fluenced and modified by local terrain, bodies of water, weather patterns, vegetative cover, and other factors. The wind flow, or motion of energy when harvested by wind turbines, can be used to generate electricity. However, the amount of energy produced depends on the strength of the wind, although a too-strong wind can destroy the wind turbines. Wind-based electricity generating capacity has increased markedly in the United States since 1970, although it remains a small fraction of total electric capacity.

Wind industry, whose prospects were gloomy only a few years ago, is seeing renewed resurgence. In Europe, Denmark's Vestas Wind Systems and General Electric's wind subsidiary have huge backlog orders. Basic economics offers an explanation. As of November 2005, electricity (most of it generated from natural gas) sold at retail for about nine cents per kilowatt-hour in most parts of the United States. Clean wind-generated power, whose costs are offset by state rebates and federal tax credits, re-tailed for less than five cents per kilowatt-hour during the same period. Wind energy has gone from being the most expensive to the cheapest, and that's why wind-power companies in California, like Santa Barbara-based Clipper Windpower, which designs wind turbine technology, are seeing so much growth. Chicago, the "windy city," could more easily support wind farms than any other American city, but nobody wants to invest in the technology there.

Europe and Eurasia accounted for almost three-quarters of installed capacity of wind-power generators worldwide; Germany accounts for almost half of that. Installed wind-power generation capacity has in-creased more than ten-fold over the last decade, growing at an average annual rate of 30 percent. By the end of 2004, installed capacity amounted to almost 48 gigawatts capable of generating around 100 ter-awatt hours a year at typical load factors. Wind now accounts for approximately 0.6 percent of world power generation. Danish consultant BTM Consult is forecasting an increase in the world's installed capacity base to 117 gigawatts by 2009, implying average annual growth of almost 20 percent between 2004 and 2009.

BP's efforts are focused on the development of wind farms at existing BP refineries and petrochemical sites, many of which are in suitably exposed locations and can offer opportunities to blend new wind facilities into already industrialized landscapes. In 2004, BP jointly owned a 22.5 megawatt wind farm near Rotterdam, The Netherlands, completed its first full year of commercial operation, and provided sufficient clean electricity to power 20,000 typical Dutch homes and displace some 20,000 tons of carbon dioxide. BP is currently examining the feasibility of developing similar projects at other selected sites in Europe and elsewhere.[1]

Biomass

Biomass energy is derived from three distinct energy sources: wood, waste, and alcohol fuels. Wood energy is derived both from direct use of harvested wood as a fuel and from wood waste streams. The largest source of energy from wood is pulping liquor or "black liquor," a waste product from processes of the pulp, paper, and paperboard industry. Waste energy is the second-largest source of biomass energy. The main contributors of waste energy are municipal solid waste or feces, manufacturing waste, and landfill gas.

Biomass alcohol fuel, or ethanol, is derived almost exclusively from corn and is currently used as oxygenate in gasoline across the United States. The United Kingdom has unveiled plans to boost biofuel use by requiring 5 percent of all fuel sold on U.K. forecourts to come from a renewable source by 2010, which would amount to a 20-fold increase of current sales. The government says the measure will save around one million metric tons of carbon dioxide emissions in 2010—the equivalent of taking one million cars off the road.

The so-called Renewable Transport Fuels Obligation in the U.K. will operate in a way similar to an existing support mechanism for renewable electricity. It will require major oil companies and importers to ensure a growing proportion of their fuel sales are from a renewable source—ethanol and biodiesel in the near term, but potentially renewably-produced hydrogen in the longer term. Companies would receive certificates showing how much biofuel they had sold. Once they reached 5 percent, they could sell certificates to companies that had not reached the target. A current 20 pence/liter (9¢/gallon) tax break on biofuels will continue, and the result is a benefit to the environment because biofuels cause less pollution of the atmosphere.[2]

Municipal Waste

The municipal waste management industry has four components: recycling, composting, land filling, and waste-to-energy via incineration. Technology is available that can convert human waste and garbage from landfills into natural gas for any kind of use. Waste-to-energy combustion and landfill gas are byproducts of municipal solid waste.

Landfills contain organic materials that produce a variety of gaseous products when dumped, compacted, and covered. Here's how that energy is produced: Anaerobic bacteria thrive in the oxygen-free environment, resulting in the decomposition of the organic materials and the production of primarily carbon dioxide and methane. Carbon dioxide is likely to leach out of the landfill because it is soluble in water. Methane, on the other hand, is less soluble in water and lighter than air, so it is likely to migrate out of the landfill. Landfill gas energy facilities capture the methane—a principal component of natural gas—and combust it for energy.

Wood

Wood or woody plants are a substantial renewable resource that can be used as a fuel to generate electric power and useful thermal output. Wood for use as fuel comes from a wide variety of sources and is common in parts of the Third World, but is a major pollutant if not properly used. U.S. forestland, or timberland, is the primary and in most cases the original resource base for wood fuel. Wood for fuel use is also derived from private land clearing and from urban tree and landscape residues. A third of major wood resource is waste wood, which includes manufacturing and wood processing wastes, as well as construction and demolition debris.

Nuclear Energy

Nuclear energy comes from nuclear fission, a process whereby a large unstable nucleus splits into two smaller fragments. Nuclear power has made a comeback in the wake of rising oil prices and concern about oil sustainability, and that's good. Many people expect it to be the main source of energy in the coming years. However, the nuclear industry has been hurt by negative public perception, dating back to World War II when a nuclear weapon was used in Japan. These fears have been accentuated by recent accidents in the U.S. and the Ukraine. Concerns have been growing about safety, waste disposal, and weapons proliferation following deadly accidents at two nuclear plants, the 1979 partial core meltdown at Pennsylvania's Three Mile Island, and the 1986 accident in Ukraine's Chernobyl nuclear plant.

Of immediate concern to many people now are the ongoing wrangles between the United Nations and Iran over Tehran's nuclear program and attempts by North Korea to resume its nuclear program. People are concerned that the two countries could use their nuclear programs to intimidate their neighbors.

Besides those concerns, everyone agrees that nuclear power is without question a necessary means of diversifying fuel supply. In Europe, there is large support for it, with the French now discussing expanding their reactors, the Germans talking about restarting their programs after many years of suspension, and the British looking for ways of avoiding closures of some nuclear plants. In 2004, sixteen countries generated at least 25 percent of their electricity from nuclear energy. China and Brazil plan to build about nine new reactors. France's Areva, the world's biggest reactor builder, is attracting investors and customers, who are betting rising oil prices will trump all memories of Chernobyl. In the United States, nuclear energy is projected to grow 9 percent over the next 20 years. Given the projected growth in demand for electricity, the use of nuclear power, like that of coal, can't be ignored.[3]

Nuclear power got such a bad name, because of the Chernobyl, Ukraine, explosion that killed hundreds of people, it's no wonder few of those who oppose it know much about how it operates. This is how it works. In providing the power for a dynamo-electric machine, or electric generator, nuclear power plants rely on the process of nuclear fission. In this process, the nucleus of a heavy element, such as uranium, splits when bombarded by a free neutron in a nuclear reactor. The fission process for uranium atoms yields two smaller atoms, one to three free neutrons, plus an amount of energy. Because more free neutrons are released from a uranium fission event than are required to initiate the event, the reaction can become self sustaining—a chain reaction—under controlled conditions, thus producing a tremendous amount of energy.

In the vast majority of the world's nuclear power plants, heat energy generated by burning uranium fuel is collected in ordinary water and is carried away from the reactor's core either as steam in boiling water reactors or as superheated water in pressurized-water reactors. In a pressurized-water reactor, the superheated water in the primary cooling loop is used to transfer heat energy to a secondary loop for the creation of steam. In either a boiling-water or pressurized-water installation, steam under high pressure is the medium used to transfer the nuclear reactor's heat energy to a turbine that mechanically turns a dynamo-electric machine, or electric generator. Boiling-water and pressurized-water reactors are called light-water reactors, because they utilize ordinary water to transfer the heat energy from reactor to turbine in the electricity generation process. In other reactor designs, the heat energy is transferred by pressurized heavy water, gas, or another cooling substance.

The nuclear industry has seized on current high oil prices as an opportunity for rebirth. Nuclear advocates are working to reshape the atom's image from that of an environmental nightmare to an affordable and Earth-friendly energy source—and a hedge against future energy shortages. Nuclear expansion is the best hope, they argue, to cut carbon dioxide and other emissions that government and many industry leaders now believe are creating a perilous climate future. U.S. power consumption is projected to increase by 50 percent by 2025, and additional reactors would be the cleanest choice. The U.S. government is on board, with a 10-year, $550 million grant program called Nuclear Power 2010 that was started in 2001 to help with the costs of new designs and licensing. That's not enough. The government needs to do more. Recently, the government stepped up its contribution, with a new multibillion-dollar portfolio of financial guarantees and incentives.

Major provisions of the energy bill that President George W. Bush signed in 2005 include federal loan construction guarantees for up to 80 percent of costs. Production tax credits worth millions to a utility once its new reactor begins operating are granted in the energy law.

Utility liability is limited, and insurance help is given to new reactors by providing a larger secondary insurance pool. Whether the inducements will convince any utility that building a new reactor is financially prudent is uncertain. The Nuclear Regulatory Commission (NRC), the federal agency that's responsible for nuclear reactors, believes that a revival is imminent and has persuaded Congress to add $20 million to its $702 million budget for a new licensing division. The plan is to deregulate the industry and allow more utilities to build reactors at an estimated cost of about $2.5 billion per reactor. By 2015, at least two reactors could be built and up to 24 more by 2025, and other experts envision up to 100 more to replace and add on to today's 103 aging reactors. But these are just plans, and their success will very much depend on a number of factors, including their economic viability. The prospect of continued high energy costs due to tight supply-demand balance, however, suggests that the economics of nuclear energy have improved dramatically. In a Winter 2006 article in *Foreign Affairs* magazine entitled "The Rise of US Nuclear Primacy," scholars Keir Lieber and Daryl Press argue that the United States is improving its nuclear capabilities because it is deliberately seeking nuclear primacy. But whether or not U.S. nuclear modernization efforts are designed to fight terrorists and rogue states, there is no denying the fact that the result would in the end benefit civilian use of nuclear as an energy source. That's because the United States has lost its oil supply security with the rise of radical governments, like the ones led by Hugo Chavez of Venezuela and Mahmoud Ahmedinejad of Iran. Both Venezuela and Iran are major oil and gas suppliers and can choose to upset the oil markets, and often do, with adverse consequences to American consumers. U.S. nuclear supremacy therefore might help the United States meet its future energy needs while preserving a sound environment. Handled carefully, nuclear power can be a reliable and economic source of electricity.

Among those planning investment in nuclear energy is Dominion Nuclear, a Virginia company that has requested a permit to place a reactor near two units now operating. That will cost about $10 million for environmental and other studies. The permit would be valid for 20 years. Dominion has also formed a consortium with reactor-maker General Electric and contractor Bechtel Corp. to prepare an NRC application for a combined construction and operating license. Estimated cost is $450 million, most for the engineering to produce construction-ready blueprints. The Department of Energy has agreed to pay half, but the exercise does not commit Dominion or the consortium to build. Dominion Chief Executive Officer Thomas Capps has noted the industry's fears in widely quoted remarks that the financial risks of nuclear plants are so high that any company agreeing to build would face an immediate downgrade in its bond rating, which could markedly increase its borrowing costs.

NuStart Energy LLC—a second consortium of nine utilities, including Exelon Corp. of Chicago, Entergy Corp. of New Orleans, and Duke Energy of Charlotte, NC, along with General Electric and Westinghouse—has also won an Energy Department grant to apply for two reactor construction and operating licenses at a total cost of over $800 million. The agency is expected to pay half and the two reactors are expected to be operational by 2015.

A current concern in the nuclear power field is the safe disposal and isolation of either spent fuel from reactors or, if the reprocessing option is used, wastes from reprocessing plants. These materials must be isolated from the biosphere until the radioactivity contained in them has diminished to a safe level. Under the Nuclear Waste Policy Act of 1982, as amended, the Department of Energy has responsibility for the development of the waste disposal system for spent nuclear fuel and high-level radioactive waste. Current plans call for the ultimate disposal of the wastes in solid form in licensed deep, stable geologic structures, perhaps in the Yucca Mountains in Nevada.

Geothermal Power

Geothermal power is energy from the earth brought to the surface by hot water or steam. Underground reservoirs of water and hot dry rocks contain a lot of energy. This is how it's tapped: Hot water or steam extracted from geothermal reservoirs in the Earth's crust is supplied to steam turbines at electric utilities that drive generators to produce electricity. It can also be used for space heating or cooling, although the heat is low-to-medium. A geothermal heat pump draws heat from the ground or ground water and discharges it out. This ground temperature at 10 to 12 feet below the earth's surface stays relatively constant at 55 degrees Fahrenheit. A turbine is driven either from hot water or by natural steam or rock that drives its energy upward through a drilled hole or a pump. This type of energy has been used in the Big Island in Hawaii, but it's not very common.

Hydroelectric Power

Water is currently the leading renewable energy source used by electric utilities to generate electric power. Hydroelectric plants operate where suitable waterways are available; many of the best of these sites have already been developed. Generating electricity using water has several advantages. The major advantage is that water is a source of cheap power. In addition, because there is no fuel combustion, there is little air pollution in comparison with fossil fuel plants, and limited thermal pollution compared with nuclear plants.

Like other energy sources, the use of water for generation has limitations, including environmental impacts caused by damming rivers and streams, which affects the habitats of the local plant, fish, and animal life. In fact, many of the first commercial electric power plants relied on flowing water from dams—like the Hoover Dam in Arizona-Nevada or Niagara Falls in upstate New York—as their primary energy source.

Fusion Energy

Fusion energy has tantalized scientists for more than half a century as a possible source of limitless, reliable power. But the technology to create the power of a star on Earth and use it to produce electricity remains at least five decades away, according to U.S. government experts. In the same way that coal-burning plants sired nuclear power plants, researchers see fusion as the next step in the evolution of electric power plants. It's all about building a better firebox: a way to consume fuel efficiently to generate steam to spin a turbine and make electricity. Scientists see great potential in fusion power: It is run on special forms of hydrogen, a plentiful, low-cost fuel that produces no long-lasting radioactive waste.

Though fusion creates a nuclear reaction, which can only be done at 100 million degrees, which in itself is a problem, a fusion reactor cannot melt down as nuke plants do. The reactors use too little fuel to explode. And unlike coal plants, fusion releases no harmful greenhouse gases. The difference between today's nuclear power plant with a fission reactor and tomorrow's fusion reactor is how they create energy. Nuclear fission reactors produce energy by splitting atoms; fusion reactors create energy by fusing atoms.

Fusion research grew out of the Manhattan Project, the massive scientific effort during World War II that developed the atomic bomb. The atomic bombs dropped on Japan more than 60 years ago released energy by fission. At the time, scientists speculated that the fusion process could be harnessed to release even greater destructive power. After the Soviet Union exploded its atomic bomb in 1949, U.S. scientists started top-secret fusion research and, in 1952, they detonated the first hydrogen bomb.

Classified research continued on bombs and fusion reactors. But it became apparent by the late 1950s that creating a controlled fusion reaction to generate electricity was a highly complex problem. In 1958, at an "Atoms for Peace" conference in Geneva, Switzerland, the United States and the United Kingdom declassified their fusion research. Other countries followed suit. Since then, fusion research has been a collaborative effort among scientists around the world. In the following decades, scientists have made advances and technical progress. The U.S. government has spent more than $10 billion on fusion research.

After about two decades of talks, the European Union and five nations, including the United States, agreed in 2005 to pool resources and create an international test reactor in France to show the feasibility of controlled fusion energy production. The $5 billion experimental reactor is expected to be operational by 2016. The goal is to achieve a fusion reaction that will release more energy than is used and be a source of safe, clean power. In turn, that research is expected to lead to building a demonstration power plant sometime after 2035. Under this optimistic timetable, the hope is that a private company will build a fusion power plant by 2050 that would provide electricity to homeowners.

Natural Gas

Drilling for natural gas has surpassed oil in the United States, according to Bakers Hughes, the rig consulting firm in Houston. The United States consumes 60 billion cubic feet of gas per day. Gas is used for power generation (24 percent), residential home heating (25 percent), commercial building heat (16 percent), and industrial use (35 percent), plus nonheating uses, such as production of petrochemicals and fertilizers. These many uses of natural gas mean there's very little left for automobile fuel. Western Europe and Iceland have natural gas filling stations, but there are not many in the United States. Honda is planning to market natural-gas-powered cars in the United States, but the prices will be prohibitive. In any case, the more we start using natural gas for automobiles, the higher the gas prices will go. The good thing is that net energy from natural gas is equal to that from oil.

Coal

Despite the accident that killed 12 miners in Sago, West Virginia, in January 2006, and focused international media attention to the issue of mine safety, coal is enjoying a resurgence, in part because of rising oil prices, but also due to new technologies that now allow for gasification. Gasification makes it easy to transport coal, while other technologies are able to reduce pollution.

Yet, coal still has a bad name because of crude production methods of the previous century, which are no longer used in the West. Instead of a dirty, smoggy, acidic, and pollutant fuel, we can now use new technologies to clean it up. The good part is that coal supply is abundant in the United States, China, India, and Latin America, and it can be used to produce methane, which is easier to transport. More than half of U.S. electricity is produced by power generators run on coal. Total U.S. electricity sales are projected to increase at an annual rate of 2 percent through 2025. That means coal use and coal prices will increase as well. One other thing: The use of coal would help alleviate fuel demand from China, but only if China can introduce new technologies that would reduce pollution and improve safety. Currently, China's coal mines kill as many as 1,000 workers each year.

Coal production in the United States increased in 2004 by 40.3 million short tons to end that year at 1,112.1 million short tons (3.8 percent higher than the 2003 level of 1,071.8 million short tons), according to data from the Energy Information Administration (EIA). Although total U.S. coal consumption rose in 2004, not all coal-consuming sectors had increased consumption for the year. Coal consumption increased in the electric power sector by 1.1 percent and declined slightly in the other industrial sectors, while coking coal consumption dropped by 2.4 percent.

United States coal exports rose for the second consecutive year in 2004, while coal imports again increased to record levels. Total coal stocks declined during the year, as electric generators used their stock-piles to help meet increased demands and missed shipments.

The rebounding economy in 2004 and 2005 helped to drive up the demand for coal during the year. Although data show that total generation in the electric power sector (electric utilities and independent power producers) in the United States increased by 1.9 percent in 2004, experts at the U.S. Department of Energy say that coal's share of generation decreased by 2.1 percent, resulting in only an 11.2 million short ton increase in coal consumed in the electric power sector. Coal use in the non-electric power sector declined slightly by 0.7 percent to a level of 89.1 million short tons.

The average delivered price of coal increased in all domestic markets in 2004. The U.S. electric utility price-per-short-ton increase was 5.7 percent, while the increase was 3.9 percent for independent power producers. Coking coal prices had the largest increase for any domestic sector, increasing by 21.5 percent, while the price for the other industrial sector increased by 13.2 percent in 2004. Average open market mine prices increased by 11.6 percent.

There are numerous challenges to coal energy, mostly regarding transportation, safety, and the environment. Transportation of coal from the mine to the consumer continues to be an issue for the industry because the majority of coal in the United States is moved by railroads and river barges. In 2004 and 2005, record levels of commodities moving around the country by railroad proved too much for the system, causing delays in coal deliveries to several utilities.

At the same time, hurricanes and flooding on the major waterways, along with river lock repairs and sunken barges, disrupted deliveries. Off-line power plant operations were affected, as well as the ability of employees to get to the mines in southeastern coal-producing states. Legal challenges concerning mining permits and the levels of environmental review needed to obtain them still have not been settled.

The wide-ranging economic expansion experienced in China in the past two years drove world markets for many commodities into overdrive and helped to reestablish the United States in Asian coal markets. Coal prices have been rising since 2004, though not as sharply as oil has. The average open market f.o.b. (free on board) mine price increased in 2004 to $19.93 per ton, an increase of 11.6 percent over 2003, a price level not seen since 1993.

Conservation

Don't drive unless it's necessary and when you do, please try to car-pool. Change to more efficient light bulbs, and switch off lights behind you. These are some of the things we've heard recently from government and oil industry officials. The U.S. government has unveiled Energy Hog to promote conservation. It has become a popular thing to urge conservation, and almost everyone realizes that we could use less fuel. You could almost call it revolutionary for President George W. Bush, a former oil man, and just about every major oil company to urge conservation, except that conservation will only lessen our energy problem. Some progress has been made over the last 30 years. Today's cars use 60 percent of the gasoline they did in 1972, new refrigerators use about a third of electricity they did then, and it now takes half the energy it did 30 years ago to generate the same national economic growth rate, or gross domestic product. We've become more efficient, using just 5 percent of our disposable income on fuel, down from 11 percent some 20 years ago. But we need to do more.

PART TWO

THE MIDDLE EAST PROBLEM

CHAPTER 4

Is the Saudi Oil Supply Adequate?

HOW SAUDI ARABIA HELPED THE MARKETS COPE WITH PREVIOUS OIL CRISES

As the world's largest producer, Saudi Arabia is the single most important oil supplier and is the major driving force within OPEC. Even more crucial, it is the only oil supplier with a spare capacity of between 1.5 million and 2 million barrels per day, which gives Saudi Arabia a small arsenal to fight higher oil prices during certain limited occasions. In an oil market where supply is very tight, having any spare capacity, as the Saudis do, is golden. Perhaps the best sport analogy is of a boxer who can use both fists equally well; he is able to jab skillfully with the left, while reserving the more powerful right punch for the knocking-out moment. In that sense, Saudi Arabia is like the ultimate supplier of oil to world markets. It's like no other oil supplier, especially in the view of an insatiable consuming nation like the United States.

Saudi Arabia's oil production started in the late 1930s and grew steadily until 1970, when the kingdom became the world's largest producer. Today, the kingdom is enjoying its hugest oil boom, with revenues for 2005 at $156.8 billion, according to Saudi officials. Saudi Arabia has the capacity to produce up to about 11 million barrels per day, but actual production typically ranges from 9 million barrels per day to 10 million barrels per day, leaving a spare capacity of about 1.5 million barrels per

73

day. But the 1970s was a very tumultuous decade for the global oil indus-try. The United States, which had become an influential global power, experienced much of the transition. After the social activism of the six-ties, society became more self-absorbed in the seventies, a period charac-terized by the novelist Tom Wolfe as the "Me Decade." As the decade wore on, the U.S. worldview became uneasy, worried, and nervous, with continuing inner-city poverty, black anger, and rising urban crime rates. The Watergate scandal and the Vietnam War were still fresh in the na-tional consciousness. Narcissism and paranoia swept other parts of the world, as violence escalated in the Middle East, leading to the 1973 oil crisis, which nearly debilitated economies in the West. As the U.S. econ-omy slipped, drug use increased by the end of the decade. But on the positive side, the feminist movement grew stronger and helped improve women's working conditions, and the green movement became a major force in the United States and Europe.

Meanwhile, in the oil industry, changes were taking place as well. U.S. oil production peaked in 1970, as per Hubbert's prediction 20 years ear-lier, and the energy crisis made a return engagement in 1979. The 1973 oil crisis started on October 17 when Arab members of OPEC, during the Yom Kippur War, announced that they would no longer ship oil to the United States and Western Europe because these regions supported Israel in its conflict with Syria and Egypt. At the same time, OPEC members agreed to use their leverage over the world price-setting mechanism for oil in order to quadruple world oil prices. The complete dependence of the industrialized world on oil, much of which was produced by Middle Eastern countries, became painfully clear to the United States, Western Europe, and Japan, requiring Western policymakers to respond to inter-national economic constraints that were basically dissimilar to those faced by their predecessors. The oil crisis of 1979 was sparked by the Iranian revolution. In the wake of protests, the Shah of Iran, Mohammad Reza Pahlavi, left his country in early 1979 (he was allowed into the United States in October 1979) and allowed the religious leader, Ayatollah Khomeini, to take political control of the oil-rich country. The protests shattered the Iranian oil industry, and oil flow became more erratic and sometimes lower, forcing prices to increase as supply dwindled.

Saudi Arabia and other OPEC countries raised output to offset the decline, but even after that, world oil supply remained about 4 percent short. Still, the panic that resulted pushed the price far higher than would be expected under normal circumstances. In the United States, President Jimmy Carter ordered price controls, resulting in long lines at the gas stations. Many people at the time believed the oil shortages were artificially created by the oil companies to drive up prices, rather than created by natural factors beyond any human control or influence. Moreover, while shortages would be expected to drive up prices in a market economy, causing demand destruction, these artificial price controls only ended up maintaining demand at a level that couldn't be sustained by faltering supply. Many politicians proposed gas rationing, but that never happened. President Carter made symbolic efforts to encourage energy conservation, such as urging citizens not to turn up their thermostats, and installing solar power panels on the roof of White House and a wood stove in the living quarters. Carter made a speech arguing that the oil crisis was the moral equivalent of war.

Other problems piled on. By 1980, following the invasion of Iran by Iraq's Saddam Hussein, oil production in Iran nearly stopped, and Iraq's oil production was severely cut as well. Yet gasoline lines did not reappear in the United States other than in a few isolated incidents. Europe also responded to the two oil shocks by rationing gasoline and diesel supply to motorists. Europe particularly depended on the Middle East for oil, and in the wake of those shocks, rich consuming countries created the International Energy Agency (IEA), a policy secretariat based in Paris, to coordinate energy issues and to counterbalance OPEC. One of the biggest and most successful projects accomplished by the IEA was to urge consuming countries to keep some amount of oil in underground storage for emergencies, a policy known as the Strategic Petroleum Reserve. In the United States, these large tanks—salt caverns—are found in Louisiana and Texas.

Oil Crisis Helped Cement Saudi Friendship with the West

The most important outcome of the oil crisis of 1979 was that it gave Saudi Arabia a chance to step in and improve its relationship with the West. Before that, Iran was the best friend the West had in the Arab Middle East. Iran, under the reformist Shah Reza Pahlavi, was the most stable country in a region that had been volatile for decades. But that changed with the Iranian revolution. Iran under the rule of religious fundamentalists has never been the same, and relations with the West have remained frosty. By contrast, relations between Saudi Arabia and the United States have grown stronger despite challenges posed by the global war on terrorism. However, it's important to remember that even before the past oil crisis, the kingdom long had warm relations with both the United States and Britain.

The friendship between the Saudis and the United States can be traced back to a meeting between President Franklin D. Roosevelt and Abdul Aziz, also known as King Ibn Saud, in 1945, during which the two leaders briefly discussed the Palestinian-Israeli question, although it's not clear whether they also talked about oil. Yet, the importance of Saudi's oil potential wasn't lost on Roosevelt, nor was Aziz unaware of how much the Americans could serve to counterbalance the growing influence of the British in the region. In any case, FDR and Aziz got to respect each other, and one might even say they became friends of some sort.[1] The British already had established a foothold in the kingdom, and had close contact with Aziz's enemies, even as early as 1902, long before the founding of the kingdom. At the time, the area that is now called Saudi Arabia was inhabited by various clans and ruled by warlords. Two of the main warlords, Hussein in the west and Abdul Aziz in the center and east, were British protégés supported by regular allowances from the British government. Hussein was King of Hejaz, while Aziz was lord of Nejd, and the two hated each other. They quarreled over oasis centers in Khurma and Turaba at the borders of their clans.

The stakes were high because whoever controlled both oasis centers also had access to grazing land for camels, which was very important for each of the pastoralist clans that survived on their animals. Moreover, sectarian differences between the two clans made relationships there highly volatile. Hussein was an orthodox Sunni, while Ibn Saud was the hereditary champion of the teachings of Muhammad Ibn Abdul Wahhab, a puritanical religious leader whose alliance with the House of Saud started in 1745. David Fromkin, in his book *A Peace to End All Peace*, writes that in early 1918, the *Arab Bulletin* had recorded Hussein's complaints that his authority was being undermined by sectarian provocations by Ibn Saud's followers. Hussein complained that he was spending a lot of resources on defending himself against Ibn Saud's marauding attackers.[2]

What's interesting to note during this period is that the Wahhabist movement took root very quickly at the end of 1910, leading to a sudden shift in lifestyle. The tribesmen sold their horses, camels, and other possessions in order to settle in cooperative agricultural communities and live a strict Wahhabi religious life. This wasn't lost on Ibn Saud, who was aware of the changing political moods and decided to harness their energies for his political ends. He very quickly installed himself as the leader of the Wahhabis, with sectarian warriors at his disposal. His authority grew as he conquered neighboring clans, one after another, over the next 30 years until he finally declared the founding of the Kingdom of Saudi Arabia on September 22, 1932, in the Arabian Peninsula. Those conquered were forced to adopt Wahhabism and to join his expanding army. Ibn Saud ruled his new kingdom until his death in 1953. Ever the strategist, he became friends with both President Roosevelt and British Prime Minister Winston Churchill during World War II and met with both leaders a couple of times, including one famous meeting in 1945 on the USS Quincy.[3]

There's a great deal of debate as to whether and how Ibn Saud was involved in the development of the kingdom's oil. For a long time, scholars gave much of the credit to Americans, the British, and Australian friends of the king. But that perception is changing. Many scholars have come to believe that the king skillfully manipulated both friends and foes to achieve his goals. He had the vision to recognize early that he could use his contacts with foreigners to build a state, and he gave initial authority for the development of the oil industry in his country.[4]

Matt Simmons, in his book *Twilight in the Desert: The Coming Saudi Oil Shock and the World Economy*, writes:

> A series of advisors and quasi-advisors such as New Zealand's Major Frank Holmes, the Arabist Harry St. John Philby, the American philanthropist Charles Crane of the Crane Plumbing fortune, the Vermont mining engineer Karl Twitchell and a group of Standard Oil Company of California geologists all played an important role in convincing Abdul Aziz to grant oil concessions that ultimately led to the discovery of the world's greatest collection of super-giant oilfields. But the king played a canny role in orchestrating the early development of Saudi Arabian oil resources.[5]

Simmons adds that when Abdul Aziz became king, the need for revenue was so urgent at the height of the depression that he was ready to sell oil concessions to foreign oil companies. The first discussions about prospecting for oil in the kingdom took place in 1923, when Holmes visited Aziz and insisted there was oil in the Arabian Peninsula. Holmes had been to the area before as part of the British army that had marched on Jerusalem and Damascus in World War I. At the time, no one knew much about the geology of the Arabian Peninsula, but Holmes had heard of oil seepage in the Persian Gulf, and so after the war he organized syndicates to find oil in the region. He obtained the first oil concession in the kingdom's Eastern Province and also in Kuwait and in Bahrain. Initially, he started with drilling for oil in Bahrain, but without money he wasn't making much headway. He tried to borrow some money to finance his drilling projects. Eventually, he sold the business to Standard Oil of California (SOCAL), which, after finding not much oil in Bahrain, turned its attention to Saudi Arabia. In 1933, SOCAL was granted oil concessions in Saudi Arabia and that set the groundwork for the kingdom's current position as the world's largest oil producer.[6]

Today, Saudi Arabia can produce up to 11 million barrels per day of oil, including between 1.5 and 2 million barrels per day of spare capacity—an excess amount by which it can supply the market if needed. The kingdom's data for oil reserves are shrouded in secrecy, but the industry typically uses the figures published by industry publication *Oil & Gas Journal*. The *Journal* puts Saudi Arabia's proven oil reserves at 261.9 billion barrels, and that includes 2.5 billion barrels in the Saudi-Kuwaiti Divided, also known as the Neutral Zone. That means the kingdom has nearly a quarter of proven, conventional world oil reserves. Some two-thirds of Saudi reserves are considered "light" or "extra light" grades of oil, with the rest either "medium" or "heavy."[7] There is very little difference between these despite the names, as all of Saudi oil has high sulfur content. Calling some of its crude light or extra light is purely a marketing ploy to appeal to foreign customers, because most refiners like light sweet crude. Lighter grades generally are produced onshore, while medium and heavy grades come mainly from offshore fields.

LEADERSHIP AND SECURITY CHALLENGES
FACING SAUDI ARABIA

Saudi Arabia has about 80 known oil fields and 20 to 22 gas fields (and over 1,000 wells), but more than half of its oil reserves are contained in only eight giant fields, including Ghawar and Safaniya. Ghawar is the world's largest oil field, the so-called king of oilfields, with estimated remaining reserves of 70 billion barrels, according to the EIA. Ghawar's main producing structures are, from north to south: Ain Dar, Shedgum, Uthmaniyah, Hawiyah, and Haradh. Ghawar alone accounts for about half of Saudi Arabia's total oil production capacity. Safaniya, on the other hand, is the world's largest offshore oilfield, with estimated reserves of 35 billion barrels, according to the EIA. Despite its gargantuan oil reserves, the kingdom is not only located in the politically volatile Gulf region, but also its internal political situation is becoming increasingly volatile because of growing public discontent, which could only get worse following the death in 2005 of King Fahd.

New King Abdullah is in his 80s, and at some time soon leadership will have to change to another one of the many Saudi princes, a situation that might cause instability and could be utilized by terrorists to cause more havoc in Middle East politics. That should be of great concern to Saudi's major customers, including the United States. A few years ago I had a long discussion with one of the many Saudi princes in England. We were classmates in a media law course at Oxford's centre for socio-legal studies, and during one of the many private chats we had, he told me that the ruling monarch in Saudi Arabia typically doles out cash to the various tribal leaders, and then goes behind the tribal leaders to find out whether they are sharing the money with the rest. It was very clear to me from those discussions that the monarch survives by pitting the various Saudi clans against each other and by bribing most of the clan leaders. In any case, the prince agreed that the grip that the monarch used to have on his subjects is tenuous right now, something that I heard again from Ahmed Khelil, the Algerian oil minister, whom I met at Columbia University in New York during the summer of 2005.

Don't get me wrong; Khelil is a diplomat and a suave operator who has dealt many times with the Western media, so he wouldn't be careless when reporters are around. On this occasion, Khelil was talking generally about the tenuous political situation in the Middle East, which has tons of oil money but lacks democratic governance. He didn't explicitly say that the Saudi monarchy was in danger of crumbling, but he was clear about the fact that the Saudi monarch bribes local tribes, which he thought wasn't a sustainable way of dealing with the political problems facing the region, including Saudi Arabia. Still, given the fact that

Osama bin Laden is more popular in Saudi Arabia than the monarch and has a huge following in the region, we can't rule out a revolution in the kingdom at some point if matters get worse. There have been numerous terrorist attacks on foreign targets—foreign embassies and apartment buildings where expatriate workers live—in the kingdom over the past three years, not to forget the Khobar Towers attack in the summer of 1996.

The Khobar Towers bombing remains by far the deadliest attack in Saudi Arabia by a terror group. Khobar is part of a housing complex in the city of Khobar, near the national oil company Saudi Aramco headquarters of Dhahran. In 1996, it was being used to house foreign military personnel, including Americans. On June 25, terrorists identified by the United States at the time as members of Hezbollah exploded a fuel truck adjacent to Building Number 131 in the housing complex. This eight-story building housed United States Air Force personnel from the 4404th Wing, primarily from a deployed rescue squadron and deployed fighter squadron. In all, 19 U.S. servicemen and one Saudi were killed and 372 wounded. This event has come to be known as the Khobar Towers bombing.

According to the United States, a group of terrorists who wanted to remove Americans from Saudi Arabia organized the attack. They smuggled explosives into Saudi Arabia from Lebanon. They purchased a fuel truck in Saudi Arabia and converted it into a bomb. It contained 3,000 to 5,000 pounds of explosives. Initially, the attackers attempted to enter the compound at the main checkpoint. When they were denied, at around 10 p.m., they drove three vehicles, two cars and the bomb truck, to a parking lot adjacent to Building Number 131. A chain link security fence separated the parking lot from the compound. Building Number 131 was adjacent to the fence. The first car entered the parking lot and signalled the others by flashing headlights. The bomb truck and a getaway vehicle followed shortly after. The men parked the truck next to the fence and left in the third vehicle. The bomb exploded between three and four minutes later.

An American sentry, Air Force Staff Sergeant Alfredo R. Guerrero, was stationed atop Building Number 131. He saw the men, recognized it as a threat, reported it to security, and began evacuating the building. His action is credited with saving dozens of lives. Many of the evacuees were in the stairwell when the bomb went off. The stairwell was on the side of the building away from the truck bomb, perhaps the safest location in the building. For his actions Staff Sergeant Guerrero was awarded the Airman's Medal, the United States' highest peacetime award for valor.

Another measure is also thought to have minimized damage. Along the security fence were Jersey barriers, concrete barriers commonly used along roadways. These deflected the blast from the lower floors of the building, perhaps preventing a total collapse. The force of the explosion was enormous. It heavily damaged or destroyed six high-rise apartment buildings in the complex. Windows were shattered in virtually every other building in the compound and in surrounding buildings up to a mile away. A large crater, 85 feet wide and 35 feet deep, was left where the truck had been. The blast was even felt some 20 miles away in the Persian Gulf state of Bahrain. On June 21, 2001, an indictment was issued in U.S. District Court in Alexandria, Virginia, charging the following people with murder, conspiracy, and other charges related to the bombing:

- Ahmed Ibrahim Al-Mughassil
- Abdelkarim Hussein Mohamed Al-Nasser
- Ali Saed Bin Ali El-Hoorie
- Ibrahim Salih Mohammed al-Yacoub
- Nine other Saudis
- One Lebanese man listed as "John Doe"

The remaining five were Sa'ed Al-Bahar, Saleh Ramadan, Ali Al-Marhoun, Mustafa Al-Mu'alem, and Fadel Al-Alawe. In 2004, the 9/11 Commission noted the possibility that Osama bin Laden may have helped the group, possibly by helping to obtain explosives, and there is strong evidence that the government of Iran was the key sponsor of the incident. So, briefly stated, another major attack on Saudi Arabian infrastructure or, even worse, a revolution in the kingdom, could very well bring another oil shock in the near future.

RELIABILITY OF SAUDI OIL DATA QUESTIONED

Saudi Arabia maintains crude oil production capacity of about 11 million barrels per day, and recently has been claiming that she was "easily capable" of producing more. In June 2005, Saudi Aramco's senior vice president of gas operations, Khalid al-Falih, said that Saudi Arabia would raise production capacity to more than 12 million barrels per day by 2009, and then possibly to 15 million barrel per day "if the market situation justifies it." Falih added that by 2006, Saudi Arabia would have 90 drilling rigs in the kingdom, more than double the number of rigs operating in 2004.

But there are many doubters in the industry and they argue that just about anything the Saudis say should be taken with a grain of salt. And even if the Saudis are right, their plans would be undermined by the fact that production from the existing fields is falling, according to the U.S. Energy Information Administration.[8] That means the country needs about 500,000 to 1 million barrels per day in new capacity each year just to compensate. State-owned oil company Saudi Aramco estimates that the average total depletion for Saudi oil fields is 28 percent, with the giant Ghawar field having produced 48 percent of its proved reserves. But Aramco claims that, if anything, their oil reserves are underestimated, not overestimated. Some outside analysts, notably Matt Simmons, have disputed Aramco's optimistic assessments of Saudi oil reserves and future production, pointing to, among other things, more rapid depletion rates and a higher "water cut" than the Saudis report.

Saudi Arabia's production volume changes from time to time, but ranges between 9 and 11 million barrels per day. For January to July 2005, the U.S. Energy Information Administration estimated that Saudi Arabia produced about 10.9 million barrels per day of total oil. That includes crude oil, natural gas liquids, and "other liquids," as well as half of the production from the Saudi-Kuwaiti Divided Zone's 610,000 barrels per day. This was up sharply from Saudi Arabia's 8.5 million barrels per day of total oil production in 2002. In addition to crude oil, Saudi Arabia produces about 1.3 million barrels per day of natural gas liquids (NGL) and "other liquids," not subject to OPEC quotas.

The Ghawar field is the main producer of 34° API Arabian Light crude, while Abqaiq, a super-giant field with 17 billion barrels of proven reserves, produces 37° API Arab Extra Light crude. Since 1994, the Hawtah Trend (also called the Najd fields), which includes the Hawtah field and smaller satellites (Nuayyim, Hazmiyah) south of Riyadh, has been producing about 200,000 bbl/d of 45°–50° API, 0.06 percent sulfur, Arab Super Light. Offshore production includes Arab Medium crude from the Zuluf (over 500,000 bbl/d capacity) and Marjan (270,000 bbl/d capacity) fields and Arab Heavy crude from the Safaniya field. Most of Saudi oil production, except for "extra light" and "super light," is considered "sour," containing relatively high levels of sulfur, and therefore not very well liked by the market.

Saudi Arabia's long-term goal is to further develop its lighter crude reserves, including the Shaybah field, located in the remote Empty Quarter area bordering the United Arab Emirates. In the spring of 2005, Saudi Arabia announced plans to increase its oil production capacity significantly. Coming at a time of tight oil supply and high fuel prices undermining economic growth, the U.S. government openly embraced that Saudi plan, but privately, they are skeptical about some of those forecasts. As oil prices have climbed over the last few years amid surging demand and tight supplies, U.S. leaders have always looked to Saudi Arabia to produce more oil so as to keep fuel prices from rising and becoming a political issue. But there are many within and outside the Bush administration who now doubt Saudi Arabia's ability to keep its promise of expanding capacity. In fact some industry analysts now treat the kingdom's assurances as not credible. And some of those doubts have been raised in a secret intelligence report and in a separate analysis by a leading government oil adviser, a federal government official who is an oil expert recently told the *New York Times*.

Moreover, the White House's expectations about oil supply from Iraq and the United Arab Emirates have been overly optimistic. The *New York Times* reported that Bush rejected the advice of credible experts who advised against relying on Iraq and the UAE for oil.[9] As everyone knows by now, Iraq is the greatest disappointment for President Bush, since its oil production will continue to be erratic for years to come. Even worse, the challenges facing President Bush on energy come at a time when oil companies are reporting record profits due to soaring prices for oil and natural gas. All of that became a political issue that the president's opponents used against him at a time when almost everything seemed to be going wrong for him: the rising death toll from the war in Iraq, the slow response to Hurricane Katrina, high fuel costs, and political scandals that tainted some White House staffers.

On top of all that, oil companies (both President Bush and Vice President Cheney are former oil executives) are now flush with money. Consider this: Exxon Mobil, the world's largest private oil company, reported a quarterly profit of $9.9 billion in October, more than companies such as Intel and Time Warner earn in a full year. When he was asked about the profits, Scott McClellan, White House press secretary, couldn't hide his embarrassment, and all he could say was that the government and the private sector both have a role to play in restoring the vital infrastructure damaged by the hurricanes along the Gulf of Mexico. At the time, gasoline prices had spiked about 20 percent after Hurricane Katrina in late August and further strained oil markets that were already tight because of the unusually low levels of spare capacity. What many White House correspondents didn't understand was that when it comes to the price of oil, there's very little the administration can do, apart from releasing government oil stored in the Strategic Petroleum Reserve (SPR) caverns in Louisiana and Texas. But releasing SPR oil is only a very temporary measure. The oil market is so global that permanent solutions to supply crunches will take time.

Even U.S. companies are limited on what they can do about supply. The world's major oil producing countries, particularly Saudi Arabia and Mexico, have kept out private foreign companies. International oil companies combined have access to just 80 percent of world reserves, and many of them are incareasingly dependent on collaboration with national or domestic oil companies of producing countries to access some of the world's oil reserves. At an oil conference in London in the fall of 2005, which was organized by Energy Intelligence, Abdallah Jumah, president and chief executive of Saudi Aramco, the kingdom's state oil monopoly, summed up the Saudi view on investment this way: "On the upstream side—particularly on the oil side—we have seen that really there isn't a need to have international companies involved."[10] What he suggested was that the Saudis wanted to keep information about Saudi geology and whatever production numbers were achievable secret. So what they are only free to do is to allow foreigners to develop the downstream—refineries and pipelines—but not to help with production of oil.

Given that kind of logic, it is clear that whatever the political repercussions from high energy costs, the Bush administration has no choice but to rely on the promises by Saudi Arabia that it will continue to provide the market with whatever is needed. Meanwhile, the market is aware that the Saudis have only 1.5 to 2 million barrels per day of spare capacity, and promises to expand that spare capacity would take a long time to be fulfilled, perhaps not until 2009. In fact, a senior U.S. intelligence official told the *New York Times* that the Saudi plans to increase production by nearly 14 percent in the next four years were not enough to meet global demand.[11]

U.S. OFFICIALS SET THEIR EYES ON IRAN
AND IRAQ FOR OIL SUPPLY

The U.S. government is now lowering its expectations about the kind of help the Saudis may offer with regard to raising oil production. The Energy Information Administration, a statistical unit of the Department of Energy, has scaled back its expectations of how much more oil the Saudis could pump in 20 years. To be sure, there is more to President Bush's energy policy than seeking to ensure surplus capacity. Bush has called for increasing domestic production and construction of more refineries in former military bases, development of alternative and renewable fuels, expanding nuclear energy, and greater consumer conservation. But Persian Gulf countries will continue to be most important in cooling an overheated market in the future. During the 2000 presidential campaign, when high gasoline prices were an issue, Bush, who was then governor of Texas, pledged to influence Persian Gulf producers to pump more oil if elected president.[12]

At the beginning of the Bush administration, White House officials were mostly concerned about ensuring that the Saudis produced more oil during the anticipated war in Iraq. And even before the Iraq war, Saudi spare capacity—what they can produce over and above the nine million barrels they typically pump daily—seemed adequate. But now it isn't, and with Iraq supply still erratic, a knowledgeable source told me recently that the administration may be trying to find ways to reach out to other producers, including Iran, which will be tricky. The idea is that Tehran won't be provoked into reducing its oil supply because that will unsettle the world oil market the same way it did a quarter of a century ago.

Senior administration officials are concerned about the new belligerent president of Iran, but they don't want to do anything that might cause him to flip and destabilize the oil market in a way that could threaten world economy, at a time when the market is already sensitive to any slight disruption because of limited spare capacity. It should be understood that this is not the first time administration officials have tried to reach out to Iran. Before the 2000 election, Dick Cheney, who was then chief executive of Halliburton, campaigned to have U.S. government sanctions against Iran lifted. In the summer of that year, just a few weeks before he was chosen by then Gov. Bush as the vice presidential candidate, Cheney told an oil conference in Calgary, Canada, which

I attended, that the sanctions were hurting American companies as well as the oil market.

Many people at the conference, including me, thought at the time that he was only trying to have Iran opened up for Halliburton, but in fact he was thinking far beyond that. It is easy now to connect his position at the time with the move to get the United States away from dependence on Saudi oil—the argument being that establishing dominance over, or at least a relationship with, Iran and Iraq would ensure a steady supply of oil for a long time. Unfortunately, the terrorist attacks on the United States on September 11 forced the plans to be changed due to the political climate. Nobody wanted to be involved with a country that had been identified as part of the "axis of evil."

Cheney's plans, supported by the oil industry, became part of the U.S. energy policy, which he started writing as soon as the Bush team took over in 2001 with him as vice-president. On April 19, 2001, reporters Peter Behr and Alan Sipress of the *Washington Post* wrote that Cheney's energy task force broached the possibility of lifting some economic sanctions against Iran, Libya, and Iraq as part of a plan to increase America's oil supply. According to a draft of the task force report, the United States should review the sanctions against the three countries because of the importance of their oil production in meeting domestic and global energy needs, the *Post* reported.[13]

The story passed without much notice, in part because no one had even followed the issue of Cheney's wanting to lift U.S. sanctions against Iran before, apart from a small story that I had written for Dow Jones Newswires following the Calgary oil conference.

The draft by Cheney's energy task force acknowledged that sanctions can "advance" important national security and diplomatic goals. But it added that United Nations sanctions on Iraq and U.S. restrictions on energy investments in Libya and Iran "affect some of the most important existing and prospective petroleum producing countries in the world." The draft added: "The administration will initiate a comprehensive sanctions review and seek to engage the Congress in a partnership for sanctions reform."[14]

The *Post*'s reporters opined that with the administration already weighing how to restructure sanctions on Iraq, Iran, and Libya, those recommendations provided the best evidence of skepticism among some Bush officials about the effectiveness of this long-standing foreign policy tool. But that view was already widespread among traditional conservatives. The Cheney task force draft report also offered a rare glimpse into the workings of one of the administration's most significant deliberations. The draft report comprised 100 pages, divided into 10 chapters, and was heavily focused on increased energy production, but it also dealt with environmental concerns and promoted energy efficiency and renewable fuels.

The draft report's recommendations came amid a brewing battle over whether Congress should reauthorize the Iran-Libya Sanctions Act for five more years when it expires in August of 2006. The oil industry was pressing for the investment restrictions to be eased, and other lobbyists wanted to keep them in place. The administration did not say whether it would support the reauthorization of the Iran-Libya Sanctions Act (ILSA), but signaled that it had some reservations about the existing restrictions. The sanctions, enacted in 1996, were designed to punish Iran and Libya for sponsoring terrorism by penalizing foreign companies that invest in their energy industries. In the fall of 2005, Senators Gordon Smith, a Republican, and Charles E. Schumer, a Democrat, sought to build support for renewing ILSA for five more years with only minor modifications. Capitol Hill staffers again told the *Post* that the measure would continue to ban foreign firms from investing more than $20 million in the Iranian energy industry, while possibly lowering the existing ceiling on investments in Libya from the current level of $40 million down to $20 million.

The clash over U.S. sanctions against wayward, oil-rich countries has a long history. The oil and gas industry has been pressing Congress and policy-makers under current President Bush and former President Bill Clinton to give them access to Libya, Iran, and Iraq. Cheney, former chief executive of Halliburton, is known to be in favor of lifting U.S. sanctions on Iran, but it appears that he has moderated those views because of an ongoing rift between Washington and Tehran over the latter's nuclear program. Bush included Iran in his "axis of evil" State of the Union speech in 2002.

OIL AND POLITICS IN THE MIDDLE EAST

How important are the three rogue oil producers? Iran, Iraq, and Libya exported a combined 6 million barrels a day in 2004 and even more in

2005, about 8 percent of total world oil demand. Iraq probably has about 10 percent of world oil reserves, second only to Saudi Arabia's 25 percent share, and Iran's reserves are close in size to Iraq's. Libya has about 4 percent of world reserves. A proposal to increase energy exploration and production in Libya, Iraq, and Iran would seem to run counter to the administration's concerns about foreign dependence. But a key conclusion of Cheney's energy task force was the need to diversify U.S. sources of energy supply as widely as possible. Colin L. Powell, who was U.S. Secretary of State at the time, led efforts to ease the economic embargo on Iraq, while tightening restrictions on imports and oil revenue that could be used to develop its military. Under the U.N. Security Council's oil-for-food program, Iraq was allowed to export petroleum, much of which ultimately was sold in the United States. But most of the profits were placed in a U.N. account and used to pay for food, medicine, and other humanitarian goods for the citizens of Iraq.

Having dropped plans to cultivate Iran as a steady source of oil supply because of deteriorating relations, Cheney and his allies turned to Iraq as the next best hope, although this, they recognized, would have to involve war because Saddam Hussein was nobody they could honestly deal with. Their initial hope was that Iraq's oil supply would increase fast enough to cool an overheated market. But the ongoing violence and the fact that rehabilitating Iraq's oil infrastructure is taking a long time have dashed those hopes. As a result, the United States is now forced to continue depending on Saudi Arabia for much of its oil supply, and this could continue for the foreseeable future, despite the kingdom's steady productive capacity.

One point needs to be made right here for purposes of clarity. Oil production capacity depends on the amount of oil in the ground as well as the infrastructure required to drill, process, store, and transport the oil. In addition, increasing capacity is very costly and time-consuming, and the Saudis don't seem to have addressed most of these issues. "The long-term capacity was not considered a problem," Robert W. Jordan, the American ambassador to Riyadh from 2001 to 2003, told the *New York Times*. The Saudis, he added, "never expressed any concern about the need to expand."[15] In April 2002, when President Bush met Crown Prince Abdullah, now the Saudi king, the focus was not on oil but on Israeli-Palestinian matters, Jordan said. The United States did not press the capacity issue because Saudi officials were publicly expressing confidence that there was no need over the next five years to add capacity.

However, the Saudis believe they can raise output to 12 or 15 million barrels per day in 2009 simply because they have about 261 billion barrels in proven oil reserves. That only makes sense if there's a political will and the financial resources to do that. They may very well have financial resources from the current oil boom, but flooding the market with additional supply doesn't make economic sense, and they know it. The Saudi promise to raise output might be a result of pressure from Washington, but there are forces within the kingdom who think it's a bad idea. In the end, very little may happen, not only because so far the numbers being floated by the Saudis are so outrageous no smart person can believe them, but also because they don't want to flood the market with oil, especially if U.S. efforts to promote alternative fuels and energy conservation oil prices to moderate or fall.

Ali al-Naimi, the Saudi oil minister, is known for giving mixed signals to the oil market, as most of his statements are often contradictory. That's in part due to the secretive nature of the oil business and it's intentional. Naimi and Saudi oil executives have been saying on various occasions that the kingdom has huge undiscovered reserves, and that they could add 200 billion barrels—from existing fields and yet-to-be-discovered resources—to its reserves, enabling production of 15 million barrels a day for 50 years or perhaps longer. Just before meeting with Prince Abdullah in April of 2005, President Bush said he wanted "a straight answer" about how much extra oil the Saudis could pump. At that session in Texas, the prince reaffirmed the previously announced expansion plans, which would expand the Saudi's extra capacity from the current 1.5 to 2 million to about 5 million barrels per day. No other producer currently has a spare capacity. The problem is that most of that expected Saudi expansion will be heavy crude, which is not very usable in the West.

Moreover, there are still some doubts about how much oil the Saudis have. Data about reserves are tightly guarded, and the Saudis dismiss skeptics as uninformed. They have dismissed Matt Simmons, who argues that "Saudi Arabia is in fact overproducing its primary resources, and couldn't possibly ramp up production for long."[16] Simmons' book, *Twilight in the Desert*, offers by far the most extensive and caustic critique of the Saudi oil supply, looking at production from oilfield to oilfield, and essentially concludes that the kingdom is overproducing its oil and cannot possibly increase production for long. In other words, the Saudi production could peak soon.

Other experts have come to almost similar conclusions, including Edward O. Price Jr., the former head of exploration for Saudi Aramco, who also was an adviser to the U.S. government on Persian Gulf oil during both Iraq wars. Price questioned future reliance on Saudi capacity in an article in the *New York Times* in 2005,[17] in which he said that he wanted to know from his former colleagues how they reached their estimate of being able to produce more than 150 billion barrels of extra oil. Price added that 20 years ago, a detailed study by geologists from four large American oil companies then in partnership with Saudi Aramco found little in the way of undiscovered oil resources. Saudi officials haven't challenged Price's claims.

Also challenging the Saudi estimates is Sadad al-Husseini, Saudi Aramco's former upstream chief engineer, who said in 2005, both at an oil conference in London and in separate interviews with *Reuters* news agency, that such a sharp increase would deplete reserves much faster than the kingdom would like. He noted that raising output above 12 million barrels per day would involve heavy crude, and that total Saudi output might exceed 13.5 million barrels per day by 2025 on this basis. He predicted that total Middle East Gulf output could rise to 25 million barrels per day by 2014 but would stop there. Predictably, the Saudi oil ministry has attacked Sadad al-Husseini for spilling the beans, but that only reflects the current split within the kingdom's elite on oil policy. But Sadad al-Husseini's view was supported by yet another former Saudi Aramco chief engineer, Bryan Bartlett, who also warned that a significant production increase would risk reducing the natural pressure and undermine the volume of ultimate recoverable oil.

The Saudi oil policy is driven by two conflicting strands of thought, pursued by different individuals within the Saudi royal family, according to William B. Quandt, a former member of the U.S. National Security Council who wrote a book entitled *Saudi Arabia in the 1980s: Foreign Policy, Security and Oil Policy*. Quandt said that the super-optimists who approach oil policy based on political considerations by certain powerful princes tend to promise more production up to the point where supplies could be depleted soon. Then there are pessimists who are more inclined to follow a rational economic approach and typically warn against over-production, which they feel has a lasting impact on the quality and quantity of future production.[18] These two groups are always at war with each other, and it will be very interesting to see how the tussle over recent promises by Naimi and King Abdullah will pan out.

According to a report in the *New York Times*, Nansen G. Saleri, who manages Saudi reserves, met with Aramco's Price in the United States in 2004, but Saudi Aramco officials declined to respond to questions about the meeting. Still, Price said to the *Times* that Saleri told him that the basis for the higher oil figures was a global study in 2000 by the U.S. Geological Survey, which estimated Saudi Arabia's undiscovered resources at 87 billion barrels. Price, relating to the Times his conversation with Saleri, dismissed those government estimates, saying that the estimates "by the U.S.G.S. had no credibility and far exceeded the detailed studies by the old Aramco team."[19] The Aramco study, unlike the survey estimate, involved detailed field work.

Questions about Saudi Arabia's long-term estimates were also raised in a report published in 2005 by the National Intelligence Council, an advisory panel that produces the government's most authoritative intelligence estimates, according to a government official who insisted on not being identified because the report was classified. On November 14, 2005, Robin Wright, diplomatic correspondent for the *Washington Post*, reported that the United States and the Saudis had "inaugurated a new strategic dialogue to expand cooperation on six key issues, including terrorism and energy."[20]

The Bush administration has been under pressure from Congress to win greater cooperation from Saudi Arabia, because 15 of the 19 men who carried out the 2001 terrorist attacks on the United States were Saudi citizens, and the oil-rich kingdom is the birthplace of al Qaeda founder Osama bin Laden. Congressional criticism of Saudi Arabia has been particularly harsh, with Senator Patrick J. Leahy, a Democrat from Vermont, saying that the Bush administration was "far too cozy" with a country whose citizens were responsible for the deadliest attack ever on U.S. soil. The six new U.S.-Saudi relations would focus on counterterrorism, military affairs, energy, business, education and human development, and consular affairs.

In addition to Saudi Arabia, the Bush administration has viewed the United Arab Emirates as a supplier with excess capacity. In 2001, the UAE planned to increase capacity to 3 million barrels a day by 2005 from 2.5 million barrels a day then. But capacity has not grown in four years, which one administration official attributes to a lack of urgency by Emirates officials and a lack of high-level attention by American officials.

CHAPTER 5

Iraqi Oil Supply and the Battle of Baghdad

The United States–led invasion of Iraq in 2003 may have been meant to impose a much-needed democracy there, but it never turned out quite that way. The conflict is increasingly costing more in lives and other resources than was initially estimated; corruption is rampant in the new Iraqi government; the insurgency against U.S. occupation is growing, and many people around the world see it as a war of choice in search of oil. These critics believe that the oil industry supported the war because it stood to gain from an Iraq that posed no threat to energy security. It's important to note, however, that whatever the reasons for the war, the oil industry, just like everyone else (except President Bush and his staunch allies), is no longer very optimistic about the outcome.

There's a growing belief that the motivation for going to war with Iraq was the thought that Iraq could play a central role as an alternative swing oil producer to Saudi Arabia, currently the world's only spare capacity holder, and that having a massive U.S. military presence in Iraq would provide the United States with much-needed energy security. Holding 115 billion barrels of oil reserves, there's no question that Iraq has great potential to supply the world with oil for years, and its new leaders have ambitious plans to boost production to about 3 million barrels per day. However, their ability is very much limited, and the possibility of harvesting those gargantuan oil reserves is very much in doubt, at least for now, in part because of ongoing violence throughout the country, but also due to a lack of financial resources to upgrade oil facilities. For now, the future doesn't look bright, as the prospect of a full-blown civil war in Iraq is growing by the day, especially following the attack in early 2006 on a Shiite mosque and religious shrine; in fact, some Iraqi officials tell me that a civil war may already be under way in Baghdad.

News reports of daily carnage from Baghdad indicate that the situation is spinning out of control into anarchy, with tens and sometimes hundreds of civilian casualties every day, and that may ultimately drive away experts who are needed to save the country. Highly educated Iraqis who could be relied on to help revive the country's oil sector either are being targeted for elimination or are leaving Iraq. Sectarian and ethnic divisions have hardened to an extent that many see the country on the brink of breaking apart, a situation some argue may not be a bad thing. "Rather than the folly of continuing a course of action of holding a country together where residents clearly don't want it, we would do much better to have a managed breakup," Peter Galbraith, a former U.S. ambassador to Croatia who has long advocated partitioning Iraq, said in early 2006.[1]

The civil war points to the failure of the Iraqi project, and that's very unfortunate for a country that has vast resources. But just as important, there may be other disturbing issues that weren't clear a few years ago at the time of planning the 2003 war that overthrew Saddam Hussein. I'm told by some of my sources that the U.S. Geological Survey (USGS) has downgraded Iraq's oil supply reserves estimate to 87 billion barrels from the initial forecast of 115 billion barrels. This revision, along with others, is expected to appear in the next USGS report due out later in 2006. As of early 2006, the downgrade hadn't been reflected in the Energy Information Administration's reports, which still have stuck with the earlier estimate of 115 billion barrels. The USGS and Energy Information Administration typically work separately, although at some point they are going to share information on the state of the world's oil and gas reserves. Regardless, what this discrepancy shows is nothing more than the lack of a definitive estimate of Iraq's oil reserves, and it suggests that all the numbers we've heard about Iraq's oil wealth may be doubtful.

After spending more than $20 billion of American taxpayer money to try to revive Iraq, including rehabilitating its oil industry, without much success, the Bush administration is almost giving up on Iraq. The administration has said it won't ask Congress for any more reconstruction funding for Iraq in 2006, and there are reports that the administration may be planning to scale back troops in Iraq. Much of the initial financial allocation was misspent during the three years since the war that toppled Saddam Hussein in 2003, according to U.S. government audit reports. At the same time, the Iraqi ministry of oil has become a den of infighting among the various factions bent on controlling the country's oil wealth, and that situation has made it even more difficult for the officials to proceed with reviving the oil industry. In conversations I had with senior Iraqi oil officials throughout 2005 and 2006, they alleged all sorts of corrupt schemes being perpetrated by senior officials, including bribery and smuggling. They say some of the shady deals involve senior members of the Iraqi leadership, including the office of the prime minister. The deals, for the most part, involve oil products—kerosene and liquefied petroleum gas—being imported into Iraq from Kuwait, Turkey, and other neighboring countries. In my two years of reporting and writing on Iraq's oil industry, I found very few people to trust (just like everywhere else) because even those officials who were telling me of the shady deals in the oil ministry—the people who were accusing their colleagues of corruption—were themselves not totally clean.

Moreover, operational and logistical problems continue to affect Iraq's oil exports. Sometimes oil tanker loadings at the Basra oil terminal, the exit point for more than 90 percent of Iraq's crude exports, are suspended because of power outages, pipeline leaks, a lack of tugboats, and falling production. The Basra oil terminal can export up to 1.8 million barrels per day, but in 2005 the flow rate was down to 1.4 million barrels per day and in early 2006 the port was handling only about 1 million barrels per day of oil exports.

The situation in the north is even more precarious. Exports of Kirkuk crude, from northern Iraq, have been very erratic, although production was down to 300,000 barrels per day by early 2006, or less than half the normal level, and all of that was used in local refineries. Total production in 2006 was down to about 1.8 million barrels per day from 2.2 million barrels per day in 2005 and 2.5 million barrels before the war in 2003. During the whole of 2005 the Iraqi oil ministry had intended to export about 913 million barrels for the year, but managed only about 511 million barrels, and those exports occurred within a small window—from June to September. There were virtually no exports for the other months. So, after all that war in 2003 and the continuing violence, Iraqi supply is still erratic at best and can't be relied on to help ease the global pain of limited oil supply. And that's for many reasons, including the fact that most of the equipment is dilapidated, electrical power supply is erratic, and security problems are abundant both in the north and in the middle parts of the country.

Output is still constrained by insurgent attacks and rusty oil facilities, especially the pipelines and oil production equipment. The oil facilities in the northern Kirkuk area have seen their share of attacks by Sunni insurgents opposed to the Shiite-Kurdish rule in post-Saddam Iraq, limiting production by almost a third on a good day. The Kirkuk export pipeline has been sabotaged several times, and Kirkuk oilfield facilities have been targeted as well.

Even in the southern Basra region, where U.S. Marines and British soldiers have mounted the highest level of security, piracy continues at the Basra oil terminal and many workers have been abducted. Moreover, there are still numerous oil tanker loading problems caused by harsh weather in the Persian Gulf, and by leaking pipes. The problem is that Iraq's oil industry has suffered decades of neglect. There can be no increase in oil production if the failure of the system for injecting water into reservoirs is allowed to continue. Water injection is needed to maintain pressure and increase oil production from mature oil wells. But in Iraq, this isn't being done properly and as a result the oil ministry failed in 2005 to meet its target of raising the country's oil production to 2.5 million barrels per day. Since production was less than had been promised, in January 2006 the Iraqi oil ministry cut oil supply contracts with foreign buyers by almost half to about 1 million barrels per day for the first half of 2006. That scaled-down contract volume is likely to continue throughout the year and into 2007 if the situation doesn't turn around.

Iraqi oil output is not down for lack of a plan. A series of plans are in the drawer, and are being dusted off. Some of these plans are unreasonably ambitious, having set a target for increasing production to 3 million barrels per day in the next couple of years, and then later to 10 million barrels per day in the long term. That's like trying to catch up with Saudi Arabia—an uphill task for the Iraqis that can't be taken seriously right now. Such a spike in production would require an injection of about $30 billion in capital investments, but money is tight in Iraq. In any case, no significant upstream developments can take place until peace and security are restored to the country—and even that expectation is overly optimistic because a peaceful Iraq is far, far away.

New exploration could probably raise Iraq's reserves. The country has high-quality crude, which is cheap to produce. Initial plans were that this kind of development would lead to a gold rush of profits for international oil firms in the post-Saddam era, but that could take longer than expected. Insurgents have inflicted heavy casualties in the past two years and there's no end in sight for the violence. And unlike its neighbors with enough capital, Iraq has none. Its new leaders are still trying to rid the country of the loan burdens incurred by Saddam Hussein during the wars with Iran in the 1980s. Those wars drained the country of its financial resources. The sanctions imposed by the United Nations during the 1990s only increased the hardship and hampered investments in the oil industry. Little wonder, then, that the oil infrastructure in Iraq is now reeling from a lack of key spare parts. Pipelines, refineries, and oil production equipment are decaying. Export terminals suffer frequent power outages, and all of these negatively impact Iraq's oil exports. In the late 1990s, Iraq tried to get the UN Security Council to approve some repairs and upgrades on its oil facilities, but the United States and the United Kingdom blocked those requests because they didn't trust Saddam Hussein, who was bribing his way around those sanctions.

The four giant U.S. and British firms—Exxon Mobil, Chevron, BP, and Royal Dutch Shell—have been keen to get back into Iraq since they were kicked out of there in 1972. But they are still prevented from doing so by the insurgency. At the same time, they face companies from France, Russia, China, Japan, and elsewhere that already had major concessions in Iraq before the fall of Saddam Hussein's regime.

For Western oil executives and their friends in the White House, the war removed the biggest obstacle to accessing the huge Iraqi oil deposits and bringing them onstream to stabilize the world oil market. That's one of the things they had lobbied the Bush administration to do as soon as George Bush was elected president, and part of their demands formed the basis for the Energy Act of 2005, which was signed into law to public fanfare in 2005. A White House document shows that oil executives met with Vice President Dick Cheney's 2001 energy task force, which critics say secretly formed energy policy favorable to the industry, as reported by the *Washington Post* on November 16, 2005. The document, obtained by the newspaper, shows that officials from four major oil companies met in the White House complex with

Cheney aides who were formulating the Bush administration's energy policy, according to the report.[2]

The *Post* wrote that the document shows that officials from Exxon Mobil, Conoco (before its merger with Phillips Petroleum), Royal Dutch Shell, and BP America met with the Cheney aides. Shell is now part of Royal Dutch Shell following a 2005 merger. The White House refused to divulge information about the task force. Just a week before the *Post* published the report, the heads of several major oil companies told members of two Senate panels that they were not involved in the vice president's energy task force. The two senior members of the Senate Energy and Natural Resources Committee, Pete Dominici, Republican of New Mexico, and Jeff Bingaman, Democrat of New Mexico, said that they had "agreed to send a joint letter to each of the witnesses involved, asking for their prompt explanation, in writing, of these apparent inconsistencies."[3]

A statement from Exxon Mobil said that the meeting in question, which took place on February 14, 2001, was not "secret" and was reported to the General Accounting Office and to both Democratic and Republican House and Senate energy staffs that same day.

New Jersey Senator Frank Lautenberg, a Democrat, asked Attorney General Alberto Gonzales to investigate whether the executives lied in their testimony to Congress on November 9, 2005, noting that the *Post* article suggested they may have given "false statements" when they denied participating in the energy policy task force.

Cheney spokeswoman Lea Anne McBride declined to comment on the document but told the newspaper that the courts have upheld "the constitutional right of the president and vice president to obtain information in confidentiality." According to the *Post*, a person familiar with the task force's work said the document obtained by the paper was based on records kept by the Secret Service.[4] Democrats asked the U.S. attorney general to investigate whether top executives from big oil companies lied to Congress when they said their firms did not take part in Vice President Dick Cheney's energy task force.

Democrats and environmental groups have fought unsuccessfully to find out which energy industry executives met privately with Cheney's group in 2001 as it prepared a broad plan friendly to oil industry interests, while excluding environmental concerns.[5]

After being kicked out of OPEC during the sanction years in the 1990s, Iraq is now back as a member, most of its oil exports going to the United States and India, but the world's oil markets have almost written off Iraqi production due to its unreliability. The United States gets between 15 million and 20 million barrels of Iraq's Basra light crude per month, most of it going to Chevron, Exxon Mobil, Koch, and Valero; Holland's Royal Dutch Shell; U.K.'s BP; Spain's Cepsa and Repsol; Italy's Eni; France's Total; Portugal's Petrogal; and the Indian Oil Company.

Developing Iraq's oil is going to be tough, but in the postwar setting, if the United States continues its military presence there, American and British companies will eventually gain the most lucrative oil deals in the coming decades. For now, international oil majors are not talking about any upstream investments they may have in Iraq, in part because of the uncertainties surrounding just about everything in that country right now.

That's not to say they won't get involved. They will jump in as soon as the security situation stabilizes in Iraq. Many of these companies already have plans in their drawers for drilling of giant oilfields in the western deserts, close to Syria and Jordan. Some of these plans are new, while others date back many years. Saddam had wanted to develop these areas with the help of French and Russian companies. Thamer al-Ghadban, who was oil minister until 2005, said restoring Iraq's oil supply capacity to pre-1990 levels of 3 million barrels per day would require tens of billions of dollars, money that's not readily available. Money is tight because most of the U.S. funding allocations instead went into beefing up security, and others were misspent. In any case, the first priority of Iraqi officials should be to rehabilitate and bring up to date all of the existing oil facilities and to manage production fields better.

If that happens and peace returns to Iraq, international oil companies would come up with money and carve up the country's vast oil and gas resources among themselves. They would then develop those reserves to benefit oil consumers around the world. For the time being, though, President Bush's democratic experiment in Iraq appears to be failing, as sectarian war ravages the country and the oil sector languishes. It's going to be an enormous task to turn things around.

Still, if the situation gets stabilized, even if that takes 10 or more years, international oil companies may eventually have what they have coveted for a long time, given that the country's new liberal constitution allows for the participation of private oil companies in the nation's natural resources.

MAJOR EVENTS THAT HAVE AFFECTED
THE IRAQI OIL INDUSTRY

Before coming to the Iraq war of 2003, I want to review the history of oil in Iraq and of conflicts over there.

The British established Iraq as a state after World War I from three separate provinces—Basra in the south, Baghdad in the middle, and Mosul in the north. In area, Iraq is only slightly larger than California and Maryland put together. But it is historically important as it embraces most of the old Biblical lands, covering the valleys of the Euphrates and the Tigris Rivers. Inside it are such ancient places as the Ur de Chaldees (or birthplace of Abraham), Hit (from where bitumen that built the walls of Babylon came), Nineveh (the tomb of Jonah and former capital of Syria), and even the traditional site of the Garden of Eden. It's a land rich in history as the birthplace of prophets and, as we shall see, oil. The Greeks called it Mesopotamia, meaning "middle rivers."[6]

Iraq in Arabic language means "banks of a river," and unlike the Nile, the world's second longest river, which cuts across Africa, floods from the Euphrates and the Tigris meander through Iraq, causing great damage to property and lives in the neighborhoods. It's said that Noah, who was forewarned of such floods, built the Ark to perpetuate life in Biblical times. With its location between the Euphrates and the Tigris, Iraq was a favored trading center. Then as now, vessels plied the Persian Gulf waters from India and China, and traveled up the rivers to the head of navigation, from where caravans of loaded camels trekked across the deserts and mountains westward to the Mediterranean Sea or northward to the Caspian Sea. Medieval Baghdad became the trading center for all the Middle East.

The Ottoman Turks conquered Mesopotamia in 1534 and dominated it until 1918, when they were driven out by the British army at the end of World War I, allowing Britain to take control of the area. In Baghdad, on October 17, 1920, Sir Percy Cox, a British representative, declared his government's intention to establish a national government of Iraq. A plebiscite was held and on August 23, 1921, Faisal bin Husayn was proclaimed King of Iraq.[7]

At the turn of the twentieth century, the Ottomans ruled a vast empire of mountains and desert lands, which has since been proven to hold the largest oil reserves in the world, covering what is now Turkey, Syria, Iraq, Lebanon, Palestine, Jordan, and the Arabian peninsula. Around 1890, Calouste Sarkis Gulbenkian, a young Armenian Turk, who had grown up mostly in England, was working as an aide to Hagop Pasha, the financial advisor of the Ottoman Sultan. He reported to his boss the prospects of oil in Mesopotamia, based on rumors from the people he met who had been to the region.[8]

As his father had been a petroleum merchant, Gulbenkian probably was aware of the economic opportunity Mesopotamia presented for the Sultan. Impressed by the report, the Sultan obtained possession of a swath of oilfield in Mesopotamia right away. Today, Gulbenkian is credited with laying the foundation for oil exploitation in Iraq and the entire Middle East in the same way George Bissell and Drake Edwin are credited with starting the oil industry in the United States.

By 1912 European and U.S. business groups—Deutsche Bank from Germany, Royal Dutch Shell Group from the Netherlands, the Chester Group from the United States, and the British D'Arcy—began to seek oil concessions in Mesopotamia. The British formed a company called the Turkish Petroleum Co. and gave a few shares of that company to the Dutch and the Germans, but froze out the Americans altogether. Turkish Petroleum Co. was charged with exploitation of oil in Mosul and Baghdad.

After World War I, Iraq was mandated to the British to administer. With Germany defeated by the allied powers, the German shares in the oil company were redistributed to the French. At that point, the Chester Group, which had the support of U.S. presidents Theodore Roosevelt and Woodrow Wilson, claimed shares of the company because the Big War was won with the help of American oil. In Washington, Herbert Hoover, the secretary of commerce, invited U.S. oil executives to his office in 1921 and told them to go get Iraq oil reserves. In August 1922, the Turkish Petroleum Co. offered 12 percent interest to the Americans, an offer that was promptly rejected because the Americans felt entitled to more.

Meanwhile, after losing oil reserves in Eastern Europe to the Russians during the war, the Western powers thought the Middle East offered the best prospects of finding new oil reserves, and Iraq in particular was the most attractive part of the region. In essence, we can see that for the first time Americans began to clamor for the Middle East, and in this case, they demanded an equal share with the British, the Dutch, and the French in the country's oil reserves.

Eventually in 1923, the Americans were given 25 percent interest in Turkish Petroleum Co., but no agreement was signed until eight years later, when the name Turkish Petroleum Co. was changed to Iraq Petroleum Ltd. This new company came to hold rights to oil in all of Iraq, but it was British in outlook and had its offices in London. From 1929 through 1953, the company's chief geologists were Americans, and they led the discoveries of new fields all over Iraq, including near Mosul in the north and near Basra in the south. By 1960, they had dug 57 wells all across the country.[9]

In the spring of 2005, I had an interview with James Paul, a man who has spent the past several years following the Iraq debate at the U.N. and elsewhere. Mr. Paul is a tall, slim, polite man, a Paul Newman lookalike, with an effortless smile on his face most of the time. Widely traveled, bookish, with a masterful grasp of policy issues, he represents the finest of what I would call an activist intellectual. Over a buffet lunch at an Indian restaurant in Manhattan later in the summer of that year, we talked at length about Iraq. He told me how he got into his advocacy work, which sounded impressively high-minded.

Soon after the first Gulf War in 1990, which drove Iraqi forces from occupied Kuwait, Paul decided to start a nonprofit organization, Global Policy Forum, based in New York, to focus on debates at the United Nations. He told me that he wanted to know what was being discussed and why, and also whether he could help inform some of those debates or get U.N. members to talk about certain issues that were not getting any attention. The more he studied Iraq, he said, the more he came to realize that he would have to learn more about oil because of Iraq's position as a major oil producer. Over the years, he has written a lot of policy papers on Iraq and its oil industry, and most of these papers are posted on the website of his organization, at globalpolicy.org. They detail the problems of oil and war as well as the close personal ties between oil companies and various U.S. governments since the 1950s, but also note that those ties are more intense in recent years, especially with the election in 2000, of George W. Bush, whom *The Economist* has called America's first second-generation oil president.

Quoting a *New York Times* report published August 16, 1990, Paul notes that following the Iraqi invasion of Kuwait in early 1990, President George H.W. Bush talked of Saddam's threat to U.S. energy security, concluding, "Our jobs, our way of life, our own freedom and the freedom of friendly countries around the world would all suffer if control of the world's oil reserves fell into the hands of Saddam Hussein."

For the next 12 years after the liberation of Kuwait, the United Nation's embargo continued, although Saddam was able to bribe his way around the sanctions, which debilitated Iraq's economy and restricted oil sales. Still, the United States declared its goal of removing Saddam, and President George W. Bush launched a military campaign against Iraq in March 2003, despite international opposition.

The war brought the United States into direct rule over Iraq and its oilfields nearly a century after America first fell in love with Iraq's oil. Because there was less resistance from Iraq's military than feared, the war initially didn't affect much of the oil infrastructure, which the United States wanted as much as possible to protect, because the United States wanted to use that oil for reconstruction. But the insurgency and sabotage that followed did just as much damage to Iraq's oil supply as military action might have.

BEHIND-THE-SCENES PLOT TO GET IRAQI OIL SUPPLY

The constant wars fought over Iraq highlight the exceptional lure of the country's oil resources. Iraq's oil is of good quality and is very much in demand around the world; that oil is very cheap to produce and profitable to refine. By some estimates, royalties on Iraq's oil could yield as much as $80 billion to $90 billion per year, although the 2005 earnings were much less at $23.5 billion, according to *Iraq Weekly Status Report*, which is published by the U.S. Department of State.

As other oilfields around the world become depleted in the next two decades, global production will increasingly depend on the enormous reserves of the Persian Gulf region. Because of its potential, Iraq's oil will in the future represent a huge part of the world's supplies, and so any sensible oil executive would want to be a player in the recovery of Iraq's oil sector.

Shortly before the 2003 war, industry experts described Iraq as a future "gold rush," where the companies would battle to gain control of key reserves. According to James Paul, at that time a well-informed diplomat at the U.N. commented bluntly: "Exxon wants Majnoun and they are determined to get it." And a longtime industry observer said: "There is not an oil company in the world that doesn't have its eye on Iraq." The future of major oil companies might at some point have to depend, to a large extent, on their control of Iraqi oil reserves.

The 1972 oil nationalization in Iraq pushed the U.S. and U.K. companies completely out of the country. In the period leading up to nationalization, international oil companies held a 75 percent stake in the Iraq Petroleum Company and also some equity in the country's oil reserves. In the 1980s and 1990s, oil companies from France and Russia began to make deals that resulted in lucrative production sharing agreements allowing companies such as French oil giant Total and Russian oil company Lukoil to gain a large potential share of Iraq's oil reserves. The 1990-2003 sanctions prevented these deals from going forward.[11]

In the oil market generally, as production from older fields worldwide has fallen, oil companies have found reserve replacement increasingly expensive. Some studies say the cost of finding new reserves is up 60 percent in the past decade. Some companies, like Royal Dutch Shell and Repsol, have had to revise their reserves downward. Other companies, including Exxon Mobil, have struggled to maintain their reserve levels in recent years.[12]

That view is supported by many analysts who believe that Iraq would help oil companies to improve their reserve replacement. Major Anglo-American companies were eager to tap Iraqi oil, but waited for regime change. Meanwhile, in 1997, as the sanctions became unpopular around the world, Chinese, Russian, and French companies struck deals with Saddam's regime for production sharing in some of Iraq's biggest fields.

But, as permanent members of the U.N. Security Council, China, Russia, and France pressed for lifting of the sanctions. Of course, one can argue that the three veto-holding members were motivated by their economic interests, but so were the United States and Britain. With Iranian fields being parceled out to their rivals in Europe and Asia, US oil executives were eager to put up shop in Iraq, and they reportedly encouraged Washington to move quickly with plans to get rid of Saddam.

But in fact the oilmen didn't have to, because the foreign policy establishment was restive and growing more hawkish on Iraq. In the late 1990s, the neoconservative wing of the Republican Party, led by William Kristol, editor of the *Weekly Standard*, formed a small think tank called Project for a New American Century to refocus U.S. foreign policy toward American hegemony.

This group argued, for example, that as the only remaining superpower following the demise of Communist Russia, the United States had become an empire and so should use its military strength to dominate world affairs. To these neoconservatives, Iraq was an unfinished business they wanted to deal with, and so they decided that the starting point would be the removal of Saddam from power. On January 26, 1998, they sent a letter to President Bill Clinton, warning that containment was a failed policy and called for "a strategy for removing Saddam's regime from power."[13]

Exiled Iraqis told reporters and U.S. government officials that Saddam was hiding large stocks of deadly weapons. Congress held hearings and then drafted legislation. President Clinton then asked the Pentagon to plan strikes on Iraq, starting 1999 through 2000.

Clinton also signed a law that provided $5 million in funding for the Iraqi opposition, and set up Radio Free Iraq. Later, Clinton signed another law pushed by Washington military hawks, accusing Iraq of reconstituting weapons of mass destruction and failing to cooperate with U.N. inspectors. A military conflict was then set in motion with the signing by Clinton of the Iraq Liberation Act of 1998, which stated that, "It shall be the policy of the United States to support efforts to remove the regime headed by Saddam Hussein from power in Iraq."

This aggressive policy was a turning point, and it showed a hardening of positions in the United States and Britain that Saddam must be pushed out by force, if it could be done through covert means. While it can be argued that the Clinton administration became more aggressive only after being pushed by conservatives, it should be noted that this came on the heels of the successful military intervention to end the Kosovo war by the North Atlantic Treaty Organization (NATO).

Neoconservatives like William Kristol supported that Kosovo war on moral grounds, and so Clinton might similarly have been persuaded to get tough with Saddam on moral grounds. But for the war in Iraq, morality may have played a very small role, and in fact traditional conservatives didn't feel strongly for the war. Those who supported it did so for different reasons, including political expediency and some form of economic benefit for their political constituencies.

For neoconservatives, however, Iraq just fell into their grand vision of American dominance, which they thought "can be sustained for many decades to come, not by arms control agreements, but by augmenting America's power and, therefore, its ability to lead."[14]

The new Bush administration came into office in January 2001, just in time to finish the job of getting rid of Saddam. Former Secretary of the Treasury Paul O'Neill says in his memoirs that the new Bush White House started planning for an invasion of Iraq almost immediately. According to O'Neill, Iraq was "Topic A" at the very first meeting of the Bush National Security Council, just 10 days after the inauguration. "It was about finding a way to do it," says O'Neill in a book written by Ron Suskind, a former Pulitzer Prize–winning reporter for the *Wall Street Journal*. "That was the tone of the President, saying 'Go find me a way to do this.'"[15]

Meanwhile, President Bush ordered stepped-up overflights and provocative attacks on Iraqi targets under a plan evidently known as Operation Desert Badger. On February 16, U.S. aircraft bombed Iraqi radar installations north of the no-fly zone and very close to the southern limits of Baghdad. Readily audible from the Iraqi capital, this attack drew wide media comment. Just a few weeks later, the National Energy

Policy Development Group, chaired by Vice President Cheney, studied the challenge posed by French, Russian, and other nations' companies. One of the documents produced by the Cheney group, made public after a long court case, is a map of Iraq showing its major oil fields and a two-page list of "Foreign Suitors for Iraqi Oilfield Contracts." The list showed more than 40 companies from 30 countries with projects agreed to or under discussion, but not a single U.S. or U.K. deal. The list included agreements or discussions with companies from Germany, India, Italy, Canada, Indonesia, Japan, and other nations, along with the well-known French, Russian, and Chinese deals. The report by the Cheney group, released in May, warned ominously of U.S. oil shortfalls that might "undermine our economy, our standard of living, our national security."[16]

The Bush administration seems to have reached a decision to go to war with Iraq in 2001, but the decision was firmed up in mid-2002 in the aftermath of the September 11 attacks on the United States, according to leaks from Prime Minister Blair's aides. According to Christopher Meyer, the British ambassador in Washington at the time, President Bush raised the issue of Iraq with British Prime Minister Tony Blair at a private dinner at the White House just nine days after September 11. Bush asked for British support for removal of Saddam Hussein from power, a clear reference to a military operation.

Meyer's account, which is similar to those of Richard Dearlove, David Manning, and Philippe Sands, says that Blair gave his silent assent to the proposal. Both Dearlove and Manning were at the meetings with U.S. officials planning the Iraq war and they made top-secret notes of the discussions, which later found their way into newspapers. Dearlove, for example, says in his notes dated July 23, 2002, that he realized during a trip to Washington that intelligence was being fixed around the policy to invade Iraq, even though the case against Saddam was thin to begin with. [17]

Manning, in his notes around the same time, says that President Bush told Prime Minister Blair during a private two-hour meeting in the Oval Office on January 31, 2003, that he was determined to invade Iraq no matter what, and the "diplomatic strategy had to be arranged around military planning." He adds that the start date for the military campaign was penciled in for March 10, 2003.[18]

Meanwhile, there was a growing sense in the oil industry that war was imminent, and preparation would have to be made to minimize the impact of the conflict on the oil market.

As war talk peaked in Washington and at the United Nations, the influential Heritage Foundation published a report on post-Saddam Iraq, which called for the privatization of Iraq's national oil company and hinted that only U.S. and U.K. companies would sign oil contracts. The companies, the Bush administration, and the Iraqi opposition held many meetings over postwar oil. The *Washington Post* reported in September that the big companies were "maneuvering for a stake" in postwar Iraq and that the war could cause major "reshuffling" of world petroleum markets.[19]

James Woolsey, former CIA director, said that the United States would use access to postwar oil to manipulate the French and the Russians into supporting the war. Around the same time, Iraqi exile leaders said that a post-Saddam government would cancel all the foreign oil contracts. Ahmad Chalabi, at the time a leader of the exile group Iraqi National Congress and a U.S. favorite as heir to the Iraqi leadership, said, "American companies will have a big shot at Iraqi oil."[20] Chalabi, who was accused of bank fraud in Jordan, is now a senior cabinet member in the postwar Iraq government and has enormous influence over the country's oil resources.

But that was still in the future.

In the early months of the Bush administration in 2001 and 2002, Russian officials told the *Observer* newspaper in London that they feared that the United States would void Russian oil contracts and award the most lucrative deals to U.S. companies. The *Observer* quoted one official in Moscow as saying that the impending conflict could be called "an oil grab by Washington." In France, state-owned oil firm Total decided to negotiate in advance with the U.S. government "about redistribution of the oil regions between the world's major companies."[21]

On Wall Street, investment banks published investor research speculating on the prospects of postwar Iraq oil, in which Western oil companies were expecting to play a role. One such report by Deutsche Bank noted that "war drums are beating in Washington" and "Big Oil is positioning for post-sanctions Iraq." It analyzed the upward stock market potential of the oil industry in light of declining world reserves and Iraq's postwar potential. Around the same time, Youssef Ibrahim, a former energy reporter for the *New York Times* and the *Wall Street Journal* who at the time was a fellow at the Council on Foreign Relations, warned in the *International Herald Tribune* that the coming war was "bound to backfire." Ibrahim wrote:

> Let us not be fooled. The upcoming war against Iraq has nothing to do with the war against terror. President George W. Bush's war is fueled by two things: bolstering the president's popularity as he attempts to ride on the natural wave of American patriotism unleashed by the criminal attacks of Sept. 11; and a misguided temptation to get more oil out of the Middle East by turning a "friendly" Iraq into a private American oil pumping station. . . . So all the talk about spreading democracy and changing the whole Middle East, starting with Iraq, does not hold water. The United States, obsessed with oil and something called "regime change," wants to create a totally pro-American Middle East. The problem is that it will not work. You don't impose democracy by installing an occupying power in a region that has no tradition for it.[22]

Meanwhile, diplomatic initiatives continued through early 2003 in Washington, London, and elsewhere, between government officials, oil executives, and Iraqi opposition leaders in various combinations. In December, there was a meeting of oil company executives at a resort near Sandringham in Scotland, which was addressed by the former head of Iraq's Military Intelligence Agency. The executives wanted information on Iraq's future oil potential and whether Iraq might pull out of OPEC after the overthrow of Saddam. In Washington, meanwhile, war planners were considering seizing Iraq's oilfields in the first days of the impending conflict. U.S.-U.K. forces invaded Iraq on March 20, 2003, taking control of the major oilfields, pipelines, and refineries almost immediately. When they later entered Baghdad, they protected the Oil Ministry, while leaving all other institutions unguarded. Looters ravaged the National Museum and burned a wing of the National Library, but the Oil Ministry remained unscathed, with its thousands of valuable seismic maps safe for future oil exploration.

President Bush immediately appointed Phil Carroll, a former high-ranking U.S. oil executive, to assume control of Iraq's oil industry, and on May 22, Bush issued Executive Order 13303 giving immunity to oil companies for all activities in Iraq and deals involving Iraqi oil. On the same day, under pressure from the United States and the United Kingdom, the U.N. Security Council passed Resolution 1483, which lifted the former sanctions and allowed the occupation authorities to sell Iraqi oil and put the proceeds in an account they controlled. Every step in the early postwar period confirmed the centrality of oil, and every argument to the contrary, however well intentioned, fails to hold up to close scrutiny. In 2006, three years after the war, the picture remained the same and, in fact, American military presence in Iraq is designed to be permanent.

Meanwhile, the companies are not in a great hurry to go to Iraq. They plan and act on decades-long time horizons and are now waiting for the insurgency to end before committing to investing in Iraq. But it is by no means certain that the Anglo-American oil majors will get their way as easily in Iraq. As they wait, the violence is escalating into a civil war, pitting Sunnis against Shiites.

After the Iraq War of 2003, it is clear that U.S. and British oil giants will gain privileged access to Iraq's oil resources only after the fighting for the heart and soul of Iraq stops. At this point, nobody knows when that will be, but the companies are still happy to wait. Having been excluded from control over Iraqi oil since the nationalization of 1972, Exxon Mobil, BP, Royal Dutch Shell, and Chevron expect to gain the lion's share of the world's most profitable oilfields when the dust settles. Few outside the industry understand the huge stakes in Iraq, which amount to tens of billions of dollars in potential profits. That's because the fate of the country's oil reserves escaped public scrutiny, even though they are central to Iraq's future economy. Iraqi oil ministry officials anticipate signing contracts with foreign oil companies in 2006. The move would open the majority of Iraq's oilfields to Western companies for the first time in more than 30 years.

In 2005, one observer summed up a debate on Iraq's new constitution this way: One key issue was how oil revenues would be managed and whether oil production would be shared between the central government and the regions. But Iraqi politicians didn't talk about whether and how revenues would be divided between Iraqi state and private companies. The constitution, which took effect later that year, says that oilfields will be developed according to "the most modern techniques of market principles and encouraging investment."[23]

That language was quite ambiguous, although it laid the groundwork for a radical change in Iraq's oil industry. Other parts of the constitution said that Iraqi oilfields that were already producing hydrocarbon should be developed by the state-owned Iraq National Oil Company (INOC), but that all other undeveloped fields should be developed by private companies. Given that only 17 of Iraq's 80 known fields—and 40 billion of its 112 billion barrels of known reserves—are currently in production, that policy potentially allocated to foreign companies 64 percent of known reserves. And if a further 100 billion barrels are found, as is widely predicted, the observer suggested the foreign companies would control 81 percent of the total.

The liberal investment policy came from guidelines issued in August 2004 by Ayad Allawi, a moderate who was installed as interim prime minister of Iraq by the U.S. government. He wanted new fields to be developed by private companies through production sharing agreements (PSAs), the contractual mechanism favored by foreign oil companies. In addition, he wanted:

- New fields would be developed exclusively by private companies, with no participation of INOC.
- The Iraqi authorities should not spend time negotiating good deals, but should proceed quickly with terms that the companies will accept, while leaving open the possibility of later renegotiation.
- INOC should be partly privatized. It is not known whether these details have been carried forward into the current draft law.

There were many people, mostly Iraqis, who didn't agree with Allawi's privatization plan, although many experts working in conservative think tanks in Washington, D.C., thought it was the best thing for Iraq. I remember that I was invited to debate the issue on a San Francisco radio affiliate of National Public Radio with Dr. Gal Luft of the Institute for the Analysis of Global Security, and he strenuously argued that total liberalization of Iraq's oil sector was necessary; by this he meant the government should play no role at all. I thought that his view was totally bogus because it neglected the fact that nationalism dominates much of Iraq's policy initiatives. In addition, the political situation there probably won't allow it because the Sunnis think such policies are politically designed to deprive them of their economic power, so they would be more willing to support the ongoing insurgency.

Details aside, the opening up of Iraq's oil resources to foreign companies is certainly going to happen and the only question is when. The oil ministry has been seeking bids for the development of 11 oilfields in the south of Iraq, and has held preliminary talks with BP, Chevron, Eni, and Total. This was happening despite a political stalemate in early 2006 because the senior oil officials argued that it would take months or even a year to negotiate contracts with foreign companies. The contracts are expected to impact Iraq's public revenue (of which oil accounts for almost the entirety) because they are likely to preclude any future regulation or legislation that damages the oil companies' profits. And once signed, the contracts will be irreversible. Some Iraqis are concerned that contracts signed while Iraq is still under foreign occupation will tie the hands of any future Iraqi government. And it is even more worrying that this happened without extensive public debate. For the short term, oil companies are still nervous about the deteriorating security situation, although this may just be what the Iraqi nationalists want because that way they still stay in control of their oil wealth. Looking at the situation, one observer wrote: "The great tragedy is that the one thing that may stop the loss of Iraq's sovereignty over its resources, and of its main opportunity for development, is the continued bloodshed."[24]

Total sent officials to Iraq soon after the war but has since stopped, while ConocoPhillips and BP have both acknowledged safety issues. Royal Dutch Shell won't send anyone there before the security situation improves. The insurgency will delay but won't prevent the companies from reentering Iraq. BP, Exxon Mobil, and Royal Dutch Shell recently struck cooperation or training deals with Iraq's new leaders. France's Total regularly invites Iraqi engineers to Paris for training. "It's a way to maintain contact and get the oil officials to know about them," said Issam Chalabi, a former oil minister who fled Saddam Hussein's regime in 1991.[25] Meanwhile, Lukoil has teamed up with

ConocoPhillips as it evaluates a 68.5 percent stake in the large West Qurna oilfield that Lukoil negotiated with Saddam's Iraq. Lukoil, based in Russia, which opposed the war, is granting a 17.5 percent stake in the southern oilfield to ConocoPhillips, giving the project a solid U.S. connection. ConocoPhillips holds a 10 percent stake in Lukoil.

PART THREE

THE OIL BOOM

CHAPTER 6

Why and How Oil Prices Soared

OIL PRICES WILL STAY HIGH AND MAY EVEN RISE TO $100 A BARREL

The world is experiencing its first demand crisis in more than two decades. We can blame China, OPEC, Iraq, and the oil peak for that, but we must also admit that the industry has gone through some structural changes that have had enormous influences on energy prices. Certainly, a case can be made that oil and gas have become asset commodities that are attracting more investors at a time when equity returns aren't great. In fact, that's why the American Stock Exchange introduced the first exchange-traded fund (ETF) tracking crude prices in April 2006. Exchange-traded funds have become hot on Wall Street because they give individual, average investors the opportunity to have control over their investments, by taking positions in crude oil rather than investing in shares of energy companies or mutual funds. In a kind of cyclical effect, these new investors have added, and will continue to add, market liquidity, causing oil prices to continue soaring, and energy companies also to make more money.[1]

Oil prices had climbed to $75 per barrel in April 2006 and were set to hit a new record, while gasoline prices passed $3 per gallon, double what they had been two years earlier in December 2004. Oil was trading at $40 and we thought that was high. Now, in retrospect, we were so wrong. In fact, we probably won't see oil that cheap again, unless there's

117

a temporary glut caused by OPEC, which is unlikely. The sharp rise has nearly everyone scratching their heads about where oil prices may be headed next. Consumers are paying through the nose and traders are asking how they can get a piece of that boom. Some think it won't be long before we get to $100 oil, while more aggressive analysts are setting their sights as high as $180 per barrel.

The oil boom has made headlines across the globe recently. Strong demand from China and India, a lack of spare capacity, or more accurately, the inability of OPEC countries—particularly Saudi Arabia—to increase oil supply by any significant margin, as well as weather-related supply shocks have fueled the crude oil rally. As a result, we have seen windfall earnings for oil companies and painfully high fuel costs for the consumer, all of which has forced politicians and oil executives into a corner as public outrage mounts.

The U.S. Senate Committees on Energy & Natural Resources and Commerce, Science, and Technology heard executives of the world's five largest oil companies at a public hearing amid charges of gouging in November 2005. But the executives offered strong defense of their companies' high profits, as national politicians pressed them to account for soaring gasoline, diesel, and natural gas prices in the months after Hurricanes Katrina and Rita struck the Gulf Coast. Later, senators heard from state officials who urged Congress to pass a federal anti-price-gouging law. The Bush administration, however, cautioned against such laws, saying competition was more effective in controlling prices.

While admitting that high oil prices were hurting consumers, the executives said their profits were not out of line, arguing in fact that prices were being driven by larger forces often out of their control. "Today's higher prices are a function of longer-term supply and demand trends and lost energy production during the recent hurricanes," said James Mulva, chairman and chief executive of ConocoPhillips.[2] But several senators, mostly Democrats along with some Republicans, appeared unsatisfied by those responses, and they demanded to know what the industry was doing to increase supplies, and whether oil companies would help promote conservation measures. "Most Americans and most of the polls show that our people have a growing suspicion that the oil companies are taking unfair advantage of the current market conditions to line their coffers with excess profits," Pete Domenici, Republican of New Mexico, said during the televised hearing. Senator Barbara Boxer, Democrat of

California, added: "Working people struggle with high gas prices, and your sacrifice, gentlemen, appears to be nothing."[3] She noted that the executives were making millions of dollars in salaries, bonuses, and stock awards. Still, calls for a windfall profits tax on oil profits that would help families pay high heating bills and other energy costs were beaten back.

Oil, gasoline, and natural gas prices soared in the weeks after Hurricane Katrina struck the Gulf Coast and shut down the vast majority of offshore production sites and 18 percent of domestic oil refining. Gasoline prices spiked past $3 a gallon in many parts of the United States, though they retreated to pre-Katrina levels by October. It was clear the economic impact across the country was going to cause problems, and it was not long before politicians such as Senator Conrad Burns, Republican of Montana, began saying high diesel prices were squeezing farmers and making American agricultural products too expensive for world markets. "Let the American people understand, agriculture is going to get shut down," he said. "We're not going to turn on one tractor to produce food and fiber for this country under these kinds of conditions. We have to do something different."

The executives of Exxon Mobil, Chevron, British Petroleum (BP), ConocoPhillips, and Royal Dutch Shell noted that they have been investing most of their profits in new production and refining. Lee Raymond, chairman and chief executive of Exxon Mobil, which reported a $9.92 billion profit for the third quarter of 2005, said that the industry's profits measured as percent of revenue were no greater than other industries. "We are in line with the average of all U.S. industry," he said. "Our numbers are huge because the scale of our industry is huge. How are these earnings used? We invest to run our global operations, to develop future supply, to advance energy-producing and saving technologies, and to meet our obligations to millions of our shareholders."[4]

The oil chief executives asserted that in the past decade their capital investments matched their profits. Asked what they were doing to increase domestic oil refining capacity and bring on additional sources of energy, they said investments in their industry can take decades to come to fruition. Mr. Raymond said that even if the government streamlined the approval process for constructing new refineries, a move the energy industry sought, it would still take years to build new plants. Instead of building new plants, Exxon has chosen to expand existing plants.

"It is much more efficient because the basic infrastructure is already in place," Mr. Raymond said. "Over the last 10 years, Exxon Mobil alone has built the equivalent of three average-sized refineries through expansions and efficiency gains at existing U.S. refineries."[5]

Raymond's argument is rather lame because acquiring another refinery doesn't increase the overall refining capacity. There has not been a new refinery built in the United States since 1976. Companies have expanded existing plants, which are also being operated closer to full capacity, but they have been coy about building new plants from scratch. In 1980, there were 425 refineries across the country; there are 176 today.

Some of the executives said Congress could help bring more energy supplies to the market by allowing the industry to develop oil and natural gas rigs and platforms in places like the Florida coastal waters, which have been declared off limits to exploration. At some point during the hearing, several senators and state attorneys general sparred with the chairwoman of the Federal Trade Commission, Deborah Platt Majoras, about whether Congress should consider a federal law criminalizing "price gouging," which some lawmakers defined as an unconscionable increase in prices. She opposed the move.

The state attorneys general and lawmakers argued that policymakers needed better tools to deal with gasoline stations and oil companies that take advantage of an emergency to increase prices and raise their profits. "I do believe that we need a federal statute that has a criminal penalty and we have to look at what the statute will be in terms of the criminal penalty," said Senator Ted Stevens, the Republican from Alaska who is chairman of the Commerce Committee.[6] But the administration rejected that. "Higher prices—as tough as they are to swallow, and they are—help curtail panic buying and the topping off," said Majoras.[7]

In this chapter, I will explain how the oil market works and then discuss in detail the reasons behind oil prices soaring since 2004 to unheard of levels.

HOW THE OIL MARKET WORKS

From Economics 101 textbooks, we remember that commodity prices are a function of demand and supply. But today's market is responding to additional pressures—geopolitical tensions as well as speculative activity. Those who look at fundamentals argue correctly that because of growing economies around the world—particularly in the United States, China, and

India—demand for oil is rising so sharply that supply cannot keep up. Current daily oil production of about 84 million barrels globally leaves us with, at the most, with just two million barrels of spare capacity, hardly enough to absorb any unplanned disruptions in the supply chain. And yet there have been and will continue to be many disruptions in the supply chain, especially in oil producing countries that are politically unstable. It's important to note that the majority of these countries are politically unstable: the Middle East, Russia, Nigeria, and Venezuela. Obviously, such a tight market causes oil and gas prices to soar, as we have seen since 2004. When you add an unexpectedly destructive natural disaster like Hurricanes Katrina and Rita, the pain becomes almost unbearable. Since 2004, oil prices have spiked in a manner that hasn't been seen since the last oil shock in 1979.

In terms of oil supply and demand balance, let's start right here at home. About 82 million barrels a day of oil are consumed globally, of which the United States accounts for one-quarter (North America as a whole accounts for a whopping 30 percent). Yet, North America—which includes Canada and Mexico—produces just 25 percent of the world's energy supply. United States demand rose by about 2 million barrels per day, or 11 percent, to about 21 million barrels per day between 1995 and 2005. The United States remains the largest consumer of oil and Canada is our largest energy trading partner, supplying us with most of the oil we need. There is also a significant oil and gas trade between the United States and Mexico.

In the U.S. oil market, everything from steel to drilling rigs to refining capacity is scarce and supply is constrained. Although the oil industry's capital investment has picked up with higher prices, those investments won't yield any more supply anytime soon and prices won't drop much unless demand eases substantially. And that may not happen. Hurricane Katrina highlighted constraints in supply by taking out 20 percent of oil production and about 14 percent of gas production in the Gulf of Mexico, and about 18 percent of refining capacity for several months. Of course, the impact is being felt through 2006, and future hurricane seasons will be just as severe.

Hedging against High Prices

Crude oil and its products, such as gasoline, heating oil, diesel, kerosene, (or jet fuel), are traded both on a spot basis and on the futures contract basis. The futures market is basically a market for risk management, where traders sell contracts for crude cargoes that will be delivered at a later date, typically two months to many months out, through 2011. The New York Mercantile Exchange, located in lower Manhattan, is the oldest and largest energy futures market, where light sweet crude from West Texas is traded. Because of its sheer size, the West Texas Intermediate crude delivered to Cushing, Oklahoma, sets prices for oil in North America, and it also influences other oil prices globally because of its liquidity. There is another electronic futures market in London—the Intercontinental-Exchange (ICE), formerly the International Petroleum Exchange—where crude from Europe is traded, with Brent crude from the North Sea acting as the benchmark. In recent years, because of the low volume of Brent (because the North Sea production is falling), the New York-based energy information firm Platts, which provides price data for oil traders, has added crude from the Forties and Oseberg fields in the North Sea as alternate benchmarks whenever Brent becomes illiquid.

Liquidity is important in the oil market because it prevents price manipulation, especially when price reporting isn't diversified. Since it has a near-monopoly on the oil price index, Platts, owned by publisher McGraw-Hill Companies, is very influential in the oil market, although there is no evidence it has used its influence to adversely affect oil trading. However, it has come under investigation over an inaccurate natural gas index. The Commodity Futures Trading Commission (CFTC) claims it has evidence that some energy companies allegedly attempted to affect prices in the natural gas market by submitting false data to Platts between November 2000 and October 2002.

Platts produces a monthly report that can influence prices, potentially affecting billions of dollars worth of natural gas transactions. Platts itself hasn't been accused of any wrongdoing, but the CFTC says the following companies have settled to the tune of $96 million in civil monetary penalties: Duke Energy Trading paid $28 million); Enserco Energy ($3 million); Williams Energy Marketing and Trading ($20 million); WD Energy Services (formerly known as Encana Energy Services, $20 million); El Paso Merchant Energy ($20 million); Dynergy Marketing and Trade and West Coast Power (Dynergy and West Coast together paid $5 million). American Electric Power Company (AEP) and its subsidiary AEP Energy Services Inc (AEPES) haven't settled yet and investigations continue.[8]

As oil prices have become more volatile, those whose business involves producing, marketing, or using oil, gasoline, and other types of energy use have resorted to managing their financial risks by buying contracts for oil and product deliveries many months or years in advance. The reason is they want to be sure of how much they will have to spend on fuel as part of their budgetary planning. At the same time, they want to lock in prices, either when those prices are low or when they think the prices will rise to more than they can afford. As with every risk, sometimes they win and sometimes they lose, when prices fall below their contracts. But at least they are paying attention to financial instruments that are available for hedging against price risk—the futures, options and swaps— which are tied to basic commodities or some underlying financial or economic entity. They do this on the Nymex and ICE, both of which were started for this kind of risk management.

Crude oil and natural gas prices have been soaring, refined products such as jet fuel, heating oil, gasoline, diesel fuel, and kerosene have become more volatile, and electricity continues to show its usual wide swings in wholesale prices. In August of 2005, crude oil prices reached as high as $70.85 per barrel, up from $33 in April 2004. The prices are expected to rise even higher in 2006 and beyond. Strong consumption of gasoline in the United States as well as growing energy use in China and India amid supply shortages caused the surge. The price of natural gas at the Henry Hub in Louisiana rose to $12 per million British thermal units by late August from $5.20 in April 2004.[9] By November 2005, the prices had come down about 20 percent, but went up again because of rising winter demand.

In such a volatile situation, the best way for an energy user or a wholesale buyer to protect against soaring prices, or for a producer or reseller to deal with falling prices, is to buy and sell the relevant futures or options contracts that trade on the Nymex and ICE, which can help offset some of the risk. This strategy is called hedging. In its simplest form, hedging involves buying or selling a futures contract, a temporary substitute for the sale or purchase of the physical commodity. When the time comes to make or take delivery of those physical crude cargoes, the futures position is liquidated. The gain or loss on the futures contract is at least partially offset by the loss or gain on the physical product, giving market participants a fairly stable sales price.

Hedging can be an effective way of allowing a trader—a seller or a buyer—to lock in prices and margins in advance, and it reduces the potential for unanticipated losses. In return for mitigating the risk, however, the trader often limits the opportunity for a profit if prices move favorably. The trader who hedges too far forward into the future can be hurt if prices move sharply in a favorable direction and he is unable to take advantage of it. Options on futures give the buyer the option, or the right but not the obligation, to buy or sell the underlying contract at a specified price within a specified time, for a one-time premium payment, allowing participation in favorable price moves. A third instrument, a swap, is typically traded over-the-counter (OTC). In essence, the buyer and the seller exchange payments based on their differing expectation of which way the commodity's market price will move, or one party may want a fixed price while the other opts for a variable price. In a typical OTC swap, parties can design the contract whichever way they want, but they are exposed to the risk that the counterparty may default.

The oil market has become increasingly dominated by hedging, which basically is a legal form of gambling, but that's important for many people. People who wait to buy fuel when prices come down are also gambling with fate. Take the plight of the airlines, some of which have been pushed into bankruptcy by soaring jet fuel prices. One of the few that has stayed solvent is Southwest Airlines, which has remained profitable by an aggressive jet fuel hedging strategy—using a combination of options, swaps, and crude and product futures to offset rising jet fuel expenses. As a result, the airline was able to keep its net jet fuel costs to crude oil equivalent of under $24 and $26 per barrel in 2004 and 2005 respectively, at a time when crude prices rose to $70 per barrel.

Hedge Funds

Increasingly, big money investors have seen there's money in oil, and they have poured as much as one trillion dollars into the energy markets, buying and selling these contracts but not looking for deliveries; instead, they make money on the price differentials from time to time. For instance, they buy contracts for future delivery at today's prices, aware that the equity on those contracts will grow sharply in a year or two. In fact, some of those investors—mostly hedge funds and mutual funds—have bought contracts for deliveries 10 years into the future, by which time the equity on those contracts may have gone up ten times or more. It's quite clear that they will make a lot of money when they ultimately sell those contracts to refiners, who will then pass on their costs to consumers. The result is that oil and product prices will continue to go up.

As I've said before, oil prices have been rising sharply because demand is rising more than supply, in part because of China's robust economy and also due to supply-side problems like hurricanes that destroy oil infrastructure in the Gulf of Mexico. But aside from that, in recent years a lot of speculators and other big money investors, including hedge funds, have turned to energy commodities as a new investment vehicle.

Most of these investors are betting that supply and demand constraints will get worse in the future, and so they are only too willing to bid up crude cargoes, thus pushing up oil prices. As a result, these speculators ignore short-term market fundamentals of demand and supply and instead go on a buying spree based on long-term probable risks of short supply, especially in the event of political problems in the Middle East, Nigeria, or Venezuela. Often these days you find that there's a divergence between fundamentals and the actual value of oil at any given time.

The situation could moderate once OPEC rebuilds its spare capacity to a comfortable level and if demand tapers off, although that's unlikely to happen soon. Natural gas prices almost doubled in 2005 as residential and utility use rose. Natural gas prices on the New York Mercantile Exchange were around $6 per million British thermal units for much of 2004 and peaked at $9 in the fourth quarter. They then started to rise again in the first quarter of 2005, getting to about $13 by the end of the third quarter, following the shutoff of Gulf of Mexico oil and gas production by Hurricanes Katrina and Rita.[10]

Part of the reason natural gas prices are high is that the United States relies completely on domestic production. Imports of liquefied natural gas are expensive and limited. There are plans to get gas from Alaska, but the issue of how to transport it to the lower 48 states has not been resolved. The governments of the United States and Canada and major oil companies that are supposed to fund the project have been discussing the pipeline project for almost a decade, but there's an impasse on funding and where the pipeline would be placed.

Natural Gas

Currently, the only way natural gas can be imported is in liquid form. That means the gas has to be liquefied and shipped in specially made large tankers. This is already happening, but on a very small scale and it takes a long time to do that. In any given month, there are about four large liquefied natural gas, or LNG, tankers trading globally, and only one or two comes to the United States, where deliveries are made either to Lake Charles in Louisiana or to New York Harbor. LNG imports are low in part because there are not enough transportation tankers and terminals where cargoes of gas can be stored. Because of that the LNG market is neither flexible nor efficient and so the price of LNG is very high for ordinary consumers.

However, additional facilities for imports are being developed. A new offshore terminal in the Gulf of Mexico received its first delivery of LNG in 2004. In Georgia and Maryland, import terminals have been taken out of mothballs after more than two decades, and more tankers are being built. In addition, a two-way trade in gas between the United States and Mexico is expected to grow. But even with the added capacity in 2004, LNG imports still accounted for less than 3 percent of U.S. consumption.

Within the financial sector, commercial banks are becoming bigger players in energy risk management, partly because they are more wiling to use their huge capital to buy and store natural gas and oil. They also can take title to physical energy assets. Typically, these banks look at the current price of energy commodities and try to figure out what the same type and quantity of assets will cost in the future, given the underlying demand and supply picture, plus any political risks that could affect supply either way. They then buy paper contracts for future deliveries of the commodity, be it oil, gasoline, heating oil, or natural gas.

Light sweet crude traded in the futures market is delivered to Cushing, Oklahoma, and natural gas futures contracts are for delivery to the Henry Hub in Louisiana. These are the two principal pricing and wholesale delivery points for the U.S. market. Numerous pipelines converge at these two locations, taking physical oil and gas from the producing regions of the Gulf Coast and distributing those supplies throughout the United States.

THE CHINA AND INDIA EFFECT: OIL DEMAND AND PRICES TO STAY HIGH

China and India are locked in an increasingly aggressive wrangle with the United States over the world's most critical economic commodity: oil. More than any other issue, this tussle will shape the economic, environmental, and geopolitical future of these three countries and the world.

Ensuring a steady flow of cheap oil has always been one of the central goals of U.S. foreign and economic policy, and Washington's preeminent position in the world is based in large measure on its ability to do this. But China and India are increasingly competing with the United States to secure oil exploration rights in Africa, Southeast Asia, Central Asia, and Latin America. India has invested more than $3 billion in global exploration ventures and has said it will continue to spend $1 billion a year on more acquisitions. China, which has already invested about $15 billion in foreign oil fields, is expected to spend 10 times that over the next decade. The motive, says Zheng Hongfei, an energy researcher at the Beijing Institute of Technology, is that "there is just not enough oil in the world" to cover China's and India's growing energy needs.[11]

By 2010 India will have 36 times more cars than it did in 1990, according to Jehangir Pocha, Asia correspondent for *In These Times*. China will have 90 times more, and by 2030 it will have more cars than the United States, according to the Energy Research Institute of Beijing. More than 4.5 million new vehicles are expected to hit Chinese roads this year alone, a far cry from the time when families saved for months to buy a Flying Pigeon bicycle. The country is now the world's largest oil importer after the United States, guzzling about 6.5 million barrels of oil a day; this figure will double by 2020, says Stephen Roach, chief economist at Morgan Stanley.[12]

India, the world's second-fastest growing economy after China, now consumes about 2.2 million barrels a day—about the same as South Korea—and this is expected to rise to 5.3 million barrels a day by 2025, according to the U.S. Energy Information Administration. With global oil production barely 1.5 to 2 million barrels per day over the global consumption rate of about 83 million barrels a day, the surge in demand from China and India could eventually lead global demand to outstrip supply, causing fuel prices to shoot up beyond the $60 to $70 per barrel range seen in early 2006, says Roach. The impact of this on the global economy, particularly in developing countries that import most of their fuel, would be severe. The International Energy Agency says that for every $1 increase in oil price, the global economy loses $25 billion.

Anxiety over this is already throwing the nervous oil market into further disequilibrium. In September, Michael Rothman, a senior energy analyst at Merrill Lynch, said rising oil prices were not so much a result of the Iraq war or political instability in Venezuela and Sudan as of extensive "hoarding" by China. According to Rothman's analysis, China and India are roiling oil markets by creating oil reserves, which are designed to provide the minimum cache the country needs to ride out a crisis, along the lines of the U.S. Strategic Petroleum Reserve (SPR). With both countries flush with foreign exchange reserves that are threatening to infect their economies with inflation, creating an oil stock seems a sensible solution. But critics say Beijing's and New Delhi's timing is unfortunate, coming just as the global economy seemed to be recovering and the United States was questioning the value of its own reserve. At 175 million barrels and 25 million barrels respectively, China's and India's estimated oil reserves are just a small fraction of the 700 million barrels held by the United States in its SPR.

China and India, which are both nuclear states, are also taking advantage of the United States' strained ties with Iran, Vietnam, and Myanmar (Burma) by extending these countries military and political support in exchange for energy supplies. A Washington preoccupied with Iraq, the war on terror, and nuclear crises in Iran and North Korea has been unable to checkmate either country as successfully as it did earlier. For example, U.S. nervousness over China's intentions in Latin America had led it to use its leverage with Panama to impede China's access to the all-important canal connecting the Pacific and Atlantic. But in December 2005, Beijing signed a landmark deal with Venezuela and its neighbor Colombia, under whose terms a pipeline would be constructed linking Venezuelan oil fields to ports along Colombia's Pacific coastline. This will allow Venezuelan oil to bypass the Panama Canal and create a new and direct route to China.

There are also signs that China is warming to the idea of a Russia–China–India axis, which, in cooperation with Iran, would turn the oil-rich Central Asian region into their domain. This proposal would put in place extensive military agreements and pipeline networks. Originally put forward by Russia's Asia-centric ex-Prime Minister Yevgeny Primakov, the proposal seems to be gaining ground with all four nations. China and India have already signed multibillion-dollar gas and energy deals with Russia, which is the largest arms supplier to both countries, and with ex-Soviet Central Asian republics such as Kazakhstan.

What worries Western powers most are China's and India's growing ties with Iran, a country Washington is trying to isolate. Both Beijing and New Delhi have recently signed 25-year gas and oil deals with Iran that are collectively valued at between $150 and $200 billion, and both countries are also deepening their military cooperation with Tehran. Iran and India conducted their first-ever joint naval exercises last September, and

India has agreed to modernize Iran's aging Russian-built Kilo-class submarines and MiG fighters.

Both China and India have also tried to thwart Western attempts to curtail Iran's nuclear program, which has largely been built with Russian assistance. In a departure from China's traditional neutrality on international issues that do not involve its own interests, Chinese Foreign Minister Li Zhaoxing flew to Tehran in November 2005 when the United States threatened to haul Iran before the U.N. Security Council and announced that China would oppose any such effort. And in January 2006, the State Department imposed penalties against some of China's largest weapons manufacturers for their support of Iran's ballistic missile program.

The potential volatility from such aggressive oil politics could bring China and India into conflict with Western, Japanese, and other regional interests, says Robert Karniol, the Asia-Pacific editor of *Jane's Defense Weekly*. "Even if China's oil consumption doubles by 2020, it will still only be half that of the U.S.," says Zheng, the energy researcher at Beijing Institute of Technology.[13] Yet the sheer size of the Asian juggernauts and the prospect that they might indiscriminately swallow global resources scare economic planners.

State-owned Indian and Chinese oil companies are investing heavily in local energy fields, such as the 200,000-square-mile Ordos Basin that stretches across the provinces of Shaanxi, Shanxi, Gansu, Ningxia, and Inner Mongolia in northwestern China, and is reported to have oil reserves of up to 60 billion barrels. To defray the substantial costs of exploration, both China and India are privatizing state-owned oil companies and using the billions raised to restructure and modernize their operations. Other public sector oil units are also undergoing massive recapitalization and restructuring, including the firing of thousands of workers. Sharon Hurst, a Beijing-based executive with ConocoPhillips, the largest refiner in the United States, says, "Western investment is helping Chinese oil companies morph into world-class players."[14]

Significantly, both nations are also opening up their domestic oil industries—previously considered strategic and therefore off limits to foreign and private investors. Companies such as Exxon Mobil, which owns a 19 percent stake in China's giant Sinopec company, are being wooed not just for their capital but also for their refining and marketing capabilities. For example, Exxon Mobil is helping Sinopec establish more than 500 gas stations across the country and build at least two refineries in southern China.

Optimists—mostly people from the corporate world such as Warren Buffett—say such common opportunity will lead to greater cooperation rather than competition between the West and China and India. But pessimists—mostly people from the security establishment—fear that China and India, two energy-hungry giants seeking access to limited world resources, will inevitably clash with the West.

China's Need for Energy Resources

Until recently, the exclusive club of major energy users was reserved for a few, with the United States as the main member and the leading oil consumer. On the other side of the spectrum was OPEC, a grouping of 11 producing countries, most of them in the Middle East, formed in Baghdad in 1960.

For much of the past 50 years, all the United States had to worry about was whether OPEC was producing enough to meet global demand, and in particular, the needs of American consumers. Often the cartel would play games on the market by limiting oil supply whenever its members chose and for whatever reason. Occasionally, the United States and other developed nations would confront OPEC. But whether the world was adequately supplied very much depended on Saudi Arabia, the world's largest oil producer.

In 2004, everything changed as China's oil consumption grew faster than anyone expected, making China the second largest importer after the United States and causing a panic in the oil market.

Continuing very high demand from China and India, Asia's new powerhouse economies, has strained oil supply and pushed up prices to record levels, with analysts at Goldman Sachs, the New York–based investment bank, forecasting a price "super-spike" to slightly more than $100 per barrel. Given that bullish broad view, hedge funds and other speculators have become more active investors in the energy markets. All of that adds another premium to the price because of the huge pile of cash coming into the sector.

Unprecedented need for energy resources now drives China's foreign policy. A booming economy, increased export processing, rapid urban growth, and a growing affluent population with a big appetite for cars are increasing the country's demand for oil and natural gas. Twenty years ago, there would have been no problem because China was East Asia's largest oil exporter. Today, China is the world's second-largest oil importer after the United States. This change comes just as China has become the world's largest workshop, where textiles, computer chips, and a host of other manufacturing activities are going on at the cheapest labor cost.

Industrial and housing construction is at full speed in cities like Shanghai ahead of the Beijing Olympics in 2008, and China's hunger for electricity and other industrial resources has soared as well. In 2004, China alone accounted for 31 percent of global growth in oil demand. And it's not just oil. China's combined share of the world's consumption of metals—aluminum, copper and iron ore—more than doubled within the past decade to 20 percent, and is likely to double again by the end of the next decade, according to Professor David Zweig, an expert on Chinese foreign relations at Hong Kong University of Science and Technology.[15]

Professor Zweig wrote an article in the September/October 2005 issue of *Foreign Affairs*, a journal published by the Council for Foreign Relations, in which he said that, despite calls by senior Chinese politicians to cut consumption of energy and other resources, there is little sign of that happening since the country's economy is forecast to grow at 9 percent per year for the next 20 years.

China currently gets 70 percent of its energy needs from coal. But as it tries to improve air quality ahead of the Beijing Olympics, a lot more oil and natural gas is going to be needed. That's why China has begun looking for steady sources overseas and will compete with the United States for oil from the Middle East, West Africa, and Russia. In the past year alone, China has been on full-scale oil diplomacy to Africa, Russia, North America, and South America, and its state oil companies have been scouting for fuel sources abroad through partnerships or buy-outs. Chinese leaders have been making rounds in oil-rich countries. Their need for oil has serious implications for the country's foreign policy.

China's Approaches to Oil-Rich Countries

China's access to oil and gas is necessary both for continued economic growth as well as for the survival of the Chinese Communist Party. With still more than 900 million people living in poverty, China can't afford a slow growth rate, which could cause political and social upheaval. Since China remains a relatively centralized, state-controlled economy, Beijing has been able to adapt its foreign policy to its domestic development strategy. Business leaders are now helping to shape foreign policy, and the government is encouraging state-controlled companies to secure exploration and supply agreements with countries that produce oil, gas, and other resources.

Chinese leaders, meanwhile, have been aggressively courting governments of these countries, building goodwill by strengthening bilateral trade relations, awarding aid, forgiving national debt, and helping build roads and bridges. In return, China has won access to key resources, from gold in Bolivia to coal in Philippines to oil in Ecuador and natural gas in Australia.

In a bold move in August 2005, the Chinese National Offshore Oil Company (CNOOC), a company based outside mainland China but with government ties, made the first foray by a Chinese company into a Western country, by pursuing a $18.4 billion bid for Unocal Corp., a small company based in California that had extensive exploration interest in Southeast Asia. But the deal flopped in part because of the intervention by powerful members of the United States Congress, who were worried about China's growing military and economic influence. In that regard, the Chinese hunt for oil and gas across the globe is also causing a great deal of concern from those who are suspicious of China.

As China struggles to manage its growth, the United States will have to learn how to coexist with an emerging power, or else a conflict is inevitable. When Professor Wangare Mathai, the Kenyan activist who won the 2004 Nobel Peace Prize for her work to renew the environment, said the next world war will be fought over natural resources, she probably didn't have these two powerful countries in mind. But it surely looks like we are heading toward a precipice unless both the United States and China can pull back.

One of the most widely recognized power theories studied in military academies holds that a superpower like the United States can keep its global dominance only by sheer force. Yet, our military interests can sometimes collide with our economic interests. But those who think the United States must declare war on such challengers as China while we are still at a military advantage are enemies of free markets. A free market economy thrives in peace, not war. Unocal eventually went to Chevron for $1.5 billion less than what the Chinese had agreed to pay, and that was a loss for American holders of Unocal shares.

Evidently, the Chinese learned a lesson on how to play high-stakes Wall Street games. Two months after the Unocal debacle, another Chinese company, China National Petroleum Corp. (CNPC), succeeded in buying PetroKazakhstan, a Canadian company that produces oil and gas in the former Soviet Republics, for about $4.2 billion.

Previously seen as a champion of the Third World, China has over the past 20 years paid a lot of attention to its ties with developing economies. But while these ties remain important, Beijing is now turning its attention particularly to oil-rich developing countries regardless of their human rights records. State-owned Chinese firms are busy seeking resources abroad, often with the support of Beijing, which courts supplier countries by cultivating bilateral relations and providing aid to those countries. Beijing keeps a list of countries and resources in which investment is eligible for state subsidies. The list is full of Third-World countries, with the exception of Norway and Russia. They include Saudi Arabia, Oman, and Iran in the Middle East; Angola, Sudan, and Congo in Africa; Vietnam, Indonesia, and Malaysia in Asia-Pacific; and Russia, Norway, and Brazil in Europe and the Western hemisphere. This list is by no means conclusive because China has lately grown chummy with Canada, Venezuela, Bolivia, and Nigeria as well.

Dependence on imported oil has made China an active player in the Middle East. More than 40 percent of China's oil is coming from that region alone. In 2004 Chinese President Hu Jintao met with members of the Arab League in Cairo to boost political and economic ties. He framed his move as "a new type of partnership" that would further increase oil shipments to China. Iran already accounts for about 11 percent of China's oil imports. In late 2004, state-controlled China Petroleum & Chemical Corp, otherwise known as Sinopec, one of the three major government oil companies, signed an oil and natural gas agreement with Tehran worth $70 billion. It is China's biggest energy deal with any OPEC producer. Beijing committed to developing the giant Yadavaran oilfield and to buying 250 million tons of liquefied natural gas over the next 30 years. Tehran agreed to export to China 150,000 barrels of oil a day at market prices for 25 years.

In Africa, which already supplies 29 percent of China's total crude oil imports, Beijing has recently extended its traditional relationships and has began to challenge the U.S. influence in some countries. In 2003, Prime Minister Wen visited several oil-producing African countries, accompanied by Chinese oil executives; President Hu toured Algeria, Egypt, and Gabon. China already has good working relationships with governments in the Gulf of Guinea, from Angola to Nigeria, as well as with Central African Republic, Chad, Congo, Libya, Niger, and Sudan.

China also has begun to make forays into Latin America. Dozens of business leaders accompanied President Hu on his four-stop trip in the fall of 2004, during which he announced $20 billion in new investments for oil and gas exploration among other projects. In the winter of 2005, Vice President Zeng Qinghong also visited Latin America and the Caribbean and signed various trade and oil supply agreements with Venezuela. The trade between China and Latin America has grown four-fold since 1999 to almost $40 billion.

Oil diplomacy also prompted China to seek access to Canada's tar sands of Alberta. The two countries have concluded a series of energy agreements since 2004, providing China with the opportunity to develop Canada's oil and natural gas sector. Yet that deal could further exacerbate tensions between the United States and China, as well, and between the United States and Canada. U.S. Vice President Dick Cheney's 2001 national energy policy emphasized the importance of Canada's tar sands to U.S. energy security. The U.S. Congress has been nervous about China fishing in American waters as well as uneasy about China's willingness to pursue oil resources in countries that are hostile to Washington, such as Iran, Sudan, and Myanmar.

The Long View

Whatever happens in Washington, it is becoming increasingly clear that China's boom can no longer be ignored or understood in regional terms alone. Although China's new energy demand need not be a source of conflict with Washington in the long term, rising demand for oil by both countries is currently driving oil prices higher, and that has begun to hurt Americans. That may be the single most important impact of China's rapid growth on the international oil market. China's demand is so great now that it will affect global supplies and prices for a while. Matt Simmons, a Houston-based investment banker and best-selling author of *Twilight in the Desert*, predicts that oil prices could soon jump to between $125 and $180 a barrel in the event of a very cold winter or another serious disruption of oil and natural gas supplies. "Everyone keeps thinking there's a ceiling [for oil prices], there's no ceiling," Simmons told Reuters on Oct. 19, 2005.[16]

For investors, China offers long-term promise, but the next five years are key. China is getting a great deal of attention from U.S. investors despite the fact that its equity market is less than 1 percent of the world total. Most money managers, including those who own oil stocks, are betting the fast growth rate will pay off because of an explosion of demand. Hedge funds like those of Franklin-Templeton have heavily invested in China's electric power stocks, while John Hancock holds a Chinese oil portfolio, including stock in oil and gas producer PetroChina, in which Warren Buffett owns a 1.3 percent stake.

HURRICANE BLUES: THE COST OF KATRINA AND RITA

The oil market already was tight, with no room for error, when Hurricanes Katrina and Rita knocked out all of the oil infrastructure in the U.S. Gulf of Mexico in the summer of 2005, sending prices through the roof. Katrina was the first to strike the region like an unruly monster on August 29. It damaged production platforms in the deep waters of the Gulf, and then shut down four refineries along the coasts of Louisiana and Mississippi. But that was just a preview for what was to come three weeks later, when Rita followed with more fury and knocked off twelve more refineries in Texas. In total, the 16 downed refineries accounted for three million barrels per day of refining capacity, or about 20 percent of the total U.S. capacity. The impact sent crude oil prices to record levels above $70 per barrel and retail gasoline prices above $3 per gallon.

Katrina was the biggest and deadliest hurricane to have hit that part of the United States in more than a century. Its impact was enormous in every way and will continue to be felt for years to come. Financial loss as a result of the two storms was assessed at more than $50 billion, up from $22 billion caused by Hurricane Ivan just a year earlier. These hurricanes changed the way we look at a number of things, least of which was the fact that weather and environment are changing for the worse, which will continue to affect the energy industry. The entire oil industry, including skeptics like Exxon Mobil and the Bush administration, has begun to accept the fact that global warming was taking place and something had to be done.

This is interesting because in March of 2000 I was at a conference in San Antonio, attended by many oil executives, where most leaders of the industry were openly castigating the Kyoto treaty and blasting the Clinton Administration for not fighting it. I remember hearing those oil executives openly call Carol Browner "the second most dangerous woman in America after [former Attorney General] Janet Reno." Browner was the head of the U.S. Environmental Protection Agency (EPA) during the Clinton presidency and was considered a zealous environmentalist, having been an activist before her appointment.

Just about every Western oil executive hated Browner's EPA, except one: John Browne of BP, who with his European sensibilities had long recognized the environment as a major issue. He had tried to get his colleagues in the industry to awaken to the fact that global warming was a reality, arguing that the idea that weather science was still inconclusive, as claimed by Exxon Mobil, was beside the point. Rather, he wanted the industry to embrace the environment as a central issue and to fight for a place at the government policy-making table, where the problem of the environment could be tackled not in an adversarial manner, but in a way that would be sensitive to the industry's goals and would be guided by market forces.

In essence, Browne wanted a marketplace where the industry sets its own rules and those rules would be considered legitimate. He didn't want a situation, advocated by his colleagues, of absolutely no rules and where the industry could do just about what they liked. It's difficult for me to know whether Browne values the environment very much. What is clear, however, is that Browne was ahead of the game, and he used that to position BP as a company for the future, a company that cares about the environment and about the communities where it does business, and a company that is already thinking of our shared future. Hence the success, as a public relations matter, of BP's name and motto, Beyond Petroleum.

At the time of the conference, other oil executives, like Exxon Mobil's Lee Raymond (who has since retired), were dragging their feet and using large sums of money to fight scientists who opposed their views, which were informed more by profit margins than by science. They tried to rewrite scientific theories on global warming when George W. Bush came into the White House. The *New York Times* reported in June 2005 that a White House official repeatedly edited government climate reports in ways that played down links between greenhouse gas emissions and global warming. The official, Philip Cooney, was chief of staff for the White House Council on Environmental Quality, a body which shapes much of U.S. environmental policy.[17]

Before coming to the White House in 2001, Cooney was a lobbyist at the American Petroleum Institute. Just two days after that article was published, Cooney resigned from the White House Council and joined Exxon Mobil. Exxon Mobil defended its hiring of Cooney by stating that they hire from both sides of the aisle. Meanwhile, an investigation by *Mother Jones* magazine found that Exxon Mobil spent at least eight million dollars funding a network of groups to challenge the existence of global warming.

In 2005, that was history. Now, Katrina had provided enough practical evidence that global warming was real and we'd ignore it at our peril. Even Exxon Mobil wasn't going to say otherwise. The company, along with others, changed its tune and started promoting conservation and a cleaner environment, with an assist from President Bush himself. They did this not in recognition of global warming, but to address shortage issues and to argue for alternative fuels that would fill supply gaps.

GULF COAST STORMS TO KEEP THE PRICE OF OIL HIGH

After Katrina, it became impossible not to acknowledge the impact weather has on oil prices. The Gulf Coast, which supplies the United States with a third of its oil and product needs, is going to suffer hurricanes for the next 25 or more years, and that could raise petroleum prices by 30 percent or more each year.

By now it should be clear to almost everyone who followed news reports about Katrina and its aftermath that there were predictions a couple of years ago that a catastrophe was looming, but almost everyone ignored them. Government and independent scientists and even journalists had written extensively about the impending doom. Oceanographers at the nearby Louisiana State University had done a number of computer simulations of what might become of the Gulf Coast region in the event of a powerful hurricane.

Nobody paid much attention, of course, or at least no one in authority who could make a difference. In 2001, *Scientific American* magazine said it was inevitable that a major hurricane would hit New Orleans, which it described as a "disaster waiting to happen."[18] And in 2002, a local newspaper, the *Times-Picayune*, warned in a five-part series of articles on the issue that the city would be washed away. Finally, in October 2004, *National Geographic* magazine published an article entitled "Gone with the Water,"[19] which opened with a prophetic description of damage, chaos, and death that would descend on New Orleans with a major hurricane.

A year later the waiting was over as Katrina arrived in the morning of August 29, sacking the Gulf Coast and creating reverberations that shook the nation. Growing from a counterclockwise swirl of winds in the Caribbean, the storm churned west and rolled over south Florida as a category one storm, then swelled with a vengeance into a category five before easing to a category four hurricane as it made landfall in Louisiana. It was disaster upon disaster as the storm swept in a deadly wall of water, erasing towns, trapping hundreds of thousands of people, and paralyzing rescue efforts.

Floodwalls around New Orleans fell apart, drowning the city, which sits on a shallow bowl that dips below sea level and is surrounded by water on three sides. Levees and floodwalls running 320 miles around the city were the main barriers against flooding from the Mississippi River and Lake Pontchartrain. But they failed that day after parts of the levees broke and let in floodwater. As a result, four refineries in the New Orleans area were extensively damaged and stayed out of service for months after the hurricane.

For the energy industry, a steady flow of supply of crude oil and crude products is key to maintaining market confidence as well as some market equilibrium—a situation where there's enough supply to meet demand. But that's going to be difficult now and for many years to come because of the hurricanes. Hurricanes run on heat and there's plenty in the Atlantic these days, which enabled Katrina to draw extra energy from the Gulf of Mexico.

Global warming may increase hurricane intensity in the future, but scientists now believe that what warms the ocean today is a natural climate cycle that has strengthened the currents flowing northward from the tropics. The same cycle also tends to calm the winds that can destroy a developing hurricane. As a result, the Atlantic has spawned twice as many hurricanes since 1995 as in the decade before, although most of them missed the United States.

Until 2004, high-altitude winds had steered most of the hurricanes away from the Gulf and East Coasts. Then the winds shifted and became more intense. "My results suggest that future warming may lead to an upward trend in tropical cyclone destructive potential, and—taking into account an increasing coastal population—a substantial increase in hurricane-related losses in the twenty-first century," says Kerry Emanuel, an oceanographer at Massachusetts Institute of Technology, in a study published in the science journal *Nature* on July 31, 2005.[20]

The source of heat that is expected to continue spawning hurricanes in the future is called Loop Current, a stream of warm water from the Caribbean that circulates through the Gulf and exits south of Florida, feeding into the Gulf Stream, then sometimes going all the way to Eastern Canada. In the summer of 2005, the loop didn't exit south of Florida but rather stretched further north, along the path of the slowmoving storms. That's what intensified Hurricanes Rita, Katrina, and Ivan a year earlier, and the same scenario could be repeated over and over in the coming years.

Now, consider the region's future, and, for that matter, that of the United States, in light of these past two hurricane seasons, and you can imagine what is in store for us. If I were an oil executive, I'd be really afraid. Ultimately, it's not whether they should be afraid; instead, they should stop disputing science on climate change and get on with the business of learning how to provide alternative fuels as the globe continues to get warmer. It's unfortunate that companies like Exxon Mobil are lagging on this issue, but it's also heartening that BP and others have fully recognized the problem and are trying to address it. We can only hope that, after Katrina, Exxon Mobil and other companies that produce oil in the Gulf of Mexico will come on board and become part of the solution to this big problem.

The Gulf of Mexico, which covers the nation's only reliable offshore oil and gas production fields, has about 800 manned and thousands of unmanned platforms, which are responsible for 28.5 percent of domestic production of oil and 19.2 percent of domestic gas supply. The Louisiana Offshore Oil Port, in New Orleans, serves 6,000 seagoing vessels a year, many of them delivering imported oil from the Middle East, West Africa, and South America.

LOOP's onshore facilities, Fourchon Booster Station and Clovelly Dome Storage Terminal, are located just onshore in Fourchon and 25 miles (40.2 km) inland near Galliano, Louisiana. The Fourchon Booster Station has four 6,000-hp (4.47 MW) pumps which increase the pressure and crude oil flow en route to the Clovelly Dome Storage Terminal.[21]

The Clovelly Dome Storage Terminal is used to store crude oil in underground salt domes before it is shipped to the various refineries. The terminal consists of eight caverns with a total capacity of 40 million barrels, a pump station with four 6,000-hp pumps, meters to measure the crude oil receipts and deliveries, and a 25-million-barrel Brine Storage Reservoir.

These oil imports, plus those from offshore Gulf of Mexico, are pumped to the various refineries in the Gulf Coast for processing into gasoline, diesel, home heating fuel oil and kerosene (or jet fuel). These products are then transported by pipelines to consumers in the East Coast and the Midwest. There are over 9,000 miles of pipelines connecting the Gulf region with other parts of the United States. Gulf Coast refineries constitute 47.4 percent of the national total.[22]

TIGHT REFINING CAPACITY WILL KEEP PRICES HIGH

As we've seen before, if there's anything we remember most from Hurricanes Katrina and Rita besides the human toll in New Orleans, it's the impact they both had on the nation's oil refining capacity. In fact, much of the price spike we saw was due to the fact that up to a quarter of U.S. refining capacity was wiped out for several weeks. We could deal with the shutdown of offshore oil production, but we could not deal with a large reduction in refining capacity. The reason for this is simple: Since the oil shock of the 1970s, the U.S. government has always kept about 700 million barrels of oil in underground salt storage in Louisiana for emergency supply. But we can't import gasoline from everywhere because of strict environmental rules.

Other developed countries do the same, as advised by the International Energy Agency. These emergency supplies go by the name Strategic Petroleum Reserve. In fact, when Katrina knocked out many of our refineries, the U.S. Department of Energy moved fast and made available 30 million barrels of that emergency oil to refineries that needed it. But with several refineries shut down in Louisiana and Texas, the department was able to release only about 11 million barrels, and in fact the actual volume refiners took was less than that.

But even before Katrina, we already had a refining capacity problem in this country. Consider this: There has not been any new refinery built in the last 30 years. In 1980, there were about 425 refineries; today there are only 147. Many refineries failed in the intervening years when refining wasn't a profitable business. Finding and extracting oil—the so-called upstream part of the business—has captured our imagination since the 1860s when prospectors descended on Pennsylvania to dig the world's first oil well.

The downstream part of the business—which transforms oil into products—has been less sexy by comparison. Those 147 refineries in the United States can process only between 17 and 20 million barrels a day of crude into gasoline. That's just not enough for the 217 million automobiles registered in this country, so we have to import about one million barrels of gasoline every week, or 30 million barrels a month, to get along.[23]

Many analysts estimated that the United States consumed almost 32 million tons of gasoline in 2005. Projections for 2006 are higher. At the same time, we are facing a shortfall of more than 10 million tons of diesel and fuel oil because we won't be able to import that high volume of products from Europe forever. Moreover, according to Edinburgh-based oil consultant Wood Mackenzie, without huge new investment in refining capacity, by 2010 Europe would be 50 million tons short of diesel, one-fifth of projected demand.

But it's not a problem in the United States alone. It's happening everywhere in the industrialized world. According to figures from *Statistical Review*, refineries have been kept extremely busy over the past few years because there are only a few left. The global refinery utilization rate—how much crude a refinery runs through the refining system—rose in 2004 to 84 percent, the highest level in more than 25 years. In the United States alone, refineries were running at 95 percent of refining capacity just before Katrina, up from about 69 percent in 1981, according to data from the Energy Information Administration.

The fact is that the value of crude oil is found not in crude itself, but in a basket of refined products that provide us with the energy we need. Just think of gasoline for our automobiles, heating oil for our homes, diesel for our trucks and farm machinery, and jet fuel or kerosene for our airplanes. That refining capacity hasn't grown all these years even as demand for products increased is a scandal the industry should be ashamed of. Oil executives knew this was a problem a long time ago, but no one was willing to spend money on adequate expansion, even as profits went up.

Sure, they have a good defense: First, investment decisions taken today could take five years or more before any returns are seen, and by then refining margins may have fallen. This would suggest that capital investment is not prudent where profits could take a long time to be realized, but they haven't stopped investing in oil exploration. Secondly, they claim that stringent environmental regulations and opposition from community groups made it impossible for them to invest in refining expansion. But the same reasons haven't stopped them from extracting oil in some of the world's most volatile countries. If they can drill for oil in Nigeria, they can as well put up a refinery there or here to process gasoline. Suffice it to say there's simply a lack of leadership on this issue.

In 2005 at an oil conference in Cape Town, South Africa, Rex Tillerson, who in early 2006 took over from Lee Raymond as chief executive of Exxon Mobil, told his fellow oil executives that there wasn't any need to use current bumper earnings to build more refineries. "At current crude prices, the reward appears great," he said, but he also warned, "This will change. Ours is a cyclical industry—what goes up will invariably come down and will undoubtedly go up again." That makes perfect sense and Wall Street seems to agree with that view.

The only problem with this line of argument is that all industries are cyclical, and business leaders are expected to look beyond that and come up with long-term plans for their companies. The point here is that refiners get more profits when product supply is tighter than demand for it, and they are willing to maintain a limited refining capacity so as to have higher margins. And that's just what most oil executives care about. It's not wrong or illegal, just unseemly.

Normally, we are used to politicians shouting at OPEC when oil and product prices go up. Politicians are smart people, so they tend to shift blame to OPEC because they know the cartel has no reservoir of goodwill among consumers. In recent years, however, OPEC has been fighting back by blaming the tight refining capacity in industrialized nations for the high oil prices. It's become a blame game.

OPEC AND CONSUMER GOVERNMENTS
PLAY BLAME GAME

When British truck drivers, angered by high fuel prices, threatened to blockade refineries in the summer of 2005, Gordon Brown, the U.K. finance minister, said only OPEC held the keys to lower prices. He asked the cartel to raise oil production. OPEC, aware of the refining bottlenecks, promptly called his bluff, proposing to make available the remaining two million barrels per day of spare capacity if anyone needed it. "We are offering everything in our pocket, and this is my message to Gordon Brown: if he would like to have it, I would be happy to sell it to him," said Sheik Ahmad Fahd al-Ahmad al-Sabah, president of OPEC.[24]

But the announcement had only a limited impact on prices. Sabah knew very well that even if OPEC were able to double its output, that incremental oil wouldn't go anywhere because there isn't enough capacity to refine the oil into usable products. OPEC's call for more refineries is more persuasive, because refining constraints have the effect of putting a ceiling on oil production. It's a problem that could take a decade to overcome because it takes time and a lot of money to rebuild a refinery. That means high fuel prices are here to stay.

The U.S. Department of Energy predicts that world refining capacity will rise 60 percent by 2025, to 130 million barrels per day from 82 million b/d in 2003. The Middle East has more than a dozen projects planned and under way, including upgrades, integration, and grassroots construction, although the extent of progress varies. All those projects would boost refining capacity by 3.2 million barrels. Other ambitious schemes are moving ahead in North Africa.

OPEC'S PETRODOLLARS HELP U.S. TREASURY

Middle East countries meanwhile are soaking in cash from oil. In March 2005, Joe Quinlan, chief market strategist for the Investment Strategies Group at Bank of America, analyzed data from the U.S. Treasury Department and found out that recycled petrodollars to the United States hit a record high in 2004.

While rising world energy prices may be an unpleasant fact of life, there is a bright side to it. Flush with cash, oil producers recycled record sums of petrodollars back into the United States last year, helping to underwrite the debtor status of the United States. These producers include Bahrain, Iran, Iraq, Kuwait, Oman, Qatar, Saudi Arabia, United Arab Emirates, Algeria, Gabon, Libya, Nigeria, Venezuela, Indonesia, Russia, and Mexico.

Taking with one hand, so to speak, while giving with another, the world's major oil producers bought $67.7 billion of U.S. securities last year, a fourfold increase from the prior year. In the fourth quarter of 2004, net purchases of U.S. securities by the oil producers soared to $23 billion, up from $9.5 billion in the prior quarter. For the year, U.S. capital inflows from the major oil producers were 25 percent greater than inflows from Europe ($54.2 billion) and 43 percent larger than China's ($47.3 billion).

Free flowing petrodollars into the United States have offset declining Chinese purchases of U.S. securities, a fact which seems to be largely ignored by investors fretting about China's and other Asian countries' plans to diversify out of dollar-denominated assets. Of total inflows in 2004, U.S. government agency bonds were the preferred assets among oil producers. Bonds totaled $26 billion, or nearly 40 percent of total capital inflows.[25]

Last year's surge follows two years of net selling and runs against the prevailing view that Middle East producers have been busy diversifying into non-U.S. dollar-denominated assets. Granted, on the margin, we suspect many Middle Eastern oil producers have increased their euro exposure. Yet, inflows into U.S. securities and the strategic shift toward owning more non-U.S. dollar-denominated assets, has been neither very dramatic nor detrimental to the United States. With oil prices hovering in the $55 per barrel range, OPEC remains flush with cash, with a sizable share that could be recycled back into the United States.

The benefits come via two channels: One is through surging net purchases of U.S. securities, while the other comes via rising U.S. exports to OPEC members. Regarding the latter, U.S. exports to OPEC surged 28 percent last year, twice the pace of overall export growth at 13 percent. They may have oil but OPEC members have to import just about everything else from us. Given all of the above, there may be a silver lining to high oil prices after all.

FOR BIG OIL, THE BEST IS YET TO COME

Australian independent oil firm Woodside is pushing the message that while 2005 was better than expected, 2006 should be an even better year for oil profits.

Woodside officials said during presentations in Sydney that investors should expect higher 2006 production figures, as well as a sharp jump in exploration spending and drilling. Woodside is just one of those that have revealed their bright forecasts. Looking farther ahead to 2008 and beyond, the company is poised to exploit the growing global need for LNG with the development of two major stand-alone projects, as well as an additional train at the North West Shelf project.

Woodside expects that production for 2005 will have totalled around 59 million barrels of oil equivalent (or 161,000 barrels per day) as a result of new oil production at the Mutineer and Exeter fields in Western Australia, production from newly acquired wells in the U.S. Gulf of Mexico, and higher-than-expected output from its existing projects. This figure was up from earlier production targets. In 2006, the company expects that production will jump by about 30 percent due to new oil and gas output at the Chinguetti field in Mauritania and the Otway and Enfield projects in Australia.

By 2008, Woodside hopes to double its production to 120 million barrels of oil equivalents, or 327,000 barrels per day, as new production comes on line from the Tiof and Tevet fields in Mauritania, and the Stybarrow, Vincent, and Pluto fields gear up in Australia. Higher production from Train 5 of the North West Shelf will also contribute to higher levels, as the company expects total output of 16.3 million metric tons per year once the unit is in production, up from earlier forecasts of 15.9 million tons per year.

The head of the company's African operating unit, Duncan Clegg, said that Chinguetti was set to begin production of 75,000 barrels per day of oil at the end of February 2006, adding that the floating production, storage, and offloading ship Berge Helene was on site. LNG will be the basis for much of the company's future growth, especially beyond 2008, with the Browse and Pluto projects the backbone of its efforts. The director for Pluto, Lucio Della Martina, said Woodside is trying to find North Asian customers interested in taking up to four million tons per year of LNG starting in 2010. Browse, located up the coast from Pluto, is looking at the same markets for its exports of between 7 million and 14 million tons per year of LNG starting after 2011.

Woodside has received engineering proposals for Pluto and began its design phase in early 2006. The Pluto-3 appraisal well was drilled in December, and Pluto-4 followed in March 2006. At Browse, Woodside will drill the Brecknock-3 appraisal well in 2006 while working on securing marketing heads of agreements. Browse Director Paul Moore pointed to the importance of the project for Woodside, noting that successful development would mean an annual production plateau of around 50 million barrels of oil equivalents, or 137,000 barrels per day.

Exploration projects will abound in 2006 with about 40 wells planned, almost double the number drilled in 2005. Woodside plans to spend about $365 million on exploration in 2006, with 85 percent of the money dedicated to proven exploration areas, and 15 percent to frontier areas. Most of the activity will be based in the U.S. Gulf of Mexico, where the company plans to drill between 19 and 23 wells, with Africa seeing 10 to 14 new wells and Australia six to nine new wells. While Woodside is small, its planning for the future is superior and should be an example to others in the industry.

CHAPTER 7

Bumper Harvest for Oil Majors

AND THE WINNER IS . . . EXXON MOBIL

By mid-September 2005, two weeks after Hurricane Katrina pounded the U.S. Gulf Coast, gasoline prices soared to an all-time high of $3.06 a gallon. Each day of that same week, the nation's top five oil companies pocketed $364 million in profit. That's the way the numbers shake out based on second quarterly earnings reported in 2005 by the Big Five—Exxon Mobil, BP, Royal Dutch Shell, Chevron, and ConocoPhillips. Together, they amassed a staggering $32.8 billion in net income in the three months that made up the third financial quarter of that memorable year, with revenue for the group totaling $378 billion.

Of course, the king of oil was no surprise: Exxon Mobil, the world's largest oil company. At the end of January 2006, Exxon Mobil reported profits of $36.13 billion and revenues totaling $371 billion for 2005, up a staggering 40 percent over 2004. To put it into context, it's more than what Coca-Cola Co., Intel Corp., and Time Warner, Inc. together earn in an entire year. It was a stunning success at beating the competition and a bittersweet payback for a company that has suffered at the hands of federal regulators who broke it up in the early part of the twentieth century against the wishes of founder John D. Rockefeller.

To put everything into perspective, from a stock price of $12 per share in 1990 to about $60 a share fifteen years later, Exxon Mobil has grown

147

fivefold, compared with Coca-Cola's share price, which rose from $11 to $42 a share during the same 15-year period, while Time Warner's share price rose from less than $1 to about $17 a share. Intel's share price, meanwhile, climbed much faster but from a very low base: from slightly over $1 a share to about $27 during the same period. Given such competition, some analysts think Exxon Mobil's strong performance is a vindication for a company that had been taken apart by federal authorities in the early part of the last century when it was known as the Standard Oil Company of New Jersey.

Smaller oil companies than Exxon Mobil haven't been left behind either, especially refiners—those whose only job is to refine oil into several usable products. Among these, Valero Corp and Sunoco Inc. represent different business approaches within the refining market. Valero specializes in refining dirty low grade oil—heavy sour crude—that is found mostly in Latin America and the Middle East. Sour crude, which has a sulfur content of about 30 degrees API, has the advantage of being easy to get and cheaper for a refiner to buy in the market, but it is also very difficult and costly to refine. Sunoco, on the other hand, specializes in refining the more pricey high grade oil—light sweet crude—found mostly in the U.S. Gulf of Mexico, Canada, West Africa, and Europe. Sweet crude is very expensive to buy and also difficult to find, but it is very cheap to refine and yields a lot more gasoline, kerosene, and jet fuel.

At Sunoco's headquarters in Philadelphia, refining has become the best part of the business, pulling in 50 percent of the company's revenue from its retail division, which includes gas stations and convenience stores. Sunoco is trading at a premium to its peers, including Valero and Marathon Oil Corp. Its share price at slightly more than $80 in December 2005 had doubled since January and had also risen more than fivefold since 2001. At Valero, meanwhile, the stock price, which was trading at $104 a share in December 2005, had roughly doubled since January and had increased about seven times during a five-year period.

RECORD EARNINGS EMBARRASS
OIL EXECUTIVES AND POLITICIANS

The buoyant refining business helped both companies to improve their position within the oil industry, culminating in Valero's being recognized by *BusinessWeek* (Jan. 17, 2006) as America's third-best company to work for. The magazine also recognized Sunoco as one of the top 50 American corporate performers for 2005. Sunoco's third quarter 2005 sales jumped to $687 million on $24.5 billion thanks to its gas station strategy, which makes a lot of sense because the retail sector adds stability to the company's earnings; when refining profits slump, gasoline profits rise.

The oil industry's profits, year after year, have been so bloated that they're becoming a public relations problem. Shareholders are cheering, as they should, but consumers of fuel are fuming. By the summer of 2005, Americans were shelling out so much money just to fuel their cars that the fallout was felt from Wall Street to Washington. New York's pugnacious U.S. Senator, Charles Schumer, summed the whole situation up this way: "Big-oil behemoths are making out like bandits, while the average American family is getting killed by high gas prices, and soon-to-be record heating oil prices. We need to fix this."[1]

Schumer called for a temporary levy on oil company profits, with the money to be channeled into Katrina relief funds to help rebuild the Gulf Coast. Schumer's red-meat rhetoric is in line with the prevailing mood in Congress, where House Speaker Dennis Hastert, whose Republican Party has a long history of close ties to oil company boardrooms, distanced his party from Big Oil's bonanza, calling on the industry to use its money in ways that would ease the squeeze on our pocketbooks.

It didn't take long before politicians bowed to public pressure and hauled oil executives to a Congressional hearing in the fall of 2005, but that was just a publicity stunt because the congressmen and congresswomen knew very well that no one could do anything to stop prices from rising. And, in fact, nobody would have raised the issue if the industry had been smart enough to have a public relations strategy that would have made the issue go away before it even started. Such an approach had been mooted by some industry experts earlier, but no one paid much attention until it was too late. After all, investment banks make tons of money all the time and no one complains. That's because they've made people think that their industry exists to serve communities.

However, in the oil industry, company executives take a long time to learn from past mistakes. That's why the public image of Exxon Mobil is tarnished, since it has been associated with corporate arrogance, epitomized by public fights with global warming scientists and victims of the

Valdez oil spill years ago. The result is an ugly picture that only obscures some of the good community service the company provides.

Regarding strong earnings, oil companies acted too late when they tried to mute some of the criticism after the media started focusing on the huge profits. Instead, the industry began to emphasize losses from the hurricanes, the high cost of repairs, and their humanitarian efforts in the aftermath of Katrina. John Browne, BP's chief executive, summed up the industry's situation, saying: "The recent hurricanes in the United States have impacted our results. However, underlying performance is strong, amplified by high but volatile prices of oil, gas, and products."[2]

Still, while all of the major oil companies operating in the Gulf of Mexico pointed to production outages, whatever money they lost at that end of the business was more than made up for in higher oil and gas prices. Since higher crude prices in the United States spread quickly through the global energy market, overseas operations of these companies swiftly benefited from the chaos in the Gulf. Spot crude-oil prices in New York were up 32 percent at the end of the third quarter of 2005. The price gains were amplified on the Amex Oil Index (XOI), which measures the share performance of oil and gas companies. The index was up 54 percent from a year earlier.

One of the biggest gainers was ConocoPhillips, whose third quarter 2005 earnings rose 89 percent to $3.8 billion on a year-on-year basis, compared with Exxon Mobil's 75 percent increase to $9.92 billion, and Royal Dutch Shell's 68 percent rise to $9.03 billion. BP saw its profit rise by 34 percent to $6.46 billion, while Chevron posted a more modest gain of 12 percent on a $3.59 billion profit. Chevron lagged the rest of the class because it was the biggest loser from hurricane damage. Chevron's biggest refinery in Pascagoula, Mississippi, with a capacity of 325,000 barrels per day, was badly flooded by Katrina and stayed idle for almost two months before resuming production.

Hurricane Katrina's punch of the Gulf Coast laid bare the oil industry's vulnerability and highlighted the nation's lack of surplus refining capacity, which was dramatized by gasoline's meteoric rise after the storm shuttered almost a quarter of U.S. refining capacity. In the middle of all that, the industry's dirty little secrets became known to the general public, such as the fact that the number of refineries has shrunk to 176 from 425 in 1980. It's been almost 30 years since a new refinery was built in the United States, much of this delay due to shrinking margins in the business during the 1980s through early 1990s and local residents' staunch opposition to new petroleum plants. But also, it's fair to say, industry leaders weren't keen to spend money on refining, which until recently was considered a money-losing operation of the oil business.

If lawmakers are going to have any success getting refiners to build more plants, their best argument might rest not with the steep spike in refining margins after last summer's hurricanes, but with some form of consumer gasoline tax, which would reduce consumption. Obviously, oil companies won't like it, but it might force them to expand refining capacity; otherwise companies would do what they know best: cut costs to ensure even higher returns to their investors. BP is already reducing its refining and marketing workforce in Europe by 9 percent just to achieve efficiency. That's not a bad move from a business standpoint, but it doesn't exactly send the right message.

BP's plan to fire workers was announced only days after the company reported a $6.46 billion net profit for its third quarter of 2005. This is a company that's already doing very well, with its share price up to about $70 from $14 a decade ago. In the third quarter of 2005, BP's refining and marketing unit in Britain posted a $316 million profit before taxes and interest, compared with an $18 million loss a year earlier. Downstream profit for the rest of Europe stood at $1.122 billion, up 30 percent.

Meanwhile, Royal Dutch Shell's annual earnings rose 37 percent to $25.3 billion in 2005, the largest by a Dutch company. In a press conference call, Shell's Chief Financial Officer Peter Voser said: "We are capturing the benefits of high oil and gas prices and refining margins."[3]

Yet, for all of their robust earnings, it doesn't do any good just to blame the companies for their cash windfall. The truth is the industry has seen some pretty rough times before, and there's credibility to their claim that they need to save money for a rainy day. Those who follow this market remember just how the oil price surge of the late 1970s went bust in the 1980s. What followed were nearly 20 years of mostly depressed prices, which undermined oil earnings and stock prices. Chevron, for example, earned no more in 1998 than it had in 1985. Coca-Cola, by contrast, earned nearly five times as much in 1998 as it had 13 years earlier.

Many of the diversification moves the energy giants made with their record earnings in the 1970s went bust in the 1980s. Mobil Oil Corp. (the former Standard Oil of New York), which at the time hadn't merged with its baby sister company Exxon Corp. (the former Standard Oil of New Jersey), bought retailer Montgomery Ward in 1974, only to dump it 11 years later. Exxon invested in an office products business that marketed word processors and electronic typewriters. Gulf Oil, since merged into Chevron, considered buying the Ringling Bros. and Barnum & Bailey circus, although its board ultimately vetoed the idea. Those were lean times for the industry, and their desperation shows in some of the decisions they made.

The common advice for the oil companies in the 1970s was to diversify away from their core energy business. Companies that hated venturing into nonenergy businesses were attacked if they invested heavily in high-risk exploration and development projects in the 1980s, only to find that tumbling oil prices made the investments uneconomical. Up until a decade ago, investing in refining was still frowned upon.

That's now history. Today, any capital spending program by an energy company is unlikely to face severe review by its shareholders, although there are lingering fears that the boom of the last few years could quickly give way to another bust. That explains why the richest companies like Exxon Mobil and BP are buying back their shares, and very soon they'll start buying other smaller companies that they believe they have synergy with.

A share buyback, or retiring shares, is very popular with shareholders because it raises the value of remaining shares as well as having tax advantages. Since 2000, Exxon Mobil has bought back, or retired, $85 billion of their own shares, and Royal Dutch Shell bought back $2.6 billion worth of shares. Smaller companies are also getting attracted to buybacks. For instance, independent oil and gas producer Anadarko Petroleum Corp. purchased more than 5.5 million shares of its common stock to complete the buyback program that began in June 2004. Through late 2005 Anadarko had bought a total of 28.4 million shares under the $2 billion plan at an average price of $70.50 each.

Anadarko reported that fourth-quarter 2005 profit more than doubled to $874 million, or $3.73 per share—easily beating analysts' consensus estimate of $3.35. Anadarko's third-quarter 2005 earnings soared 50 percent despite hurricane-related losses off the Gulf of Mexico, and its second quarter 2005 earnings of $596 million, or $2.51 a share, were up from $399 million, or $1.58 a share, in 2004. Annual revenues for the company rose to $7.1 billion in 2005 from $6.08 billion in 2004. Its share price rose from $88 a share in November 2005 to $105 a share in February 2006.

According to the U.S. Energy Information Administration, revenues and earnings for oil services companies increased with higher drilling rig counts. Net income of U.S. oil drilling companies jumped 143 percent, as revenues rose 22 percent. The earnings strengthened on the bank of an 18 percent increase in the worldwide rig count to 2,979 rigs in 2005, according to Baker Hughes data. Total earnings of the independent refiners, like Valero, also rose because of an increase in average refining margins of 60 percent from 2004 to 2005. Yearly total earnings also showed strong growth, increasing from $236 million in 2004 to $566 million in 2005.

OIL COMPANIES RAISE CAPITAL SPENDING TO INCREASE CAPACITY

As I said earlier, capital expenditures are going to pick up again in 2006 despite reservations, thanks to robust demand that has kept oil prices high. This is good for the consumer, as the increased investment in drilling and refining will eventually ease the current tight market and eventually bring fuel prices down. The question now is whether that's good for the oil investor. In the short term, all these capital expenses could eat up some of the money that should have gone into dividend distribution. But in the long run, oil investors will gain from a stable market that will avoid what economists call "demand destruction"—a permanent loss of demand as consumers opt for alternative fuel sources. In a way, it's very much like when you have a convenience store and you are trying to keep your customers happy so they can keep coming rather than have them go to your competitor.

In 2005, oil companies spent about $86 billion on capital expenditures in the United States, up from $81 billion in 2004 and $76 billion in 2003, according to the American Petroleum Institute, the industry's lobby in Washington. Exxon Mobil's total capital and exploration expenditures rose to $17 billion in 2005 from $14 billion in 2004. The company expects to spend $17 billion to $18 billion per year from 2007 through 2010. Chevron, meanwhile, is involved in more than 20 exploration projects worldwide that will require outlays of about $1 billion or more, compared to a handful of such projects a few years ago. Whether the company will get new reserves is difficult to tell, given the declining rate of reserve replacement. Chevron in 2005 approved a new deepwater oil drilling project in a Gulf of Mexico field known as Blind Faith, where it believes more than 100 million barrels of oil may lie.

One of the most high-profile acquisitions recently is Chevron's purchase of Unocal for $17 billion, or $62 a share, edging out the offer from China's CNOOC despite a lower bid price. Chevron's chief executive, David O'Reilly, has long argued that the time to invest in expansion of reserves is now, before demand for fuel goes higher. "The time when we could count on cheap oil and even cheaper natural gas is ending," he says.[4] For a long time, he was the sole high priest of capital spending in the industry. Now, many are coming around to his view.

Two recent surveys found that worldwide exploration and production spending increased about 14 percent in 2005. Lehman Brothers, which conducted one of the surveys, found that 356 companies planned to spend a combined $192 billion in 2005. Citigroup's Smith Barney unit, which conducted the second survey, sees spending rising to $169.4 billion. Much of the increased spending reflects the higher costs of doing business at a time when equipment and labor are scarce. But again it would take years to add enough new oil production to ease current supply constraints.

Most of the money is going into oil drilling and buying or leasing of oil rigs. The global rig count is rising every day; in 2005 the average number was up 13 percent to 2,500 on a year-on-year basis. There are currently many active rigs, with a large concentration in the Middle East, the United States, and Asia Pacific. The rig count in the United States is 1,400, up 15 percent, compared with 9 percent for the Middle East and 14 percent for Asia Pacific, according to Baker Hughes, a rig consulting firm in Houston. Chevron, Royal Dutch Shell, and ConocoPhillips are spending more money in the United States. Others expect to spend under $1 billion to expand, including Burlington (up 48 percent), Chesapeake (up 71 percent), Denbury Resources (up 67 percent), Occidental Petroleum (up 39 percent), Houston Exploration (up 46 percent), Plains (up 69 percent), and XTO Energy (up 25 percent).

There are other reasons why capital spending should continue to rise. Oil companies are valued on Wall Street in most part by their oil and gas reserves. As long as earnings remain strong, the companies will be forced to replace the crude they pump out of the ground, because they'll go out of business if they don't. That requires taking some risks—financial, logistical, political, and marketwise. Consider the case of ExxonMobil's project in Russia's Sakhalin Island. With reserves estimated at 171 billion barrels, a fifth of the world's supply, Russia has the largest oil reserves outside the Middle East. Its deposits in eastern Siberia are especially attractive because they are close to the fastest growing Asian markets. But investing in Russia can cause heartburn, and in the case of Exxon Mobil, prospects of a $4 billion loss.

Exxon Mobil signed its first deal there in 1995 and launched its operations after Vladimir Putin took over as president in 2000 and appeared to stabilize the country's chaotic economy. Sakhalin is a former penal colony off the east coast of Russia and north of Japan. It has 14 billion barrels and the largest natural gas deposits in Russia. Exxon Mobil formed a consortium with Russian, Japanese, and Indian companies to produce both oil and natural gas, retaining a 30 percent stake in the project. After cumbersome negotiations with the Russian government, development began in 2001.

The project was supposedly one of the largest foreign investments in Russia, but it has turned out to be a nightmare for Exxon Mobil. The consortium committed $4.5 billion before pumping the first barrels in 2004, but the cost is rising, and investments are now expected to jump to $12 billion. The company expects the project to produce 250,000 barrels per day, which would equal less than 10 percent of the company's global production. But that's a breathtaking bet in a country so volatile. If anything goes wrong, Exxon Mobil's crude replacement strategy would disappear into thin air, and that could affect the company's finances as well.

Lehman Brothers' survey, which I talked about earlier, shows that two-thirds of oil executives want to increase capital spending in the coming years by more than 10 percent, which would push the spending for exploration and production above $200 billion in 2006. That spending will circulate within the industry. It is good news for oil services companies because their earnings will get a boost from these new projects in the future. Halliburton, Transocean, and Schlumberger all reported bumper earnings for 2005. And all of that has changed the mood in Wall Street and executives are looking upbeat, planning to expand their companies through mergers and acquisitions.

At the moment, the mergers and acquisitions (M&A) market is concentrated on minnows—the mid-size companies—and most of them have production projects abroad: U.S. oil firm Occidental, Canada's Talisman, and Norway's Norsk Hydro are out shopping for their dream mates. But major leaguers, like Exxon Mobil and BP, have decided to stand by for the moment. Exxon Mobil doesn't believe in buying at the top of the market, and BP has been busy selling off downstream assets. But Royal Dutch Shell could do with a major acquisition, which would improve its long-term growth prospects. A major league acquisition is not out of the cards yet, and in fact you should expect to see most M&A activities occurring down the road as midlevel players absorb minnows, especially in the upstream sector.

While upstream is looking up in terms of investment, the downstream sector isn't getting too much attention. So far, the only plans out there are for Marathon Oil Co. and Saudi Aramco to expand their U.S. refineries. But the plans are still in very early stages and it's not clear they will ever be accomplished. That's because enthusiasm for downstream investments is lacking despite the tight refining capacity. We probably shouldn't expect refiners to expand refining capacity merely to deflect public criticism about soaring fuel prices and profits.

Oil executives insist that in spite of the supply crunch that has kept oil prices high for much of the past two years, demand and prices are fickle. True warriors for keeping spending down include Exxon Mobil chairman Lee Raymond and John Hofmeister, who's currently president of Shell's U.S. unit. Hofmeister in 2005 told Associated Press reporter Brad Foss that: "A surplus of supply is not good for the industry. Just as a surplus of demand is not good for industry, we strive for balance."

Hofmeister added: "We will continue to work as an industry to increase supplies to the American people."[5] But he said Shell executives were still debating whether it makes economic sense to expand the capacity of Motiva refineries, which it owns jointly with Saudi Aramco, the state-owned company of Saudi Arabia. For Exxon Mobil, there was nothing to debate because the case for resisting downstream investment was already clear. Shell and Aramco, for their part, said that they planned to add 100,000 to 300,000 barrels per day of capacity to Motiva plants in Louisiana and Texas. Keep in mind that "high-priced" oil at $60-plus has not led people to seriously question their use of energy. If as they question that use of energy, they would use less.

INDUSTRY'S SUPER EARNINGS IMMEDIATELY
AFTER KATRINA SPARK PUBLIC DEBATE

Complaints that the market might not be working well exploded into the open after hurricanes Katrina and Rita exposed the industry's vulnerabilities. The backlash reached a crescendo when Exxon Mobil, BP, Shell, and Chevron reported combined third-quarter profits of $29 billion. A congressional hearing on energy prices and profits was held on November 8, 2005, because politicians were not only worried about the economic hardships soaring energy costs are placing on average consumers, but also about their political careers.

With oil rising above $60 a barrel and home-heating costs surging ahead, some people thought the industry would have no choice but to work with government to make the world's largest petroleum-consuming market more secure and less volatile. Bill Frist, majority leader in the U.S. Senate, who is believed to be eyeing the Republican presidential nomination for 2008, threw his support behind a federal anti-price-gouging law. Not to be outdone, Senator Schumer, typically not a shy fellow in front of cameras, rushed to introduce a bill that would place additional taxes on oil company profits to help reduce the deficit and pay for hurricane relief. The whole thing became political football. Even the industry-friendly White House acknowledged that something must be done to fix the supply imbalances that underpin today's high prices.

President George W. Bush repeatedly stressed conservation after Katrina. That's a complete change for someone considered to be a second-generation oil president. His Energy Secretary, Samuel Bodman, said the administration was considering a wide range of proposals, including the creation of an emergency reserve of gasoline, diesel, and jet fuel. Bodman also encouraged the industry to increase refining capacity to make the United States less dependent on imports of gasoline and diesel. But he did what most couldn't do at the time. He opposed the so-called windfall profits tax that Schumer had proposed. That needed courage to do. Remember, it was the first time Wall Street analysts had fielded calls from investors who were increasingly concerned about the pressure in Washington to do something about high prices and record profits. Of course, Wall Street was dead opposed to any tax that would punish companies for living up to their fiduciary responsibilities. "If they take the profits away from us, it is fundamentally not going to help consumers," said John Felmy, chief economist at the American Petroleum Institute, the Washington-based lobby for the oil industry. "It will only drain investment budgets."[6]

In Europe, governments were willing to use legislative fiat to impose taxes if Big Oil refused to toe the line. The French government didn't waste time in ordering Total and other oil companies to invest in refining. In London, BP and Royal Dutch Shell, both active in North Sea oil production, pled with her majesty's government against a windfall tax. BP Chief Executive John Browne reportedly met with his friend Gordon Brown, who is Chancellor of the Exchequer, the British equivalent of a finance minister and second most powerful political figure after Prime Minister Tony Blair. Dow Jones Newswires reported that industry executives were more concerned about public opinion in Britain and they felt the need for regular contacts with the U.K. Treasury, especially because they remembered a similar situation in 2002 when the British government slapped them with a windfall tax. They argued that a tax would affect investment.

Other Wall Street firms came to the aid of the oil industry. Ernst & Young, the tax consulting and accounting firm, warned against the tax, but it also recognized that there was little that could be done, as the U.S. Treasury was likely to approve some kind of windfall tax. Still, the accountants suggested that the Treasury should adopt a "progressive tax rate based on commodity prices" as a way to "to deal with any opposition to higher rates of corporation tax," according to the Dow Jones report.

In Washington, the White House started looking for creative ways to deflect the political heat from high oil prices. Secretary Bodman mulled the creation of a strategic refined products reserve among a variety of initiatives. "There are a number of initiatives that are being considered by the White House," Bodman told reporters following his appearance at a Senate Energy Committee hearing. "These are initiatives to help the situation with respect to the price of energy and the availability of energy to our citizens."[7]

The secretary said that conservation was the only short-term strategy that can protect consumers and ruled out mandatory oil company contributions to the federal Low Income Home Energy Assistance Program

(LIHEAP). "It's not something I would be in favor of," he said of proposals that would force oil companies to chip in. "It's the equivalent of some sort of windfall profits tax. And we learned in the 1970s and '80s that this didn't work."[8]

After Katrina, Senate Democrats tried several times to pass legislation that would double LIHEAP funding to $5 billion, but every time they were voted down by the Republican majority. The Democrats argued that more LIHEAP money would be vital in helping millions of Americans pay for increasingly expensive winter fuel.

But as Bodman downplayed the idea of taxes on windfall oil profits, he also indicated that plans for a refined products reserve were preliminary. "You've got to understand that keeping refined products in long-term storage is more difficult than holding crude," he said. That's because of the numerous product specifications that vary from state to state. And unlike crude oil, products need to be rotated regularly through the system to maintain quality.

Some major consuming countries, including Germany and France, hold gasoline and distillate as part of their emergency reserves. Apart from the Strategic Petroleum Reserve, the United States also has a small two-million-barrel heating oil reserve in the northeast, but that's just enough to last 10 days. The SPR caverns in Louisiana and Texas have nothing but oil in them. But Bodman agreed with Congress that oil companies should fund more infrastructure projects. "These companies are showing record profits," Bodman said. "They are doing well. It is time for them to demonstrate to the American public that they are going to be responsible in running our country's business."[9]

The energy bill signed into law in the summer of 2005 includes a lot of tax incentives through 2011 for refiners willing to expand their plants. However, there are a couple of problems that will have to be dealt with before refiners can expand refining capacity significantly:

- In the U.S., they face difficulties getting permits to expand refineries, let alone build new ones, and petroleum-rich acreage in the Rockies and the Gulf of Mexico remains off-limits
- Around the world, public oil companies are finding foreign governments less eager to have them as investment partners, since they are reaping huge sums on their own, thanks to high prices.

- Because of years of underinvestment when prices were low, the industry faces a shortage of everything from drilling rigs to oil tankers to petroleum engineers.

John Hofmeister, the chief executive of Shell in the United States, said the groundwork for the current energy crisis was laid long before back-to-back hurricanes knocked out Gulf of Mexico oil and gas supply. That's a stunning admission for a man in his position, but it was the plain truth. Hofmeister blamed underinvestment by the industry in the 1990s as well as faster-than-expected economic growth in China and India. Both of those reasons, he said, led to a virtual disappearance of excess capacity that the industry had come to depend on in case of a disruption in supply. But he also cautioned against making long-term policy or business decisions in the midst of a crisis, and predicted that as the industry recovers from the hurricanes, oil and gas production will rise, market tightness will ease, and the pressure from Congress will fade.

Some downstream investments are already in the pipeline. For instance, Marathon Oil Corp. plans to expand its Louisiana refinery and is weighing additional refinery projects. Marathon, the fifth-largest U.S. refiner with seven plants, is "also looking at other conversion capacity strategies," Gary Heminger, president of Marathon's refining division, told analysts recently. "We're certainly studying it, but we're a ways off."[10] Marathon wants to expand the 245,000-barrel-a-day Garyville, Louisiana, refinery to 425,000 barrels per day. The project, estimated to cost $2.2 billion, would be completed in late 2009 or later. The Garyville plan is very encouraging because the company already owns the necessary land in Louisiana. In fact, Marathon executives recently told Wall Street analysts that additional refinery projects could come in the Midwest, where the company has the majority of its capacity. In late 2005 the company completed a $300 million expansion of its Detroit refinery from 74,000 barrels per day to 100,000 b/d. The Detroit refinery is now up and running, according to Marathon spokesman Paul Weeditz.

At least two other refiners, Shell and Valero, have announced major refining expansions in the United States in recent months. Others are considering small upgrades over the next four years that may only have minimal impact: BP's refinery at Pascagoula, Mississippi, plans to expand its main gasoline processing unit, or the fluid catalytic cracker unit, by late 2006. Valero wants to expand its refinery at St. Charles, Louisiana, but no timing has been given for that project. While Marathon's plans for the Garyville refinery are in the earliest stages, executives describe the project as a building-out from the existing site that wouldn't require significant retrofitting. Marathon doesn't foresee extensive downtime to current production once construction gets under way, which is expected in the 2007 time frame. The company says it will essentially build an entirely new refinery at the site.

Meanwhile, ConocoPhillips' earnings surged 89.4 percent in the third quarter of 2005 from a year earlier. The third-largest U.S. integrated oil producer posted net income of $3.8 billion, or $2.68 a share, up from $2.01 billion, or $1.43 a share, in the third quarter of 2004. Revenue climbed 43 percent to $49.7 billion from $34.7 billion. In the exploration and production business, income from continuing operations jumped 61 percent to $2.29 billion from $1.42 billion a year ago, fueled by commodity price hikes. Amerada Hess's third-quarter 2005 profit rose 53 percent, bolstered by higher refining revenue and an increase in the selling price of gas and oil. Hess said net income rose to $272 million, or $2.60 a share, from $178 million, or $1.74 a share, in the year-ago period, and quarterly revenue rose 52 percent to $5.96 billion.

At the same time, Oklahoma City-based oil and gas producer Kerr-McGee saw an even bigger jump with net income of $359.3 million, or $3.09 per share, up from $7.4 million, or five cents per share, in the third quarter of 2004. Excluding items and discontinued business, Kerr-McGee's earnings reached $294.1 million, or $2.53 per share, from $143 million, or 95 cents, last year. And Diamond Offshore Drilling's third-quarter earnings more than doubled, helped by a 49 percent rise in revenue and a gain from insurance proceeds. Diamond, which provides contract drilling services, had its income rise to $82 million, or 60 cents a share, from $2.9 million, or 2 cents a share, a year earlier. Analysts expected earnings of 40 cents a share.

Analysts See Upside in Booming Oil

Convinced that there's more upside in the booming oil industry, Prudential Equity Group has initiated coverage of major oil companies with a favorable overall rating, based on the strength of the underlying energy market. "We have a favorable rating on the integrated oil sector. While energy-commodity prices have pulled back from their September highs, along with the equity names, the fundamental operating environment remains strong," Prudential analyst Jason Gammel wrote in a research note in the winter of 2005.

Among market trends pointing toward sustained growth, Gammel cited oil prices that are managing to hold at around $55 a barrel, resurgent U.S. demand for refined petroleum products, and the likelihood of continued strong natural gas prices going into the winter, due to lingering production outages in the Gulf of Mexico. "In this environment, we expect that the integrated oil companies should continue to post outstanding results: We expect earnings will grow by about 9 percent in 2006 vs. 2005, and that the average return on capital employed will be 28 percent in 2006," said Gammel, touting Exxon Mobil as the best performer in the group.

The analyst believes the company's share price still has room to grow; he also thinks that Exxon Mobil will continue to reward shareholders through strong dividends and share buybacks, and that it will top the industry for return on capital while it continues to keep pace with demand by replenishing reserves. "Based on our 2006 oil price forecast of $55 a barrel, we expect the company will generate a 36 percent return on capital employed, best among the integrated oil companies," Gammel said. As for BP, Gammel was especially impressed with its ability to boost reserves in the face of rising world demand, and predicted that Chevron would post a 30 percent return on its investments, slightly ahead of the 28 percent average expected for the group. Chevron and ConocoPhillips were rated neutral due to a shareholder yield that he estimated at 5 percent in 2006, slightly trailing its bigger rivals.

Similarly, Morgan Stanley has also forecast that an upside to earnings in 2006 for several of the European oils could reach 35 percent, driven by refining margins. The brokerage firm likes Poland's PKN Orlen, MOL Hungarian Oil and Gas, Spain's Repsol (REP), and the Anglo-Dutch giant Royal Dutch Shell (RDSA) for their exposure to margin gains from refining. "PKN Orlen and MOL have the most potential upside to price targets (about 25 percent) in our European universe, as the emerging markets selloff brought local markets down," analyst Joseph

Mares said in a note to clients. "Both could see 20 percent-plus earnings upgrades if refining margins average US$10 a barrel in 2006."

He also raised price targets on Austria's OMV (OMVKY) and Finland's Neste Oil (NTOIF) by 5 percent and upgraded Neste to equal weight from underweight. "While Neste is still expensive versus its peers, it is also the most exposed to the highest possible earnings upgrades on 2006 and mid-cycle forecasts," Mares said.

CHAPTER 8

The New Frontier in Oil Investments

BRIGHT FUTURE FOR ENERGY INVESTMENTS

There's been a great deal of talk—and some whining too—about the new energy crisis. You should by now be aware of the gloom and doom forecast by some very smart people (maybe smarter than I am, I should say) for the end of oil. Also, you've heard the opposing view that we'll somehow come up with some kind of solution, something new, either in the form of additional oil supply or an alternative to oil. Forgive me if I disagree with both lines of rhetoric, because they are both very simplistic ways of looking at the issue and virtually guarantee that nothing will be done to alleviate what we know is a problem ahead of us.

Let's be honest and agree that there's no universal answer to this problem, but I'd like to suggest that the truth lies somewhere in between those two lines of reasoning. We can be sure of one thing: We've seen the rising oil and gas prices and how they affect our everyday financial choices. We have been upset about all those billions of dollars the oil industry is earning just as mother nature gives us a thorough drubbing in the form of deadly hurricanes. That trend toward frequent harsh hurricanes will continue. The U.S. Gulf Coast, which is still recovering from Hurricanes Katrina and Rita, will see another busy hurricane season in 2006, according to the U.S. National Hurricane Center (NHC) and other independent storm forecasters. The NHC forecasts 18 to 21 tropical storms in 2006, only slightly down from 26 in 2005. In the long term, says Mark Saunders of Tropical Storm Risk (TSR), a credible forecasting center based at University College London, the Gulf Coast will see above-normal hurricane seasons over the next several years.

The question you should be asking yourself is whether you are going to take advantage of the situation to save and get rich or at least make enough money through various energy investments. In traditional personal finance advice literature, the advisers used to say that to be rich you have to be frugal—give up all your money-wasting habits and save whatever pennies you have left over. Get rid of your debt, pay off your mortgage early, and buy distressed assets, they'd say. More recently, they have been telling you to retool your thinking so that you can think like a millionaire.[1] The only problem is they don't tell you whether they've successfully done that, and how changing your thinking is related to the millions of dollars that are allegedly up for grabs. The truth is some of the advisers gambled, and they are not going to tell you that.

I don't want to put down some financial consultants, but here's one important thing you should know as an investor: it's a good thing to gamble, but it's even better to be sure about which market you intend to gamble in. As I speak, there's no better market to invest in than energy, and it doesn't matter whether you want to invest in small cap energy stocks or big cap energy stocks.

To understand why energy is such a hot commodity, you ought to take a look at industry trends, starting in the summer of 2004, when Chinese demand hit the market like a thunderbolt and Hurricane Ivan ravaged the Gulf Coast like a furious beast. Then came the summer of 2005 when Hurricanes Katrina and Rita snowballed in the Atlantic and blew ashore a new energy crisis, sending crude oil prices to record levels above $70 per barrel, and gasoline, heating oil, and natural gas prices followed higher, increasing the cost of almost everything from filling your car's tank to heating your home.

Some smart people had seen it coming all along. In the spring of 2005, Arjun N. Murti, an analyst with New York-based investment bank Goldman, Sachs & Co., released a report forecasting a "super-spike," with prices rising to $105 per barrel. It was a shocker to the oil community since oil was trading at $54 at the time; many analysts condemned it as far-fetched. But that was before Katrina, which sent oil prices up 20 percent to $70 per barrel within five months. So, it turns out after Katrina that Murti may have been right after all, and no one is laughing at him now. Murti has become something of a prophet in the industry. Since that time, a number of analysts have either reached similar conclusions or have been even more bullish.

The "super-spike" theory was based on an assumption of a continued tight balance between global supply and demand, plus the likelihood that a supply disruption could occur anytime overseas, upsetting the market. It only missed one thing: that the disruption occurred in the United States. The hurricanes created additional problems and shook the oil market by taking out 1.5 million barrels per day of oil production and 3 million b/d of refining capacity, which is equivalent to roughly 20 percent of total U.S. refining capacity. As a result, gasoline supply was terribly reduced. In an interview with the *Wall Street Journal* in October 2005, Murti stuck by his view of multiyear oil price shock.[2]

My advice to any investor is that the increase in fuel prices need not prompt feelings of helplessness, as energy inflation can be offset through savvy investing and consumer purchasing. All you need to know is how and where to invest, whether to invest in small or large caps, domestic or international, and most important, in which sector to do business.

BASICS OF INVESTING, RISK MANAGEMENT AND GAME THEORY

First, the basics: the most fundamental reason for investing is to make more money than you get from your day job. But let me start by warning you that buying an oil stock or two will not necessarily make you any richer instantly, nor make up for your gushing energy bills. As you probably know already, investing is much like other forms of gambling, the only difference being that you are more in control. Because of that delicate ability to control, you can structure the gamble to suit your specific needs and concerns, and make it appropriate to your level of income. I will skip traditional investing, which includes putting your retirement money away and other similar types of savings. That's not my concern here.

I'm just going to deal with secondary investments, or what others call discretionary investments, where you simply want to make money as an add-on to what you already have. Like any venture, this type of investing involves risks. In any case, life itself is a risk, so ideally what we are talk-ing about here should be appropriately called risk management. As the psychologist Peter L. Bernstein tells us, the concept of risk management isn't new. Like much of our civilization, risk management dates back to 800 years ago, but it became more commonly used during the Renais-sance and is rooted in the Hindu-Arabic numbering system.[3]

The issue boils down to what does the past tell you about the future, and armed with that knowledge, can you change your future even if only slightly? In investing, the past of an industry or a company is what you'll be looking into. For readers of this book, the job is partly done, because energy is the industry we have been looking into. Because risk manage-ment is a numbers game, we can use past data to quantify the future of any company and what that means to the investor.

As with everything else in life, nothing is certain and neither is the market. Investors should know that. Fischer Black, a pioneering theoreti-cian of modern finance who moved from MIT to Wall Street, said, "Markets look a lot less efficient from the banks of the Hudson than from the banks of the Charles." Similarly, Nobel laureate Kenneth Ar-row once noted, "Vast ills have followed a belief in certainty."[4]

As I have said before, the only sure thing is that investing in a single se-curity concentrates risk in one company and doesn't give you protection or the total performance of the sector, which includes several industries that produce, transport, refine, and manufacture energy-derived products. As an example, you won't save much money simply by shopping for cheaper gasoline. But you can ease the pain by adding inflation-hedging energy funds to your holdings. And the more aggressive you are the better are your chances of making more money, especially if you are a younger investor, because the rewards can be tremendously huge. But first, you have to do your own homework. I hope this book has given you the back-ground and the tools to help you make informed investment choices.

STUDY INDUSTRY TREND

For starters, if you have some free money, or money that's not tightly bud-geted, which you want to invest in energy, the first thing is to go and read about that industry, so as to get an idea of the trend. Pay attention to news, both business and other types of news, because company decisions are informed by many issues, including legislative politics and technology. You must keep up with news, it helps you to decide when to get in and out. Company news is important for sound investment, but that news must be received by legal means. That's why the government prosecutes insider trading, because they know that if someone gets a tip about a company before that information becomes known to the public, that person can make or save a ton of money, sometimes to the detriment of the investing public.

Insider information is illegal, and I have to advise you against it, but getting to know that particular information when it breaks as a news item on radio, television, newspapers, or the Internet is perfectly legal. So keep up with news. In other words, do your homework; the Internet, especially search engines like Google and Yahoo, will be your biggest asset. Get some basic understanding of securities law, especially Regulation FD. That rule, available to the public for free by simply going to the U.S. Securities and Exchange Commission (SEC) web site, deals with everything that can be known about a company without being an insider.[5] In the energy sector, perhaps the best time to invest is now. You can invest as an individual, by yourself, or you can use a money manager; it doesn't matter because you still have to keep track of your investments. The next question is whether to invest in a small company or a big one, and whether to invest in a high or low stock price. I would say, though, that the choice of whether to invest in a small cap or a large cap energy stock will depend on how much money you have. A small investor doesn't have the money to invest in an expensive stock, for example. A useful avenue for investing in the energy industry right now is through an index fund like the Vanguard Energy Index Fund (VENAX), which replicates a basket of stocks in a given industry. The fund grew nearly 40 percent in 2005, more than Standard & Poor's 500 Index's gain of nearly 3 percent during the same period.

As an investor, don't get worried about high oil prices and the fact that they cause inflation. Let other people get anxious about such things; your job should be to use the opportunity to make money for yourself. In my view, energy prices are a relatively small component of the larger inflation matrix because energy expenditures have fallen to 5 percent of consumer disposable income from 11 percent since early 1980s. General inflation is the larger enemy because it erodes our purchasing power, especially if incomes don't keep up with higher consumer prices. That could erode demand and turn the economy on its head. I'm told that the one thing to keep in mind is that overall consumer inflation in the

United States—including food and energy costs—is low at around 3 percent. That's important because, as an investor, the gain on your portfolio should be higher than that inflation number, and if it isn't, you're not making any money; in fact you could be losing instead.

One other thing: Inflation erodes the prices of most bonds as well, and bonds are your safety net. To deal with that, you probably should take a look at Treasury Inflation-Protected Securities, or TIPS, which are debt instruments that reward you when inflation is rising. One of the best ways to own TIPS is through the PIMCO Real Return Fund (PRRDX). That fund compensates you for higher inflation through a variety of U.S. and foreign TIPS, and it serves as a hedge should stock prices fall due to rising consumer and energy prices. When inflation threats were said to have pressured the stock market in the summer of 2005, the PIMCO fund gained 2.1 percent compared with a decline of 1.1 percent in the S&P 500.

To better understand the equity market, let's review a few things on investing before we dip into energy stocks. First, investing for a profit takes some discipline and common sense. You could take a big risk, but you don't have to; instead, manage a small risk. You don't have to be Einstein to invest well. It's just a matter of getting proper information about various companies, and applying your common sense to determine which stocks are better than others, and whether you can efficiently manage risks by spreading out your investments. That's even more true if you invest in funds—mutual funds, index funds, or hedge funds for large investors. It might be better for you to hire a smart money manager, because that would free you to monitor only his or her performance.

DON'T PANIC BECAUSE THE BOOM WILL LAST, BUT HAVE A PLAN

It's also important to time the market very well, usually before it gets red-hot, as the energy markets are now. But even if you are late, don't give up. Go right ahead and try to cover the distance lost. I don't have to tell you that you only get a benefit if you do something. No one ever gets anything for doing nothing, so you'd better be late than never invest at all in energy stocks.

Stocks are important to successful investment plans because their annual returns are double what you can get in bonds. With the U.S. inflation rate at about 3 percent, you are left with a 7 percent rate of return per year when you invest in stocks, as opposed to 2 percent when you invest in bonds. Stock investments grow faster, almost doubling every ten years, but they are also very volatile, and you could lose your money if the market goes south. Stocks bounce around from month-to-month and year-to-year, and it matters whether you are investing for the long haul or not.

Here's something you should know: stocks typically move up and down in five-year cycles, so long haul investors are cushioned from market volatility. Someone who has ten years ahead of him is different from another person with a much shorter time before he has to start spending his money. If you have a longer time frame in which to invest, look for high return energy stocks—mostly smaller or midsized stocks—because you have time to play the market. But remember also that they are some of the most vulnerable to short-term swings. Still, you can load up most of your money in small to medium-sized company stocks. If you don't want to risk your money because you are just a few years from retirement, then consider investing in large caps and steady performers like Exxon Mobil.

One thing you should do first as an investor is to develop some spine, because you are going to be taking big chances. But don't panic—you'll be glad at the end. That's because the strategies discussed in this chapter, while concentrated on energy markets alone, are meant to help you hedge any risks to an oil downturn by spreading your portfolio to include alternative fuels as well, which could become popular in the near future.

Certainly, I don't think the oil boom will burst soon, but if that happens, you'll have a safety net to continue making you some money. Nevertheless, I'd expect you to be an aggressive investor rather than a safe one. If you panicked during the 2001 bear market, don't panic again this time around. If you viewed the bear market as an opportunity to buy neglected, undervalued stocks and you kept throwing money into them, you should now take a comprehensive look at the energy markets, starting with oil and product companies and going on to power companies, natural gas pipeline companies, and then on to non-fossil renewable energy firms.

Wise investment requires a strategy, a good plan, which sets out what you want to achieve, when you want to achieve it, and how you want to go about achieving it. Give some thought to picking funds the same way you do to any important thing in your life. Think of it the same way you think of, say, your flower garden—you prune, you nurture the plants. A good investment strategy must be well thought out, so that it takes into account your short-term needs, your medium-term needs, and your long-term needs. The trick is to minimize those risks, while expanding opportunities for success. One sure way of doing that is by diversifying your investments. How do you go about doing that? There are very many ways to diversify, depending on what your goals are, and what time frame you have for the investments.

Remember also that the market is cyclical, and Wall Street has a habit of getting carried away by one type of stock or another for three to five years, before suddenly changing course and chasing after a different stock. For example, in the late 1990s, all that mattered to most investors was technology stocks. Then at the start of the new millennium, some time around 2001, the investment tune changed to banking stocks. Now, it is oil stocks, although I do encourage people to look at the whole gauntlet of the various energy markets—oil, gas, oil services, renewable fuel, and electricity. Often, people say there's no proper rationale for sudden shifts, but if you look closely, there's usually some sort of micro or macro fundamental to back up those rallies. The market is not as capricious as some might want you to think.

GAME THEORY SHOWS YOU HAVE TO BE OPTIMISTIC

Staying ahead of those changes is the best way to play the market. If you choose a stock fund, you might want to leave the job of picking it in the hands of someone else, the manager of that fund, a smart professional—smart, because there are stupid money managers, too—who tracks the record of the best and the worst performing companies for you to see each day or each week or two. You also have to find out which stock sectors will stay strong and which ones will ease, or are already showing signs of cooling off. If you diversify, some of your funds will be better than others, but you probably won't be losing a whole lot, because you'll be cushioned from a hard landing.

I learned a long time ago that if you want to succeed, the best approach is to learn from the best, past and present. Jack Welch, the former chief executive of General Electric, is such a person. He once told a story about his hard-driven mother that should be a lesson to us all. "We'd sit [together] for hours and talk," Welch told writer Janet Lowe in her book *Jack Welch Speaks*. "I was very close to her. She was a dominant mother. She always felt I could do anything. It was my mother who trained me, taught me the facts of life. She wanted me to be independent, to control my destiny—she always had that idea . . . no mincing words. Whenever I got out of line, she would whack me one. But [she was] always positive, always constructive, always uplifting. And I was just nuts about her."[6]

It's the same advice I'd like to give to anyone, especially those trying to invest in the hot energy markets. You've got to take advantage of opportunities that come along. Doing that requires having a positive attitude, a go-getter attitude, a winner's state of mind, and you've got to take action at the right time, even within minutes. Think fast and be decisive. These aren't empty phrases; they've worked for me time and again.

Dr. Christopher Hart, a leading psychologist in Nairobi who has studied what makes optimists achieve their goals, says that when it comes to choices you make in life, you are really the one in control. If it feels to you like everyone is out to get you, then you've actually chosen to see things that way. You could just as well have decided to be in charge of your destiny, Dr. Hart said in a recent essay published in Nairobi's *Sunday Nation* newspaper. Things somehow seem to work out for optimists, and not because optimists don't work hard; quite the opposite. They work pretty hard just like the rest of us, and to have that kind of attitude is a tough job in itself—an attitude that makes things work out for you.[7]

I know you are now asking, "Oh, how could that be?" Well, the truth is that optimists achieve more because they are more persistent and more resilient. When you are assured of victory at the end, nothing in between can stop you. That's the nature of the human spirit. There are unlimited reservoirs of strength, determination, and stamina in us. We just need to tap them, and there's no better way to do that than to stay positive.

Optimists tend to see a silver lining in every bad situation. Where pessimists think things will go wrong, optimists think the problems are manageable, so they stay in control rather than melt under pressure. One might say optimism is a self-fulfilling prophesy because if you think life will get better, that's generally the way it turns out. And there's another scientific explanation for thinking positive, rooted in game theory. Game theory, which is based on rational and positive thinking, is the study of the ways in which *strategic interactions* among *rational players* produce *outcomes* with respect to the *preferences* (or *utilities*) of those players, none of which might have been intended by any of them.

I'm not much of a scholar. However, in order to understand how game theory can help us in deciding whether and how to make certain investments, here's how Don Ross, a real scholar, an economic philosopher holding joint appointments at the University of Alabama and the University of Cape Town in South Africa, explains it in "Game Theory" in *The Stanford Encyclopedia of Philosophy*.

> Game-theoretic insights can be found among philosophers and political commentators going back to ancient times. For example, Plato, in the *Republic*, at one point has Socrates worry about the following situation. Consider a soldier at the front, waiting with his comrades to repulse an enemy attack. It may occur to him that if the defense is likely to be successful, then it isn't very probable that his own personal contribution will be essential. But if he stays, he runs the risk of being killed or wounded—apparently for no point. On the other hand, if the enemy is going to win the battle, then his chances of death or injury are higher still, and now quite clearly to no point, since the line will be overwhelmed anyway.
>
> Based on this reasoning, it would appear that the soldier is better off running away regardless of who is going to win the battle. Of course, if all of the soldiers reason this way—as they all apparently should, since they're all in identical situations—then this will certainly bring about the outcome in which the battle is lost. Of course, this point, since it has occurred to us as analysts, can occur to the soldiers too. Does this give them a reason for staying at their posts? Just the contrary: the greater the soldiers' fear that the battle will be lost, the greater their incentive to get themselves out of harm's way. And the greater the soldiers' belief that the battle will be won, the more they'll stay to fight.
>
> But if they think they can win without the need of any particular individual's contributions, the less reason they have to stay and fight. If each soldier anticipates this sort of reasoning on the part of the others, all will quickly reason themselves into a panic, and their horrified commander will have a rout on his hands before the enemy has even fired a shot![8]

Game theory works best between two armies that follow the argument and come to different conclusions, one giving up the fight for the other to win. Long before game theory came along to show people how to think about this sort of problem systematically, it had occurred to some actual military leaders and influenced their strategies. Thus Ross, in his explanation of game theory, gives the example of the Spanish conqueror Hernado Cortez when landing in Mexico with a small force. Cortez's men had good reason to fear their ability to repel attack from the far more numerous Aztecs, but Cortez removed the risk that his troops might retreat by burning the ships on which they had landed. Ross adds:

> With retreat having thus been rendered physically impossible, the Spanish soldiers had no better course of action but to stand and fight—and, furthermore, to fight with as much determination as they could muster. Better still, from Cortez's point of view, his action had a discouraging effect on the motivation of the Aztecs. He took care to burn his ships very visibly, so that the Aztecs would be sure to see what he had done. They then reasoned as follows: Any commander who could be so confident as to willfully destroy his own option to be prudent if the battle went badly for him must have good reasons for such extreme optimism. It cannot be wise to attack an opponent who has a good reason (whatever, exactly, it might be) for being sure that he can't lose. The Aztecs, therefore, retreated into the surrounding hills, and Cortez had his victory bloodlessly.
>
> This situation, as imagined by Plato and as vividly acted upon by Cortez, has a deep and interesting logic. Notice that the soldiers are not motivated to retreat just, or even mainly, by their rational assessment of the dangers of battle and by their self-interest. Rather, they discover a sound reason to run away by realizing that what it makes sense for them to do depends on what it will make sense for others to do, and that all of the others can notice this too. Even a quite brave soldier may prefer to run rather than heroically, but pointlessly, die trying to stem the oncoming tide all by himself. Thus we could imagine, without contradiction, a circumstance in which an army, all of whose members are brave, flees at top speed before the enemy makes a move. If the soldiers really are brave, then this surely isn't the outcome any of them wanted; each would have preferred that all stand and fight.
>
> What we have here, then, is a case in which the interaction of many individually rational decision-making processes—one process per soldier—produces an outcome intended by no one. Most armies try to avoid this problem just as Cortez did. Since

they can't usually make retreat physically impossible, they make it economically impossible: they shoot deserters. Then standing and fighting is each soldier's individually rational course of action after all, because the cost of running is sure to be at least as high as the cost of staying.[9]

It's not clear, however, that Cortez was conscious of game theory. As Lewis Lord says, Cortez believed deeply that "fortune always favors the bold," and as one of his officers said later, his intent was "to inspire fear and terror."[10] Still, we can see that he used game theory with a fantastic outcome even without his knowledge.

SINCE THE ONLY THING YOU HAVE TO FEAR IS FEAR ITSELF

What I have tried to show above can best be summed up in one famous statement made by President Franklin D. Roosevelt during the Great Depression: "The only thing you have to fear is fear itself." In practical terms, it means we have to be perceptive and aggressive (without violence, of course) in what we do, including in planning our energy investments. Recent events have given the oil market a new paradigm in which the direction of the market would be ever skyward. Oil prices are primed for an "überspike" and oil stocks will follow up. Oil stocks have done well in the past two years, making it natural to hedge against the rising cost of oil by acquiring stocks of oil and oil-related companies. There's a lot of data to back that up. The Amex oil index basket of 12 oil industry stocks surged about 60 percent in 2005.

Top oil companies have seen standout quarterly earnings. On the New York Stock Exchange, U.S. oil giant Exxon Mobil, representing the oil industry, saw its stock rise about 30 percent in 2005. On the Standard & Poor's 500, Chevron stock rose 28 percent and ConocoPhillips rose 70 percent—the average gain for the entire S&P 500 was only 11 percent during the same period, meaning that energy stocks carried the exchange higher. These are great returns for any sector, and investors who got in at least two years earlier are better off now because they have made tons of money.

There's still time to get in right now because the oil market could stay buoyant for a while. I disagree with those who think this is the top of the market, because I believe the market still has some way up to go. As any good analyst knows, oil prices still have an upside given forecasts for rising demand and lagging oil production, or what's likely to be an oil peak in the coming years. Take my word for it, and if you don't trust me, then here's someone you can trust. "The recent correction in energy stocks has created an investment opportunity, especially for the long-term," Fadel Gheit, an oil analyst at Oppenheimer & Co., wrote in a note to clients. "Despite their large gains this year and in the last three, five, and 10-year periods, we believe the upside potential in energy stocks remains greater than the downside risk associated with a sharp drop in oil and gas prices."

One thing to expect in the short term is that we'll continue to deal with fuel supply interruptions due to political instability in producing regions of the Middle East, Russia, Latin America, and West Africa. In the Middle East, the security situation is getting worse, not better, in Iraq, Iran, and Saudi Arabia. In Nigeria, Shell will continue to have problems with militants, who are more organized than in the past. And in the Western Hemisphere, the perceived failure of free market economics has strengthened left wing politics across Latin America, personified by the rise of Venezuela's belligerent president, Hugo Chavez, who has made known his distaste for the U.S. government. After the general strike of 2003 that affected much of Venezuelan oil flow for several weeks, prospects of further political turmoil remain real, given that Chavez opponents are still scheming to topple him. Both Bolivia and Ecuador have also seen their share of instability.

Moreover, even if supply interruptions are kept to a minimum, global fuel demand is rising faster than supply. In fact, there's no cushion in oil supply capacity, and if there's a disruption of any nature anywhere for a week or so, it would create a terrible squeeze on the system.

Additional demand is coming from the United States, China, and India. Both China and India have been out in the market shopping for supply sources because they are unsure supply will keep coming to their satisfaction. The new Asian economic powers are trying to guarantee themselves oil reserves in Africa and the former Soviet Republics, especially in Kazakhstan, where Chinese National Petroleum Company made an upstream acquisition in the autumn of 2005.

CHECK OUT TOP COMPANIES WITH STOCKS
WITH LOW P/E RATIO

The current oil boom is creating a cash flow windfall for oil companies and that improves their fundamentals. It plays a part in the upward movement of a company's stock. You should ask yourself a few questions: "What's the health of the company and that of its stock?" "Has this company been discovered?" and "Is it an undervalued stock?" Put all of these things together and if the answers to most of these questions are positive, then you are in luck.

As an investor, don't wait it out for long once you have successfully gone through that vetting process. With whatever money you've got, look for such a company, especially one with large enough quantities of oil and gas reserves. The best ones are those with most of their reserves in North America and Europe, where political risks are low. Repsol, which has a lot of its reserves in Latin America, has been forced to revise down its reserves estimate because of political problems in that region—a wave of re-nationalization is sweeping across oil- and gas-producing Latin American countries. Also, look for stocks trading at a fairly low price/earning ratio, i.e. company stocks that are cheap but have high returns, because such companies have low risk, and if oil prices come off, they are more likely to profit from stock buybacks or restructuring. Such companies are also more likely to be the target of mergers and acquisition, which increases their stock value. By this standard, attractive stocks would include Apache Corp. and Anadarko Petroleum Corp., both of which have substantial energy holdings in North America, especially in the Gulf of Mexico.

Over the past five years, Apache has enjoyed compound earnings of about 20 percent per year and growth is projected at 10 percent per year for the next five years, yet it is trading at $69 a share, less than 10 times estimated earnings for this year and next. Likewise, Anadarko is trading less than 10 times earnings for this year, but its profits are up about 10 percent per year, and are projected to stay firm over the next five years. Anadarko has done aggressive restructuring, selling off less desirable assets and using the proceeds to pay down debt and buy back stocks. So, it has the opportunity to evolve into a slightly smaller producer with a higher growth rate.[11]

Since last year, there have been several acquisitions, ranging from Chevron's purchase of Unocal ($17 billion) to Total's buying of Alberta oil sands producer Deer Creek Energy ($1.1 billion), to the purchase of

Vancouver-based Terasen by Kinder Morgan ($5.6 billion). Outside North America, Chinese National Offshore Oil Co., or CNOOC, acquired MEG Energy ($126 million), while PetroChina purchased 200,000 barrels per day of oil supply from Canada. That Canadian oil will flow through an Enbridge pipeline from Alberta to Canada's West Coast, from where it will be shipped to China. China's Sinopec also bought a 40 percent stake in Syneco Energy for $84 million.

The prices of company stocks normally follow earnings, which, in turn, are dependent on sales—the more sales the larger the profits. At the start of 2004, analysts were predicting a conservative gain of about 8 percent for the third quarter earnings for the S&P 500 stock index from a year earlier. But they got more than they expected, as S&P 500 profits doubled the forecast. Then in April 2005, analysts were expecting earnings of 9 percent, but the profits actually grew 12 percent for the second quarter. Despite hurricane damages, third quarter 2005 earnings were way above expectations, with most oil majors reporting anything from 50 percent to 90 percent profit increases. That's higher than the historical growth rate.

By contrast, portfolios lacking energy have performed poorly. Compared with other industries, energy is doing wonderfully well. For instance, the technology-laden NASDAQ Composite index was down 1 percent during the third quarter of 2005 and the Dow Jones Industrial Average was down 2 percent. But the S&P 500 stock index, which is heavily weighed toward energy, was up, and energy stocks were on a roll. Energy represents 10 percent of the S&P 500's total market capitalization, while just one of the companies on the Dow Jones index is energy: Exxon Mobil. NASDAQ has some energy stocks, but they tend to have small market capitalizations.

Oil equities continued to rally during the second quarter of 2006, thanks to the big momentum in the growth of oil prices. Light sweet crude contracts on the New York Mercantile Exchange went up 50 percent to $70 per barrel in April of 2006, and is expected to target $80 by the summer. Geopolitical concerns in Iran and Nigeria that threatened to cut oil supply were pushing up oil prices. The fear among many traders was that confrontations over Iran's nuclear fuel program were getting out of hand and Iran could very well decide to retaliate against the United States and its European allies by cutting its oil exports, which would lead crude prices way up towards $100. Energy shares, meanwhile, rose on the S&P 500 more than 40 percent. Of the S&P

500's remaining nine other sectors, only utilities and healthcare were moving up by a similar magnitude. Without energy, the S&P 500 would have been down by 2 percent, on a par with the Dow Jones Industrial Average. The most profitable companies now happen to be refiners because the margins are so high. This means that for every barrel of crude that a refiner buys and processes into various petroleum products—gasoline, diesel, jet fuel and other products—the refiner gets more than $20 in profit. The reason is there are few refineries in the United States—just 147, down from 425 about 25 years ago. The few refineries we have can't make enough gasoline and diesel to meet rising domestic demand, and that causes gasoline prices to soar.[12]

Outside of the United States, we've seen growth in Asian and European energy stocks as well. In fact, foreign markets—the emerging markets—may even be growing much more than here at home because our market is weighed down by a weak dollar. In short, investors who are avoiding energy stocks are doing themselves a disservice. To catch up, they would need to make tough decisions, none more important than embracing this bullish energy market. Here's an interesting example: a senior investment strategist was bullish on energy until 2004, when he switched to other sectors. That was a bad bet on his part. He recently told the *Wall Street Journal* that he's regretting that decision.[13]

Oil stocks have been trading in lockstep with crude prices, making energy stockholders feel like they own their own crude oil. A Merrill Lynch survey recently showed that 13 percent of U.S. fund managers are bearish on energy, while 60 percent are bullish. Another survey by International Strategy & Investment, a New York-based firm, showed that hedge fund managers are similarly bullish. To be sure, there aren't many people in Wall Street fixated on a possible boom-bust soon; but there are a few who have advised against energy investments, arguing that oil production will start rising as new incremental barrels come on line. These people are on the fringes and they are wrong for the most part.

Mine is a bullish view. I think prices will continue to rally because demand is outstripping supply; there's no question about that. My job doesn't allow me to invest in energy for ethical reasons, but if I were allowed, I'd be buying standout stocks like ConocoPhillips, Williams, Grant, Prideco, and Exxon Mobil. If you have Exxon Mobil stock, you are blessed because you are able to maintain exposure to the high side while avoiding the risks. That's because Exxon Mobil is a large, integrated company. The other kind of energy stock that's related to oil is power. An assortment of power utility companies like NRG Energy, Southwestern Energy, and Reliant Energy have been doing very well in the stock market.

BUSINESS OUTLOOK AND BALANCE SHEET:
THE DEVIL'S IN THE DETAILS

There's a broad range of oil and oil services companies that can suit anyone's investment strategy. But you have to know first if there is growth of earnings and sales, both of which tell you whether the business is financially sound. Look at the balance sheet of each company you want to invest in and see if there's too much debt and what is the collateral for that debt, whether they are doing accounting right, whether the company has pending litigation or labor action, or less insurance coverage. These are red flags for potential trouble, unless they are thoroughly explained.

One of the best ways to know whether to invest in a company is to see whether insiders are buying the company's stock. Because of recent corporate scandals, investors worry a lot about how companies are run. Any small sign of trouble will send investors rushing for the door. And we can blame Enron, WorldCom and Refco for that. But all those problems and the bad publicity generated have obscured something interesting: a new study by George Mason University researchers has established that investors need to pay attention to what insiders do. The study, by James Hsieh, Lillian Ng, and Qinghei Wang, concludes that when insiders and analysts disagree on a company's financial standing and earning prospects, the insiders are often right, and so investors should ignore the analysts. However, I'd invest in such a company only if the insiders also are investing there. The study was going around academic circles in 2005 and can been found at papers.ssrn.com/so13/papers.lfm?abstract-id=687584. So, here's my advice to investors: don't be discouraged by analyst forecasts.[14]

Halliburton is the largest oil services company around and Kerr-McGee is one of the largest oil drillers. Both are great to invest in. But there are also many smaller ones involved in neighborhood drilling across the country. For example, Bass Energy, which is based in Akron, Ohio, is drilling for oil and natural gas behind Town Hall, in cemeteries and schoolyards—directly benefiting local landowners and communities. Bass has eight wells producing oil and natural gas in two municipal golf courses in Cleveland, generating $50,000 per month in royalties. The city will use the money to fix up the popular golf courses. Bass also drilled three other wells in Mayfield Heights, a Cleveland suburb, on empty land within Knollwood cemetery. Knollwood wants to use the gas to heat the mausoleum and cut prices for the locals. There are many communities like that reaping small benefits from neighborhood drilling, such as Williston, North Dakota, and Cleburne, Texas. A dozen drilling companies planned 200 wells all across Texas in 2005, which will bring $400 million in tax dollars to towns such as Cleburne.[15]

As you can see, high oil prices may not be all bad, especially to these communities. Moreover, if high oil prices restrain economic growth, that's not at all bad because it eases pressure on interest rates, which can help keep mortgage rates lower and bolster the real estate market. Even if you don't have a well in your backyard, you can still be a winner. Capital gains and fat dividends from oil company stocks and royalty trusts and mutual funds can help make up for the high gasoline price. In Katrina's aftermath, a lot of attention has gone to restoring the Gulf region's oil infrastructure. That is helping engineering firms like Nabors Industries, which rents out its 1,500 rigs to oil companies involved in exploration at rates ranging from $10,000 to $200,000 per day. As the market for rigs has soared, so have Nabor's earnings, doubling in mid-2005 to $259 million on $1.58 billion in revenue.

Nabors has been signing up customers to longer rental contracts at higher prices and in the process locking in future profits. Analysts see Nabors earnings growth at 30 percent annually over the next few years. Of course, a crash in oil and gas prices could hurt the company's stock, but that's not coming soon. Companies like Nabors, Transocean, Diamond Offshore, and other drillers will continue to have work as exploration picks up pace in the coming years, and their earnings are seen rising at a 38 percent average rate.[16]

If you are too busy to invest in stocks on your own, here are additional strategies to consider.

Mutual Funds

Yes, there are mutual funds that invest in energy, and you should seek them out. But before you start to invest in them, try to find out what kind of managers are running the funds and whether their clients are reputable. Consider the case of Charles Ober, who manages T. Rowe Price's New Era Fund, which invests in natural resources. He told the *New York Times* that stock research routinely takes him to hot spots like Libya, Nigeria, and Venezuela, where the political situation is volatile. Ober's fund is known as a steady investor in a volatile sector, and that's because he knows his stuff. He knows that you can't throw your money at something you don't understand, so he does his homework with a lot of zeal.[17]

Data from Lipper, the fund tracking firm, shows that a net $14 billion entered natural resources funds in the two years ended August 2005. Oil stocks' popularity stems from their double digit returns during the past two years and recent developments—the war in Iraq, China's economic growth, and the devastation caused by Hurricanes Katrina and Rita—that have pushed up oil prices to record levels. Oil stocks lagged behind the broader market during the 1990s, but they posted 28 percent gains in 2005, according to tracking firm Morningstar. For example, an investor who bought into Guinness Atkinson Global Energy Fund when it began in June 2004 would have had a return of more than 10 percent through September 2005. The Guinness Atkinson Global Energy Fund seeks long-term capital appreciation primarily through investments in equity securities of companies engaged in the production, exploration, and discovery or distribution of energy, including the research and development of alternative energy sources. In 2005, T. Rowe Price's New Era rose 36 percent, below the 50 percent average total return for natural resources funds tracked by Morningstar.[18]

Those who quit energy around 2003 because they thought the market would hit reverse are having second thoughts. A typical example is Vanguard Energy, which after liquidating its energy portfolio in 2004 came back in 2005. Meanwhile, several mutual funds invest in commodities indexes that offer diversified investments and far more protection against risk of loss than we realize. For a long time, people didn't know how good commodity investments were relative to stocks. But a recent study by Gary B. Gordon, a professor at the Wharton School of Business, University of Pennsylvania, and Geert Ruwenhorst, a professor at Yale University, suggests that when stocks and bonds slump, commodities, like energy, do not.[19]

The two best known commodities indexes, the Goldman Sachs

Commodities Index and the Dow Jones AIG Commodities Index, are both heavily weighted toward energy, 30 percent to 40 percent. One of Dow Jones' clients is Pacific Investment Management Company (PIMCO), which likes to diversify its portfolio. PIMCO's portfolio resembles that of a bond fund, which serves as a collateral for its commodities swaps or derivative securities for futures investment. Another mutual fund that invests in energy is Hennessy Focus 30 Fund, which returned $16 per share during the second quarter of 2005. The fund's manager, Neil Hennessy, uses computer analysis to select stocks from among 9,700 companies with market capitalization of $1 billion to $10 billion. He evaluates stocks based on their price/sales ratios and looks for rising earnings and stock prices. But since Hennessy's fund holds only 30 stocks, it's more susceptible to volatility than other more diversified portfolios. One of Hennessy's holdings is Tesoro, a refiner based in San Antonio, whose shares rose 45 percent in the second quarter of 2005.[20]

Besides investments in large oil companies, investors who prefer small cap companies could check out Brandywine Advisors Fund, whose portfolio is 21 percent energy stocks. The fund's stocks rose about 15 percent in the second quarter of 2005. Brandywine manager William F. D'Alonzo built the energy portfolio by seeking out reasonably priced companies with large earning potential. The fund has a minimum investment of $10,000 and prefers to invest in oil service companies—the firms that typically are hired by oil majors to do maintenance or drilling work. There's dire need for exploration and production right now, and service companies should do very well over the next couple of years no matter what happens to oil prices.

Exchange-Traded Funds

These are low-cost funds that have suddenly become popular with investors, although they are less well understood. Like traditional funds, exchange-traded funds (ETF) hold baskets of securities and other investments, but rather than get priced once a day, like traditional funds, they trade throughout the day like the stock market or futures market for commodities. They get priced like stocks. You can also invest in exchange-traded funds for as low as $8, by using part of your mutual fund investments. Exchange-traded fund assets have more than doubled over the past two years to $251.5 billion. But they remain small compared with traditional funds, which have $8 trillion in assets.

Many banks and brokerage firms have added ETFs to their investment portfolios, including Morgan Stanley, UBS, Smith Barney, Raymond James, and the Vanguard Group. Because ETFs trade like stocks, investors pay a brokerage commission each time they buy or sell part of their equity, which makes this type of investment very expensive for people who like to add regularly to their investments.

To get this type of investment, you can approach brokerages like Vanguard Energy's VIPERS and Dow Diamond. These brokerages have shares on index that carry lower fees than traditional mutual funds, but also they offer the ability to instantly diversify a portfolio by tracking everything from the broad S&P 500 stock index to indexes that focus on sectors or geographical regions or countries. It's the cheapest way to get investment diversity. Charles Schwab is one of the biggest distributors of exchange-traded fund accounts to individual investors and it has started offering free information about exchange-traded funds on its web site. Fidelity Investments, which launched an exchange-traded fund center on its web site in December 2004, also provides an overview of what exchange-traded funds are and how they work.[21]

To recap some of the advantages and disadvantages of exchange traded funds: first, they offer hedging opportunities at lower cost than traditional mutual funds, with most brokerages charging a smaller management fee than traditional index funds, and even smaller than the fee charged by managed mutual funds. Secondly, exchange-traded funds cam limit your capital gains tax.

SPACs and STARTs

For those without a lot of money, Special Purpose Acquisition Companies (SPAC) and Specified Term Acquisition Reserve Trust Security (START) are powerful investment instruments that can help you get started. They are basically blank-check companies to raise money from the public to later invest in another company. Here's how it works: a couple of investors want to buy a company in China, but they need $30 million to pay for the company. What do they do? In the old days, they'd look for a venture capitalist to lend them money. These days, they hire a firm like Eagle Bird Capital, an investment bank in New York which has been busy raising money from the public for SPAC management. These firms are typically priced at $6 per unit, which includes one share of common stock and two warrants with an exercise price of $5.

If all goes well, the offering generates $30 million to the managers, who are then given 12 to 18 months to find a company to buy. The underwriting bank collects a fee of 10 percent for the offering; that's more than the standard 7 percent for a normal initial public offering. The SPAC then puts 80 percent to 90 percent of the money in a trust, sets aside a small part of the money, typically less than $1 million, and tries to find a company. If one is found and all shareholders approve the deal, the management gets 20 percent of any profits eventually generated. Shareholders get ownership of the company, which they may or may not want to own. If they don't, they can sell the shares. However, if in 18 months the managers haven't found a company yet, they'd be required to give back the money, minus fees and expenses.

SPAC and START both have become the latest techniques in investment banking for taking a company public; the two closely-related techniques are now attracting marquee names. Lawyers and bankers who construct the deals call them "reverse mergers"—an initial public offering (IPO) for companies that have no operating business, but fetch tens of millions of dollars from the public on the expectation that they will find a business to acquire.[22]

Best-selling author and former White House counterterrorism chief Richard A. Clarke is chairman of Good Harbor Acquisition Corp., a START that filed registration documents with the Securities and Exchange Commission (SEC) on September 15, 2005. Other officers and directors in companies trying the trendy SPAC method are Apple Computer co-founder Steve Wozniak, who filed on September 2, 2005, with two former Apple executives to go public with Acquicor Technology Inc., and Daniel Burstein, who wrote *Secrets of the Code: The Unauthorized Guide to the Mysteries Behind the DaVinci Code*. Burstein is on the board of Juniper Partners Acquisition Corp.

So, what do these guys know that the rest of us don't? SPACs and STARTs take the concept of an IPO and make the process simple, quick, and painless. A group of hedge fund and private venture operators get together with executives who have operating experience, often adding star-power by including a well-known author or "adviser." The company files to go public, with the intention of purchasing an unknown target within 12 to 18 months of the IPO date, an effort to meet SEC rules governing blank-check companies. Investors who take part in the IPO presumably have limited risk because 80 percent to 90 percent of the proceeds are put in escrow—awaiting an acquisition.

The idea is that if no appropriate target is found, you get the escrowed portion of your money back. Read the regulatory filings all the way through, though, and you learn that the escrow accounts can be tapped for litigation claims. While the legal structure of a START is very similar to a SPAC, a START is typically registered to sell more classes of securities. The upside: management has additional incentive to get a deal done because many START securities expire worthless if no acquisition is made. Good Harbor, a START, registered to sell 14 classes of securities in 2005, compared to nine by a SPAC.

SPACs had a popular run in the mid-1990s, but they languished after 1996, when bankers saw that it was easier to put a dotcom at the end of a company's name and sell a straightforward IPO. Today, the easy dotcom deal is over and SPACs are back, because there is a lot of private equity and hedge fund capital out there having a tough time finding a home—there's just too much money chasing too few deals. Because SPACs and STARTs promise to complete a deal within a specified number of months, target companies know not only that the purchaser faces a deadline but also exactly how much money is in the kitty.

However, investors who consider joining the experts in SPACs and STARTs had better consider how the smart money might be treated differently from the dumb. Those deadlines to find a deal, or give investors most of their money back, might be at odds with incentives given to officers and directors. An unfamiliar procedure may not matter to some investors, but here's free advice for those buying shares in someone's SPAC: If you love the SPAC because it's loaded with geniuses, don't be disappointed if management buys a chain of hopeless companies. Some 50 SPACs filed for registration with the SEC to go public in 2005 and many more will follow in the coming years. They are hoping to raise billions of dollars for their startups.

Hedge Funds, Superfunds and Private Equity

Hedge funds are investment firms that try to profit by making bets on commodity and exchange futures. This is how they work: They buy financial instruments, or contracts, today and then sell them later at higher prices and pocket the difference. They generally trade on arbitrage, or the price difference of contracts. Hedge funds are a growing industry right now, with about $1 trillion invested in the oil market in the past two years. Most hedge funds are large private capital placements, but some are small, particularly when they are structured as a superfund, which is technically not a hedge fund but a managed futures fund. Superfunds are great for the little investor because the managers charge you less, typically 8.75 percent, in brokerage and management fees. Super-wealthy investors have private equity funds that invest large sums of money in all manner of sectors and are the hottest investment tools currently in the energy markets. Blackstone, Battery Ventures, and General Atlantic are among those active in energy.

Alternative Energy Investments

The oil market is not the only one looking up. Alternative fuel stocks are also attracting many investors. Because oil and gas are expensive, Americans are looking for cheaper nonfossil fuel and that demand is boosting the alternative fuel stocks as well. This is especially good for anyone who cares for the environment—the greens. If you consider yourself an environmentalist or a preservationist, this is perfect for you, for you are now able to support efforts to preserve the environment while at the same time profiting from those efforts. It's a win-win situation. Consider this: Pacific Ethanol Inc., a small ethanol-producing company started in 2003 by Bill Jones, the former secretary of state for the state of California, has trebled its stock price on NASDAQ to about $30 a share within a year of going public in March of 2005. Like many other similar renewable fuel start-ups, millions of dollars in private equity money are being thrown at Pacific Ethanol like the world is coming to an end. Billionaire Bill Gates, the chairman of Microsoft, is one of those investing in renewable fuel stocks. Gates' investment company, Cascade Investment, has agreed to pump $84 million in Pacific Ethanol.[23]

The U.S. government has recognized alternative fuel as the fuel for the future and has included a number of tax incentives in the Energy Policy

Act of 2005, the energy law signed in the summer of 2005, to spur growth in the alternative fuel sector. If you haven't already, you should give alternative stocks a try as it will make you feel morally stronger. It's been nearly three decades since efforts to promote alternative fuel floundered after the 1973 oil crisis, but it's making a comeback. Still, alternative fuel remains a small industry, with small cap companies dominating. Since 2005, 15 of the 36 companies in the WilderHill Clean Energy index have made huge profits. That includes hydroelectric power and wind energy, solar energy, and fuel cells.[24]

Some of the most successful companies in the renewable fuel sector are huge conglomerates, like General Electric and Germany's Siemens, and also big oil companies, like BP, that are hedging their bets. Investing in these companies offers a chance to own a clean energy stock. Here's some information about GE worth knowing: It made close to $2 billion in sales from production of wind-powered turbines in 2005, treble what it made from that business unit in 2002. However, that's only 1 percent of GE's revenues.

There's a lot of hope that alternative fuel technologies developed by some of the smaller companies will become commercially viable and help support the sector. As a result, stocks for these companies are expected to soar. WilderHill Clean Energy Index gained 26 percent in the past 12 months alone, compared with 50 percent for oil. That's not bad, considering this is not an established sector in the United States.

Moreover, since continued oil supply is uncertain, a lot more consumers are going to turn to coal, which is abundantly available in the United States, China, and India. Coal used to be frowned upon because of its dirt, but technology has improved enough to make it just as clean as other fuels. Shrewd investors could buy shares in U.S. coal producers, including the two biggest, Peabody Energy Corp. and Arch Coal Inc., both based in St. Louis, Missouri. Coal companies have profited from the current oil boom.

Investing in coal doesn't mean that Big Oil isn't safe anymore. It only means that you are on much firmer ground when you have a diversified portfolio. If you look at both types of stocks, the difference isn't large. Exxon Mobil, for instance, returned 36 percent to its shareholders in market appreciation and dividends in 2005 and BP returned 21 percent. Peabody Energy stockholders, meanwhile, did far better in the same time period. They more than doubled their money, and Peabody shares have risen more than three and a half times since the company's initial public offering in 2001. Arch Coal stock returned 65 percent in 2005 as well.

Coal producers have benefited from increased demand from power plants and steelmakers in the United States, China, and India. Massey Energy Co. of Richmond, Virginia, for instance, said its average selling price for coal used in steel-making jumped 38 percent in 2005. Consol Energy, Inc. of Pittsburgh, the third largest U.S. producer, plans a $500 million mine expansion to keep up with orders.

Soaring prices for natural gas have given coal demand another lift. Many electric power plants have switched from gas to coal, which costs about half as much. In the spring of 2006, Duke Energy Corp. closed on a deal purchasing Cinergy Corp. for about $9 billion, in large part because of Cinergy's coal-fired plants.

Back to oil, we've also seen that the market has been good to minnows as well. In fact, some smaller oil companies also have outperformed the giants. For instance, Apache Corp. of Houston produced a 12-month total return of 51 percent for its stockholders, helped by increased first-quarter selling prices of 51 percent for crude oil and 11 percent for natural gas. Apache recently bought property from Shell, BP, and Exxon Mobil and its profit rose tremendously in 2005. Oil transport companies have not been left behind. Overseas Shipholding Group of New York made an acquisition in 2005 that made it the world's second-largest oil tanker company. The bigger fleet, combined with higher tanker rates, boosted the company's 2005 earnings by about 40 percent. The world's biggest owner of oil tankers, Teekay Shipping Corp. of Vancouver, Canada, capitalized on high energy prices in yet another way. In the fall of 2005, Teekay raised $132 million through the public sale of a 20 percent interest in Teekay LNG Partners LP, whose ships carry liquefied natural gas and crude oil.

Is it too late to buy energy stocks, large or small? BlackRock, Inc., which manages $391 billion, doesn't seem to think so. It reported to the SEC in late summer of 2005 that after $870 million in purchases, it owned stakes in Peabody, Arch, Consol, and Massey ranging from 3.3 to 8.8 percent. The money manager also has a 4.7 percent stake in Newfield Exploration Co., an oil-and-gas company that returned 49 percent to its shareholders in 2005.

The bottom line is this: The world needs a lot of energy, but supply is getting tighter; an "überspike" in oil prices is in the making and the potential rewards for the savvy energy investor are huge.

Fuel Facts

Did you know that all crude oil is not the same?

Crude oil is called "sweet" when it contains only a small amount of sulfur and "sour" if it contains a lot of sulfur. Crude oil is also classified by the weight of its molecules. "Light" crude oil flows freely like water while "heavy" crude oil is thick like tar. There can be a combination of these types of crude oil from any given production oilfield.

Did you know that "bbl" is the abbreviation for a barrel of oil and it actually stands for "blue barrel"?

Barrels for transporting oil were originally painted blue to assure buyers that these were 42-gallon barrels, instead of the 40-gallon barrels used by some other industries. The extra two gallons was to allow for evaporation and leaking during transport (most barrels were made of wood). Standard Oil began manufacturing 42-gallon barrels that were blue to be used for transporting petroleum. The use of a blue barrel guaranteed a buyer that this was a 42-gallon barrel.

Did you know that about 27 percent of the energy we use goes to transporting people and goods from one place to another?

In 2001, there were almost 217 million vehicles (cars, buses, and trucks) in the United States—that's more than three motor vehicles for every

191

four people. Gasoline is used mainly by cars, motorcycles, and light trucks; diesel is used mainly by heavier trucks, buses, and trains. Together, gasoline and diesel make up 85 percent of all the energy used in transportation.

Did you know that personal vehicles, like cars and light trucks, consume almost 60 percent of the total energy used for transportation in the United States?

Commercial vehicles account for the rest. Gasoline that fuels vehicles is made from petroleum formed from plants and tiny animals that lived hundreds of millions of years ago, way before dinosaurs.

Did you know that nine of every ten tons of coal used in the United States are used for electricity generation?

Coal is burned to heat water into steam in an electric power plant, and the steam turns a turbine that drives a generator that produces electricity. In the course of this process, about two-thirds of the energy in the coal is used up to make electricity, or becomes waste heat, and only a third winds up being delivered to users as electricity.

Did you know that when natural gas is burned, it produces mostly carbon dioxide and water vapor?

These are the same substances we exhale when we breathe. Natural gas is odorless but has an organic compound that is added to give it an odor. That way, we can easily detect possible leaks.

Some Questions to Test Your Energy Knowledge*

1. Most of the energy we use originally came from:

   a. the sun
   b. the air
   c. the soil
   d. the oceans

2. Electrical energy can be produced from:

   a. mechanical energy
   b. chemical energy
   c. radiant energy
   d. all of the above

3. Which uses the most energy in American homes each year?

   a. lighting
   b. water heating
   c. heating and cooling rooms
   d. refrigeration

---

*Reproduced here courtesy of the Energy Information Administration, which is part of the U.S. Department of Energy.

4. The U.S. consumes lots of energy. Which fuel provides the most energy?

   a. petroleum
   b. coal
   c. natural gas
   d. solar

5. Coal, petroleum, natural gas, and propane are fossil fuels. They are called fossil fuels because:

   a. they are burned to release energy and they cause air pollution
   b. they were formed from the buried remains of plants and tiny animals that lived hundred of millions of years ago
   c. they are nonrenewable and will run out
   d. they are mixed with fossils to provide energy

6. Gasoline is produced by refining which fossil fuel?

   a. natural gas
   b. coal
   c. petroleum
   d. propane

7. Propane is used instead of natural gas on many farms and in rural areas. Why is propane often used instead of natural gas?

   a. it's safer
   b. it's portable
   c. it's cleaner
   d. it's cheaper

8. What sector of the U.S. economy consumes most of the nation's petroleum?

   a. residential
   b. commercial
   c. industrial
   d. transportation

9. Natural gas is transported mainly by:

   a. pipelines
   b. trucks
   c. barges
   d. all three equally

10. Global warming focuses on an increase in the level of which gas in the atmosphere?

   a. ozone
   b. sulfur dioxide
   c. carbon dioxide
   d. nitrous oxide

11. Solar, biomass, geothermal, wind, and hydropower energy are all renewable sources of energy. They are called renewable because they:

   a. are clean and free to use
   b. can be converted directly into heat and electricity
   c. can be replenished by nature in a short period of time
   d. do not produce air pollution

12. Today, which renewable energy source provides the United States with the most energy?

   a. wind
   b. solar
   c. geothermal
   d. hydropower

13. Electricity is the movement of:

   a. atoms
   b. molecules
   c. electrical power
   d. neutrons

14. How much of the energy in burning coal reaches the consumer as electricity?

a. one-third
b. one-half
c. three-quarters
d. nine-tenths

15. In a nuclear power plant, uranium atoms:

a. combine and give off heat energy
b. split and give off heat energy
c. burn and give off heat energy
d. split and give off electrons

Answers
(1) a (2) d (3) c (4) a (5) b (6) c (7) b (8) d (9) a (10) c (11) c (12) d
(13) c (14) a (15) b

Notes

INTRODUCTION

1. David Goldstein, *Out of Gas* (New York: Norton, 2004), 16, 31–35.
2. Samuel Beckett, *Waiting for Godot* (New York: Grove/Atlantic, 1997; first edition 1953), Act 2.
3. Goldstein, *Out of Gas*, 26.
4. Kenneth S. Deffeyes, *Beyond Oil: The View from Hubbert's Peak* (New York: Farrar, Straus & Giroux, 2005), 179.
5. John Roberts, "What Is 'Peak Oil' and Why Should We Worry," *Platts Energy Economist*, June 1, 2005 (available at plats.com/oil/resources/news%20features/peakoil/index.xm/?s).

CHAPTER 1   The End of an Era?

1. Thomas L. Friedman, *The World Is Flat: A Brief History of the 21st Century* (New York: Farrar, Straus & Giroux, 2005). The book argues that globalization is generally a good thing.
2. Daniel Yergin, *The Prize: The Epic Quest for Oil, Money and Power* (New York: Simon & Schuster, 1992), 176–181, 194–196.
3. Craig Bond Hatfield, "Oil Back on the Global Agenda," *Nature* 387 (1997): 121.
4. Richard A. Kerr, "The Next Oil Crisis Looms Large—and Perhaps Close," *Science* 281 (1998): 1128.
5. Colin Campbell and Jean Laherrère, "The End of Cheap Oil," *Scientific American* (March 1998): 78–83.
6. Colin Campbell, interview with Global Public Media, December 18, 2002 (available at www.peakoil.net/colin.html).

7. Adam Porter, "Is the World's Oil Running Out Fast?" BBC News, June 10, 2004 (available at www.countercurrents.org/peakoil-bbc 10064.htm), a report based on deliberation during the Peak Oil Conference in Berlin, June 2004.
8. Ibid.
9. Mike Swanson, "High Oil Prices Create Investment Opportunity," online newsletter, WallStreetWindow (available at www.wallstreet window.com/oil.htm).
10. Campbell and Laherrère, "End of Cheap Oil," 78–83.
11. Kenneth S. Deffeyes, *Beyond Oil: The View from Hubbert's Peak* (New York: Farrar, Straus & Giroux, 2005), 179.
12. John Vidal, "The End of Oil Is Closer Than You Think," *The Guardian* (London), science features, April 21, 2005. (available at www.guardian.co.uk/life/feature/story/0,13026,1464050,00.html).
13. Ibid.
14. Ibid.
15. Ibid.
16. David J. Lynch, "Debate Brews: Has Oil Production Peaked?" *USA Today*, October 16, 2005, Money section (available at usatoday .com/money/industries/energy/2005-10-16-oil-1a-cover-usat_x.htm).
17. Matt Crensen, "Experts: Petroleum May Be Nearing Peak," Associated Press, March 28, 2005 (available at commondreams.org/headlines 05/0528-03.htm).
18. Vidal, "End of Oil."
19. Ibid.
20. Ibid.
21. "Drop in Exploration Drilling Saps Reserves Growth," *Petroleum Intelligence Weekly*, April 17, 2006, 1.
22. Associated Press, "Are We There Yet? Oil Joyride May Be Over," *USA Today*, May 28, 2005, World News (available at usatoday.com/news/world/2005-05-28-oil-shortage_x.htm).

CHAPTER 2   Consequences of an Oil Peak

1. James Howard Kunstler, *The Long Emergency: Surviving the Converging Catastrophes of the Twenty-First Century* (Boston: Atlantic Monthly Press, 2005).

2. Daniel Yergin, *The Prize: The Epic Quest for Oil, Money and Power* (New York: Simon & Schuster, 1992), 208–209.
3. Kunstler, *Long Emergency*, 18–19, 239.
4. Richard Heinberg, *The Party's Over: Oil, War and the Face of Industrial Societies*, 2nd ed. (Philadelphia: New Society Publishers, 2005), 223.
5. Colin Campbell and Jean Laherrère, "The End of Cheap Oil," *Scientific American* (March, 1998): 78–83.

CHAPTER 3 Alternative Fuels

1. British Petroleum, *Statistical Review* (Annual Report), 2005.
2. United States Energy Information Administration, www.eia.doc .gov/fuelrenewable.html and U.K. Department for Transportation (DfT), www.dft.gov.uk/stellent/groups/dft_roads/documents/page/ dft_roads_610329.03.hcsp.
3. Alan Katz, "Nuclear's New Glow," *Bloomberg Markets Magazine*, December 2005, 87.

CHAPTER 4 Is the Saudi Oil Supply Adequate?

1. Matt Simmons, *Twilight in the Desert: The Coming Saudi Oil Shock and the World Economy* (Hoboken, NJ: John Wiley & Sons, 2005), 12–13.
2. David Fromkin, *A Peace to End All Peace* (New York: Avon Books, 1989), 424–434, 494–509.
3. Daniel Yergin, *The Prize: The Epic Quest for Oil, Money and Power* (New York: Simon & Schuster, 1992), 283–285.
4. Ibid., 289–291.
5. Simmons, *Twilight in the Desert*, 9.
6. Ibid.
7. United States Energy Information Administration, www.eia.doc.gov.
8. United States Energy Information Administration, www.eia.doe.gov/ cabs/saudi.html.
9. Jeff Gerth, "Some Doubt Saudi Pledge to Increase Oil Output," *New York Times*, October 27, 2005, C1.
10. *Petroleum Intelligence Weekly*, September 26, 2005, 7.
11. Gerth, "Some Doubt Saudi Pledge," C6.

12. Ibid.
13. Peter Behr and Alan Sipress, "Cheney Panel Seeks Review of Sanction: Iraq, Iran and Libya Loom Large in Boosting Oil Supply," *Washington Post*, April 19, 2001, A13.
14. Ibid.
15. Gerth, "Some Doubt Saudi Pledge," C6.
16. Simmons, *Twilight in the Desert*, 337.
17. Gerth, "Some Doubt Saudi Pledge," C6.
18. William B. Quandt, *Saudi Arabia in the 1980s: Foreign Policy, Security and Oil Policy* (Washington, D.C.: The Brookings Institution, 1981).
19. Gerth, "Some Doubt Saudi Pledge," C1.
20. Robin Wright, "Saudi Plan Aims to Expand Relations," *Washington Post*, November 14, 2005, A14.

CHAPTER 5   Iraqi Oil Supply and the Battle of Baghdad

1. Philip Shishkin and Yochi J. Dreazen, "Goal of Iraqi Unity Fades as Fissures Harden into Place," *Wall Street Journal*, March 14, 2006, A1.
2. Dana Milbank and Justin Blum, "Documents Say Oil Chiefs Met with Cheney Task Force," *Washington Post*, November 16, 2005, A1.
3. Greg Simmons, "Dems: Oil Execs Lied at Senate Hearing," Foxnews.com, November 17, 2005.
4. Milbank and Blum, "Documents Say Oil Chiefs Met," A1.
5. Ibid.
6. Charles W. Hamilton, *America and Oil in the Middle East*, (Houston, TX: Gulf Publishers Co., 1962), 77–78.
7. Ibid., 79.
8. Ibid., 80.
9. Ibid., 99–100.
10. James A. Paul, "Oil Companies in Iraq: A Century of Rivalry and War," Global Policy Forum, November 2003, and interviews with Mr. Paul at his New York City office.
11. Ibid.
12. "Merged Giants Get Stuck on Upstream Ladder," *Petroleum Intelligence Weekly*, February 27, 2006, 3.
13. Elliot Abrams et al., "Letter to President Clinton on Iraq," Project for the New American Century, January 26, 1998. www.newamerican century.org/iraqlintonletter.htm.

14. William Kristol and Robert Kagan, "Reject the Global Buddy System," *New York Times* (Op-Ed), October 25, 1999.

15. Ron Suskind, *The Price of Loyalty: George W. Bush, the White House and the Education of Paul O'Neill* (New York: Simon & Schuster, 2004), 174–175.

16. Charlie Christensen, "War for Oil: The Connections Between Policy and Practice," DowningStreetMemo.com/warforoil.html.

17. Walter Pincus, "British Intelligence Warned of Iraq War," *Washington Post*, May 13, 2005, A8.

18. Don Van Natta, Jr., "Bush Was Set on Path to War," *New York Times*, March 27, 2006, A1.

19. Dan Morgan and David B. Ottaway, "In Iraqi War Scenario, Oil Is Key Issue," *Washington Post*, September 15, 2002, A1.

20. Ibid.

21. Ed Vulliamy, Paul Webster, and Nick Paton Walsh, "Scramble to Carve Up Iraqi Oil Reserves Lies Behind U.S. Diplomacy," *The Observer* (London), October 6, 2002.

22. Youssef M. Ibrahim, "Bush's Iraq Adventure Is Bound to Backfire," *International Herald Tribune*, November 1, 2002.

23. Platform Newsletter (London), "Iraq Constitution Lays Ground for Oilfield Sell-off," October 1, 2005, 2.

24. Ibid.

25. Laurence Frost, "Oil Companies Hopeful on Iraqi Politics," Associated Press, March 14, 2005.

CHAPTER 6   Why and How Oil Prices Soared

1. David Hufton, "The Price of Oil Market Transparency," *Petroleum Intelligence Weekly*, April 10, 2006, 7.

2. Jad Mouawad and Carl Hulse, "An Oil Price Duel on Capitol Hill: Two Senate Committees Interrogate Wary Oil Company Executives," *New York Times*, November 10, 2005, C1.

3. Ibid.

4. Ibid.

5. Vikas Bajaj, "Oil Executives Defend Profits at Senate Hearing," *International Herald Tribune*, November 10, 2005.

6. Ibid.

7. Mouawad and Hulse, "Oil Price Duel on Capital Hill," C1.

8. Commodities Futures Trading Commission, a federal agency, at www.cftc.gov/cftc/cftchome.htm.

9. Al Karr, "Managing Energy Risk Becomes a Necessity in Volatile Markets," *Managing Global Energy Risk* (a Nymex company magazine), November 2005, 34.

10. Stephanie Cooke, "North American Energy Prices Are Driven by Many Factors," *Managing Global Energy Risk* (a Nymex company magazine), November 2005, 48.

11. Jehangir Pocha, "The Axis of Oil," *In These Times Magazine*, January 31, 2005. (available at www.inthesetimes.com/site/main/article/1909).

12. Ibid.

13. Ibid.

14. Ibid.

15. David Zweig and Bi Jianhai, "China's Global Hunt for Energy," *Foreign Affairs* (September/October 2005), 25.

16. Randall Palmer, "Oil Guru Says Crude Could Hit $190 This Winter," Reuters, October 19, 2005.

17. Andrew C. Revkin, "Bush Aide Softened Greenhouse Gas Links to Global Warming," *New York Times*, June 8, 2005.

18. Mark Fischetti, "Drowning New Orleans," *Scientific American*, October 2001.

19. Joel K. Bourne Jr., "Gone with the Water," *National Geographic*, October 2004.

20. Kerry Emanuel, "Increasing Destructiveness of Tropical Cyclones over the Past 30 years," *Nature* 3906, no. 436, August 4, 2005.

21. Louisiana Department of Transportation and Development, www.dotd.state.la.us/ or www.dotd.louisiana.gov/programs_grants/loop/loop.shhtml.

22. U.S. Energy Information Administration, www.eia.doc.gov.

23. U.S. Department of Energy figures at the department's website at www.eia.doe.gov.

24. Thomas Catan and Kevin Morrison,"The Blockade in the Oil Pipeline," *Financial Times* (Comment and Analysis), September 29, 2005, 13.

25. Joe Quinlan, "Who Needs China? Recycled Petrodollars to the U.S. Hit a Record High in 2004," March 15, 2005. A report written by Joe Quinlan, chief market strategist, for the Investment Strategies Group at Bank of America.

CHAPTER 7 Bumper Harvest for Oil Majors

1. Jad Mouawad and Simon Romero, "Big Rise in Profit Places Oil Giants on the Defensive," *New York Times*, October 28, 2005.
2. Marc Tran, "BP Boosted by High Oil Prices," *The Guardian* (London), October 25, 2005.
3. Steve Quinn, "Exxon Mobil, Shell Post Record Profits," Associated Press, October 28, 2005.
4. David J. O'Reilly, "U.S. Energy Policy: A Declaration of Interdependence," speech delivered at an energy conference in Houston, Texas, February 15, 2005 (available at www.chevron.com/news/speeches/2005-02-15_oreilly.asp).
5. Brad Foss, "Profits Likely Won't Mean New Refineries," Associated Press, October 28, 2005.
6. Ibid.
7. U.S. Senate Energy Committee hearing on Capitol Hill, Washington, D.C., on October 27, 2005, at www.energy.senate.gov/public/index.cfm?Fuseaction=search.
8. Ibid.
9. Ibid.
10. Marathon Oil Company press releases dated October 27, 2005, and September 29, 2005 (available at company web site, www.marathon.com/press_releases/2005).

CHAPTER 8 The New Frontier in Oil Investments

1. Damon Darlin, "Get Rich Quick: Write a Millionaire Book," *New York Times*, November 12, 2005, C1.
2. Peter A. McKay, "Goldman Analyst Has Last Laugh After Oil Soars," *Wall Street Journal* (Weekend Edition), October 1–2, 2005, B1.
3. Peter L. Bernstein, *Against the Gods: The Remarkable Story of Risk* (New York: John Wiley & Sons, 1996), 3–8.
4. Ibid.
5. James J. Cramer, *Jim Cramer's Real Money* (New York: Simon & Schuster, 2005), 33, 67.
6. Janet C. Lowe, *Jack Welch Speaks* (New York: John Wiley & Sons, 1998), 12.
7. Christopher Hart, "What Makes Optimists Among Us Achieve," *Sunday Nation's Lifestyle Magazine* (Nairobi), October 9, 2005.

www.nationmedia.com/dailynation/nmgcontententry.asp?premium id=0&category_id=33&newsid=58874.

8. Don Ross, "Game Theory," *Stanford Encyclopedia of Philosophy*, Winter 2005, http://plato.stanford.edu/archives/win2005/entries/game-theory/.

9. Ibid.

10. Lewis Lord, "Hernando Cortes: The Painful Birth of Mexico," *US News & World Report* (special edition), 2005, 54–55.

11. Michael Sivy, "Cashing In on the Oil Boom," *Money*, August 9, 2005 (available at money.cnn.com/2005/08/09/commentary/mkt commentary/sivy).

12. Justin Lahart, "Can Energy Help Investors Running on Empty?" *Wall Street Journal*, October 3, 2005, C11.

13. Ibid.

14. Mark Hulbert, "The Analysts vs. the Insiders," *New York Times*, September 25, 2005, B6.

15. Anne Kates Smith, "Oil Where You Least Expect it," *Kiplinger's Personal Finance Magazine*, October 2005, 21–22.

16. Christopher Helman, "Drilling for Dollars," *Forbes*, October 3, 2005, 108.

17. Tim Gray, "Is It Too Late to Ride the Energy Bandwagon?" *New York Times*, October 9, 2005, B25.

18. Ibid.

19. Ibid.

20. Ibid.

21. Arden Dale, "Building Portfolios with ETFs," *Wall Street Journal*, October 4, 2005, R1.

22. Jenny Anderson, "Crave Huge Risks? This Investment May Be for You," *New York Times*, September 23, 2005, C7.

23. Parmy Olson, "Bill Gates Goes Green," Forbes.com, November 17, 2005.

24. David Landis, "Clean Power Gets a Lift," *Kiplinger's Personal Finance Magazine*, October 2005, 54.

Index